This picture emphasizes several important practices still necessary in modern agriculture—planting young plants and taking care of them and developing young people. These plant roots are soaking in 2 to 3 inches of water, the adequately sized hole is freshly dug, the soil is moist, the plant is carefully placed into the hole, the roots are spaced evenly and straightened and then gently hand packed with loose friable soil. These plants will respond in kind—and hopefully, the young man will continue his interest in agriculture.

APPROVED PRACTICES
IN FRUIT
AND VINE PRODUCTION

by

ARNOLD H. SCHEER

Formerly Associate Professor of Fruit Sciences
California Polytechnic State University, San Luis Obispo
Currently Manager, Grower and Consultant
Fruit and Grape Industry

and

ELWOOD M. JUERGENSON

Teacher Educator, Agriculture
University of California, Davis

THE INTERSTATE
Printers & Publishers, Inc.
Danville, Illinois

APPROVED PRACTICES IN FRUIT
AND VINE PRODUCTION, Second Edition.
Copyright © 1976 by The Interstate Printers
& Publishers, Inc. All rights reserved. First
edition published under the title *Approved
Practices in Fruit Production*, 1964. Printed in
the United States of America.

Library of Congress Catalog Card No. 74-30870

Reorder No. 1704

PREFACE

The purpose of this book is to furnish a comprehensive list of activities which involve approved practices, with information on how they should be done in the fruit industry, which throughout this book will include grapes and other vines, related crops and small fruits and nuts. An approved practice in fruit production is a farm practice which has been tried and tested by state agricultural experiment stations and/or successful farmers in the community and found to be desirable to follow for most efficient fruit and vine production. Consequently, it is important that the producer know what these approved practices are and how to carry them successfully to completion, in order to attain the greatest success in the fruit business.

The primary aim of this book has been to include all of the more important activities involving approved practices in the fruit enterprise. The information has been carefully selected, in order to determine the best methods and procedures to follow in carrying the practices to successful completion, and has been condensed to a minimum to conserve space and eliminate a vast amount of reading. A considerable amount of the information has been taken from state agricultural colleges, experiment stations and other research sources in order to provide the reader with the latest information which has been tested and proved successful. However, in many situations the authors have described their own experiences, as both are from farm families and one of the authors presently is actively involved in a farm-management partnership of 6,000 acres of diversified farming in California. Labor-saving devices have been highlighted throughout the book.

One of the authors' chief purposes in presenting this material has been to tell how each activity should be done in order to accomplish the approved practices involved. Consequently, wherever possible, specific information has been given. There are many activities and approved practices which are common in the fruit enterprise and which, with minor local adaptations, can be used in most areas in the United States. Hence, much of the information in this book can readily be adapted and used throughout this country, as well as in the countries where similar type plants are grown. Many copies of the first edition of this book were purchased by students and representatives of other countries and either taken or sent to their native lands.

This book should be useful for orchardists, viticulturists, farmers, farm managers, bank appraisers and real estate salesmen, including full-time, part-time and suburban; students of agriculture; teachers of agriculture; county agricultural agents; and other persons interested in efficient fruit production.

THE AUTHORS

ACKNOWLEDGMENTS

The authors wish to express their appreciation to those who granted permission to use photographs, sketches and information. In many situations where a suggestion or recommendation is made, it is difficult to credit the proper source for bits of data or even total information used. Experience, education, observation, interviews, reading, research and experiments by others also all become one's accumulated information source. However, in the case of one of the authors, it certainly begins with being raised on a farm by a father who challenged the elements of nature by attempting to grow trees and vines with some degree of success in a climate and under conditions highly "not recommended," let alone using his six sons as the total labor source (non-union).

Special acknowledgment is given to commercial companies, U.S.D.A. and the following state colleges and universities for the numerous materials and quotations:

Arizona	Kansas	Missouri
California	Michigan	New York
Colorado	Mississippi	North Carolina

| Ohio | South Carolina | Virginia |
| Oregon | Texas | Washington |

Credit has been given for materials as they are presented. This book would not have been possible without the constant reference and evaluation of materials already written and the numerous interviews with fruit and grape growers and colleagues.

Of special significance is the contribution of pictures, research, chapters on Kiwi and on small fruits and nuts and up-to-date statistics by Ronald E. Scheer, a bio-scientist, Director of Research and Development for Pacific Agrilands, and the son of one of the authors. Also extensive use was made of facilities, materials and personnel from Pacific Agrilands, a diversified farm management company in Modesto, California.

TABLE OF CONTENTS

INTRODUCTION

Agriculture is a fantastic, fast changing, wonderful industry to study as well as one offering many opportunities to enter as a career.

Your grandfather, even your father, may have farmed with a walking plow and a harrow, implements which many present farmers may have never seen.

In 1850, about two-thirds of the power on farms in the United States came from men and animals; today less than 2 per cent of the power comes from these sources. Much of the hard work has been taken out of farming because of sprayers, tractors, harvesters, cultivation equipment, pruners, irrigation, facilities, airplanes and a host of other labor-saving equipment. There are new gas and liquid fertilizers and improved solid fertilizers. New varieties of disease-resistant, high-yielding trees and vines are developed each year, and new methods of propagating virus-free plants are being discovered. Weeds, insects and diseases are being conquered. Improved labor-saving equipment appears each year with more to come. Irrigation gives protection against drought and improves yield and quality. The tensiometer, gypsum block and dendrometer help tell when plants need water.

A modern piece of farm equipment operating in a healthy, high-producing orchard. Improved labor-saving equipment appears each year, and its use is necessary to obtain highest yield and profit.

You will be a successful farmer when you become a practical plant scientist, soils expert, mechanic, weather forecaster, marketing analyst, irrigation expert and a businessman and you "have learned how to work"; and remember, too, that "the hand that is soiled with honest labor is fit to shake with any neighbor."

Farm progress is no accident. It is the result of the same educational system that produces know-how teachers, scientists, engineers and businessmen. Education enables farmers and others with a desire to improve themselves, their families and their people to farm better and derive more pleasure from farming. Each of many kinds of specialists has had his part in helping the farmer to do his work faster and better and yet supply the consumer with a cheaper, convenient, higher quality product.

Fruit industries have significant economic effects upon the position and welfare of other industries. Many business firms depend upon the production and merchandizing of fruit. When these are considered, the full impact of these crops can be seen more clearly.

Major associated businesses are packing, shipping and processing. Distribution firms as well as ice companies, transportation, terminal markets, truckers and advertising agencies are a few who are dependent on the fruit grower.

Equipment firms serving growers are numerous, such as lumber mills, box factories, farm equipment companies, irrigation suppliers, insecticide firms, machinery makers and fertilizing supply industries.

Oil, gas and other fuels sold to producers of fruit products comprise a large part of the sales for many companies.

Markets and marketing are constantly changing. The consumer has an insatiable appetite for quality and convenience, which the producer must recognize. Producers must meet this demand by producing superior quality in economic quantity. The producer should know he has a market for his product before he attempts its production.

There are so many ways of doing things wrong that we hope this book will help you in doing them right.

Farm Review

The technological and economic changes that have occurred in U.S. agriculture the last 20 years will continue to affect U.S. and world markets for another 20 years and more. By virtually every measure, farm production has increased immensely. Output per unit of input has risen 28 per cent, output per man-hour 210 per cent and crop production per acre, 54 per cent. Twenty years ago one agriculture worker provided farm products for himself and 15 other persons. Today, 48 other persons benefit from his output. Total crop production has increased more than one-third, while cropland used has declined by 11 per cent.

Major changes in scale and mix of production resources are closely associated with the rapid increase in farm output and resource productivity. Nationally, the number of farms has decreased by 47 per cent since 1950, and the average farm size has increased from 216 to 381 acres. The increase in farm size is continuing. In the past 10 years the size of the average farm in the United States was increased by 24 per cent, while the size of California's average farm was increased by 67 per cent to a total of 578 acres in 1975.

Capital in machinery, buildings and equipment has been substituted for labor. National farm employment dwindled from 9.9 million (20 years ago) to 4.5 million at the present time, while agriculture wage rates rose $2\frac{1}{3}$ (upwards to 4) times for specific agriculture skills.

Farm Changes

During this same past 20-year period, farms became increasingly integrated with agricultural supply and marketing elements in the economy. Moves are also being made whereby farmers are demanding a part in determining prices for their product. Farm management companies increase production and cut overhead costs by their farming and marketing expertise, volume purchasing and maximum use of equipment. Purchases of supplies have increased sharply; some manufacturers and suppliers have converted entirely to the production of commodities for agriculture. Direct farm product purchasing and various integrated arrangements between farms and the marketing systems have also developed rapidly.

Some Present and Future Problems

Large amounts of cultivable lands being converted to non-agricultural uses, increased costs for marginal farm land as well as problems of available labor as farms move farther into the foothills are part of these present and future problems. Problems of the "rural-urban fringe," intense competition for land and water resources; increased taxes; air and water pollution; conflicts with odors, insects and waste disposals; sources of low-cost energy; demands of various "back to nature" groups demanding access to private property, often unsupervised, that increases the already senseless vandalism and cleanup so costly to farmers; and, of course, the ever-increasing struggle between labor and unions, growers and workers.

Many agriculture editors, statisticians and arm-chair philosophers combine their vast sources of information, and trends predict an exciting change and prosperity in the next dozen years in the United States and foreign countries for those in the food business.

People are demanding and insisting on better diets worldwide, and many are able to pay either privately or by government action. Foreign populations will continue to increase, and incomes will boom. Although U.S. families will produce two children instead of three, it will result in more money to spend on specialty foods, much of it already prepared. This will and is resulting in increased agriculture specialization, larger units, yet family and/or specialized management. U.S. markets will be worldwide. The field of food and agriculture will take its rightful place in the industry instead of becoming something to be solved by government and politics. Farmers must establish firm, steady markets for exports, not just in surplus years. Foreign incomes have also soared, therefore it's better that Americans produce food for these foreign countries than for them to buy our land and produce it for themselves.

Inheritance—"Keep 'em down on the farm"

Whom do you wish to inherit your farm? Your family or government?

Farmers must face these facts now. Take just a

minute and let your mind wander over the areas of your farm, the equipment, the buildings and your plans. Who knows the little problems with the irrigation system or the part of equipment that's wearing out or the sandy or low spot where water stands better than you and your family? And what is your most prized possession? Your family. Yet, if something happened to you right now, where would your family stand? Chances are, members of your family would be faced with a heap of financial trouble with the farm you want them to inherit, along with the possibility that they might have to move. Estate planning does not result in your losing your farm or control of it, but how you own your farm may be one way that your heirs may lose both!

Present laws permit a husband or wife to leave half of the property to the survivor free from federal estate taxes. In addition, the first $60,000 of each estate is exempt. A good plan will avoid all estate taxes.

A Midwest survey revealed that 9 out of 10 farm owners would not leave sufficient liquid assets to pay settlement costs and death taxes. Twelve per cent of the cases indicated that the only way for heirs to pay the bills would have been to sell at least some of the farm assets.

Your family banker or lawyer is a good source for estate planning information. Think carefully before you make a decision. Many times heirs know nothing of their benefactors' plans; sometimes they can be very disappointed and may lose their entire inheritance because of poor arrangements by the experts. Why not talk over the package with your heirs? Making their decisions after you have retired or have passed on is not usually appreciated, profitable or even perhaps your intent.

Fruit Classification

Before one can clearly understand a science or an art, it is necessary that the terms and expressions be defined and understood. If the terms described in the following paragraphs are strange to you, plan to master them fully.

At one time agriculture was defined as the business or science of raising plant and animal products from the land. Now we must add "and from the water," and in the future perhaps, "from air and space." Agriculture is usually divided into two major fields (1) animal science and (2) plant science. Fields such as agricultural engineering, agricultural economics and agricultural chemistry serve both areas.

The plant sciences we are interested in are separated into two departments: (1) *agronomy,* which embraces the raising of field crops, including grains and fibers, and possibly cover and intercrops and (2) *horticulture* (from *hortus,* meaning garden, and *cultura,* obviously meaning culture) which takes in the raising of fruits, vegetables and ornamentals.

Chandler defines the science of horticulture as a special part of the general field of botany connected with orchard (from the English word *ort-yard*) and garden plants. But as is true with most scientific classifications, horticulture is broken down into even more specialized areas: (1) *olericulture,* the science of vegetable production; (2) *ornamental horticulture,* primarily the art of growing flowers and shrubs used to beautify the landscape; (3) *floriculture,* the operations and practices relating to the care of plants cultivated or grown for their flowers or foilage; and (4) *pomology,* the science of fruit growing. It is this last classification with which we are most concerned in this book.

Pomology (from *pome,* meaning fruit, and *ology,* meaning branch of learning) is itself divided into three types: (1) *practical pomology,* often referred to as fruit production—modern scientists refer to pomology as the "actual growing" of fruits—; (2) *commercial pomology,* primarily the marketing and disposition of fruits, including their storage, preparation for market and, in many areas, transportation to outlets; and (3) *systematic pomology,* the knowledge of plants as they grow, their distinctions and their habitat in growth.

Perhaps the most important term to be defined is the one which constitutes the basis for our study, fruit. *Fruit* is simply a ripened ovary, or the result of a fertilized flower. Fruit plants are divided into the following categories: (1) *Deciduous fruit plants* (*hardwood*) are those which drop their leaves, usually in the winter months, and go through a period of apparent inactivity or rest. These include: (a) *pome fruits*— apples, pears and quinces; (b) *drupes* (stone fruits)— peaches, plums, apricots, cherries and almonds; (c) *small fruits*—grapes, strawberries, blueberries, brambles, currants and cranberries; (d) *nut crops*—walnuts, pecans, filberts and chestnuts; (e) *miscellaneous crops* —figs, mulberries and persimmons. (2) *Evergreen fruit plants* (*softwood*) are those whose leaves remain on the trees at all times, including the dormant season. These include such fruits as oranges, lemons, grapefruits, tangerines, olives and avocados.

THE FRUIT INDUSTRY

Agriculture is a dynamic industry. Fruit production is no exception, and in many respects, it is more dynamic than many of the other segments of the agricultural sector. The fruit industry includes nut crops, citrus, avocados, bramble and vine crops and deciduous fruits. There is one economic factor to consider that is of prime importance. Generally speaking, we have enough fruit and nut crops to supply our markets, and quite often we have too much. Yet, by 1980 to 2000, we will have to increase substantially our present production to supply the projected demand. All this on the same, or possibly even less, acreage! Present and prospective farmers will help do it. A few states control much of the fruit industry. Let's look at one.

California has 100.2 million acres. Of that, 36.4 million acres is farm land, 19.0 million acres is range land, and 11.0 million acres is cropland. California has been losing 65,000 acres to non-agricultural uses per year.

California has about 1,802,000 acres in fruits (including grapes) and nuts. California grows all almonds, apricots, dates, figs, nectarines, olives, persimmons, pomegranates, prunes and walnuts that are produced in the United States to any extent. Also, nationwide, California produces 85 per cent of the grapes, 78 per cent of the avocados, 80 per cent of the lemons, 58 per cent of the peaches, 44 per cent of the pears, 65 per cent of the plums and 21 per cent of the sweet cherries.

Because of the high production of so many crops, farmers in California and other leading states set the pace in many fields.

Farmers in most parts of the United States face a number of major challenges that will require foresight, judgment and assumption. Many of these problems are in the following areas:

1. "Keep 'em down on the farm" estate planning.

2. Mechanization which will cut down unit costs and eliminate some labor problems.

3. Replacement of present trees and vines. Many of our plants are old, and some varieties have lost their demand.

4. Increase or decrease of present acreage.

5. Financing of the farm operation.

6. Type and variety of fruit to plant.

7. Increase of market outlets.

8. Growing of trees and vines in less desirable locations.

9. Farmers continually being forced into developing less productive land.

10. The good or bad of processors offering long-term contracts with minimum price guarantees, quality requirements, some specified cultural practices demanded, delivery schedules and how a product is to be harvested.

The only certainty about fruit production is that it will be characterized by continual changes. Yet farmers and businessmen in related industries must also make decisions based on changes. Some changes are for the better; others may not be.

When one thinks of fruit production there comes to mind soils, fertilizers, water, tractors, airplanes, temperature, labor, pests, trees, vines, weeds, cover crops and a vast array of other conditions and situations affecting agriculture. Fruit production exists for the purpose of supplying our human needs for food and in some cases, food by-products. The local, national and international needs are all significant.

Many fruits and nuts are shipped outside state boundaries and sold on national and international markets. With these markets clamoring for food products, the future is assured. Many persons feel they have found their place if they own or work on a good farm. Most won't emphasize a tremendous financial return but think better perhaps the personal satisfaction of doing God's bidding—for God said "Let there be trees that bear fruit and produce each after its kind" and He called this the third day. So the history of fruit goes back a "fer piece."

Farm Finance and Records

The decreasing number of farms and the expanding acreage of those farms will nearly double between 1970 and 1980. The rest of the nation's farm investments will increase also, but to a lesser degree.

Agriculture's capital requirements will continue as such forces as mechanization, technology, commercialization, growing farm size and the impact of inflation move ahead.

Lending agencies will demand positive and realistic attitudes toward farm financing. Farmers must understand and accept the necessity of supplying lending agencies adequate and accurate financial information about their operations, precise and realistic projections of yields and expense data. All farmers should adopt a workable accounting system. The farmer and lender

Fig. 1.1—Sprinkler irrigation system in operation. This approved practice is becoming a popular way of applying water in many areas.

must work together, establish a relationship of confidence, and the farmer must not forget that in many cases, the lender has more operating capital invested in the operation than he has.

To secure needed capital, farmers will have to show lenders their competence in farm technology and business management. Computers for farm managers are a must. For the family farmer it is something realistic to be looking into, perhaps on a cooperative basis with a computer oriented farm management firm in the area.

Factors in Favor of Fruit Production

1. Population growth.
2. Per capita changes:
    a. Higher real income. The price level can expect to increase gradually.

b. More use (per capita) of foods such as fruits, juices, vegetables and less of calories and starches.

3. Foreign market outlets. This is reasonably certain because it profoundly affects our balance of trade.

4. Structural changes in marketing, locally, nationally and internationally.

5. Shifts in its location of production.

6. Technological, mechanical and variety progress.

7. Well trained young men and women in related fields as well as fruit production.

8. Exports of fruit products are greater than imports.

Fig. 1.2—A mechanical nut harvester in operation. Machines such as this reduce harvesting costs and speed up the operation.

9. In general, high value crops, such as fruit crops, can out-compete hay and feed grains for use on irrigated land.

10. Private enterprise can out-produce government farms.

The steady development of fruit production through better methods, new products, promotion, equipment, technical skills, new high-keeping quality varieties, storage, market outlets, grower organizations, long-term processor contracts and marketing orders assures the fruit grower a stimulating and profitable experience.

Fruit production, which remains a basic industry in our way of life, is not asleep nor is it self-satisfied. It is making giant strides and carrying this country along with it.

The whole agricultural picture is changing rapidly and gives promise of tremendous new potential for the future, especially for the college graduate and other types of informed persons that are willing to work. There is a shortage in "source of supply" for agriculturally oriented young people. As farms get larger, there are fewer farms, and that means fewer farm families. However, there is our increasing source of young people from non-rural areas. They seek employment away from the crowded, smog-polluted cities. They are heading for the quieter rural environment and spacious recreation.

Fruit production is one agricultural field in which it is becoming increasingly difficult to learn the business by getting directly into it, or by buying a farm and learning as you go. There are too many complex problems for which the solution must be planned ahead. You will learn all right, but it will be costly.

The fact that we have fewer farmers today illustrates that we must have the best minds possible in agriculture if 90 per cent of our people are going to depend upon 10 per cent of the people to grow their food. Thus, the financial and employment opportunities in fruit production, under a carefully planned operation, will provide growers a promising future.

Factors That Determine Successful Fruit Growing

Is that farmer down the road a better grower than you? If he is, then a check list may explain why.

When all natural and psychological factors are equal, and in the same relative area, why is it that one grower is more successful than another? Inevitably the answer must lie in the decisions he makes. In order to be successful, a fruit grower must:

1. Be well informed on horticulture facts.
2. Choose a variety to fit the temperature and location.
3. Select a suitable soil.
4. Choose a crop, then manage the crop and soil properly.
5. Have most of the trees and vines of bearing age.
6. Obtain abundant yields of good quality.
7. Grow commercial varieties in demand or those having ready market. Establish himself with a market.
8. Establish sound financing.
9. Be well informed on safety (OSHA) and environmental regulations.
10. Not spend too much time in the "shade of the old apple tree"!
11. Have efficient overall management.
12. Recognize and meet changing conditions affecting his business and those relating to it.

The most successful and profitable farms are those operated by someone who invariably devotes most of

Fig. 1.3—This old, poor selling variety has been grafted to a new popular hybrid.

his attention to that operation. In studies made, nearly all successful orchards and vineyards were directed by either resident owners or experienced managers with expertise who were in almost constant attendance throughout the year.

One-Man Fruit Farms

How much orchard can one man and his family manage efficiently and make a suitable living? Some pomology economists suggest between 125-175 acres is maximum, the range depending upon the section of the United States, varieties selected and diversity of species. For example, if apples and peaches or grapes are grown on the same unit, this may be too much.

Size no assurance of success

Even though "bigness" is the trend of United States agriculture, it is the small, intensified grower who is the most successful. If he produces a high quality fruit and above average yields consistently, he will find a profitable market. However, we must keep in mind that the larger the enterprise with a given profit per acre, the greater the total profit for the fruit grower.

Specialize in a few varieties

Research has indicated that growers who concentrated on a few varieties and did an efficient job with their farms made the greatest profit. Perhaps one of the best ways to learn about farming fruit for profit is to carefully examine records from a number of growers that make money year after year. What combination of management practices made them successful? How did they differ in their operations from those that were less profitable?

It has been found by researchers that success or failure in orchards often depends upon factors closely identified with the management rather than the farm. There is a definite association between skill of management and profit, as there is between the less profitable orchard and the less skilled human element.

In 1942 Gaston of Michigan drew up a list of qualifications for a successful fruit grower. They apply as much to present day success factors as they did then. "The successful fruit grower," he said, "must be industrious, be a keen observer, a wise economizer, able to get along with employees and customers, and able to make the most of his orchard's assets, and either a good salesman or wise enough to market effectively."

MAJOR FRUIT- AND NUT-PRODUCING STATES, SHOWING RANKING OF CROPS*

State	Fruit or Nut	Rank		State	Fruit or Nut	Rank
Alabama	Figs	3		Colorado	Apples	16
	Peaches	9			Apricots	4
	Pecans	4			Cherries	10
Arizona	Grapefruit	4			Peaches	11
	Grapes	6			Pears	6
	Lemons	2		Connecticut	Pears	10
	Oranges	3				
Arkansas	Grapes	8		Florida	Figs	8
	Peaches	10			Grapefruit	1
	Pecans	7			Oranges	1
California	Almonds	1			Pecans	8
	Apples	4		Georgia	Figs	5
	Apricots	1			Grapes	12
	Cherries	3			Peaches	3
	Figs	1			Pecans	1
	Grapefruit	2		Hawaii	Macadamias	1
	Grapes	1		Idaho	Apples	12
	Lemons	1			Cherries	8
	Olives	1			Grapes	16
	Oranges	2			Pears	9
	Peaches	1			Plums	3
	Pears	1		Illinois	Apples	13
	Pecans	11			Peaches	15
	Pistachios	1		Indiana	Apples	15
	Plums	1			Grapes	15
	Walnuts	1				

(Continued)

State	Fruit or Nut	Rank	State	Fruit or Nut	Rank
Kentucky	Peaches	19		Grapes	13
	Pecans	11		Peaches	4
Louisiana	Figs	6	New Mexico	Apples	22
	Pecans	5	New York	Apples	2
Maine	Apples	17		Cherries	4
Maryland	Apples	18		Grapes	2
	Peaches	16		Peaches	17
Michigan	Apples	3		Pears	5
	Cherries	1	North Carolina	Apples	7
	Grapes	4		Figs	9
	Peaches	6		Grapes	11
	Pears	4		Peaches	7
	Plums	4	Ohio	Apples	9
Minnesota	Apples	23		Cherries	11
Mississippi	Figs	4		Grapes	7
	Peaches	20		Peaches	13
	Pecans	6	Oklahoma	Pecans	3
Missouri	Apples	20	Oregon	Apples	10
	Grapes	9		Cherries	2
	Peaches	18		Filberts	1
	Pecans	10		Grapes	14
Montana	Apricots	5		Pears	2
New Jersey	Apples	11		Plums	2
				Walnuts	2

(Continued)

MAJOR FRUIT- AND NUT-PRODUCING STATES, SHOWING RANKING OF CROPS   (Continued)

State	Fruit or Nut	Rank	State	Fruit or Nut	Rank
Pennsylvania	Apples	5		Cherries	7
	Cherries	6		Pears	7
	Grapes	5	Vermont	Apples	14
	Peaches	5	Virginia	Apples	6
	Pears	8		Peaches	8
South Carolina	Figs	7	Washington	Apples	1
	Grapes	10		Apricots	3
	Peaches	2		Cherries	5
Tennessee	Pecans	9		Grapes	3
Texas	Figs	2		Pears	3
	Grapefruit	3		Plums	5
	Grapes	14	West Virginia	Apples	8
	Oranges	4		Peaches	14
	Peaches	12	Wisconsin	Apples	19
	Pecans	2		Cherries	9
Utah	Apples	21		Filberts	12
	Apricots	2			

°There are some types of nuts, plums, apples and berries grown in limited amounts in every state.

Fruit-producing Areas of United States

Some fruits are limited to certain sections of the country; however, some kind of fruit is grown in all parts of the United States. Certain fruits grow better in some sections than others and, therefore, become more popular. Fruits such as strawberries can be found in every state whereas the commercial production of lemons is largely localized in California and that of limes to Florida. It is wise to plant the kind of fruit that is grown successfully in a particular area. However, if you have developed a special market for a particular fruit, the state experiment station will supply you with information regarding its possibilities. Often local farmers, agriculture instructors and others interested in fruit crops can give you invaluable information that will aid you in making a decision. Occasionally, fruit trees and vines are grown in areas not recommended by pomologists. Generally, these are not grown on a commercial scale and are grown locally for ornamental use and for the small amount of fruit that they produce. Some people have reasonable success with home orchards in marginal areas, and it does provide diversion and an interesting challenge to battle the elements of nature. Besides, there is no greater personal reward than to harvest one's own fruit. Is there a man, who, after picking his own home-grown fruit or making his own wine, has not invited the neighbors over for a taste and perhaps prematurely, beamed as he anticipated a resounding response to his accomplishments?

In order to emphasize the diversity of fruit-growing areas of the United States, the following table was prepared, listing certain fruits and the states leading in production. Keep in mind that a particular fruit is not always grown in all parts and locations of the state named.

FRUIT PRODUCTION, BY STATES

Pome Fruits

Apple:

Washington	New York	California
	Michigan	Pennsylvania
		Virginia

Pear:

California	Oregon	Michigan
	Washington	New York

Drupe Fruits

Apricot:

California	Washington	Arizona
	Utah	Oregon

Peach:

California	S. Carolina	New Jersey
	Georgia	Pennsylvania

Plum:

California	Oregon	Michigan
	Idaho	Washington

Cherry (Sour):

Michigan	New York	Pennsylvania
	Wisconsin	Washington

Cherry (Sweet):

California	Washington	Michigan
	Oregon	Utah

Small Fruits

Grape:

California	New York	Washington
	Michigan	Pennsylvania
		Arizona

Strawberry:

California	Oregon	Louisiana
	Washington	Michigan

Brambles:

Michigan	New York	Oregon
	Washington	Texas
		Ohio

Exports

The United States is the world's largest exporter of farm products. World exports have been rising, with fruit products showing marked increases. United States' farmers supplied one-fifth of the total volume. United States' agricultural exports required financing, inland transportation, storage and ocean shipping for 41 million long tons of cargo—enough to fill over one million freight cars or 4,000 cargo ships. In moving these exports, an average of 11 ships weighed anchor each day. For example, the little known country of Mozambique imported over $5 million in agricultural products. So did Macao! Total United States agricultural exports set new value and volume records each year.

The produce of one acre of every six harvested is

Fig. 1.4—A high quality pack of nectarines. Fruit that is to be exported must be of the best quality and harvested at the proper time.

Fig. 1.5—A high quality product, such as the grapes shown, is one reason for the increase in per capita consumption of fruit products.

exported. The output of 60 million acres of United States' cropland moves abroad.

Fruits and fruit preparations supply the second highest export value. A staggering amount moves to foreign markets, and of this less than 1 per cent value moves under government programs.

Fruit export values range roughly 20 per cent of the United States' commercial sales.

Primarily during the winter months the United

Fig. 1.6—Bulk handling of apples. One important trend is the bulk handling of fruit, which tends to lower costs and get the product to market sooner and in better condition.

Fig. 1.7—An agriculture training center. New structures, such as the one shown, demonstrate the interest in and need for up-to-date training in agricultural fields.

States imports fruits and preparations, principally from Spain, Mexico, Canada and the Philippine Islands. With proper timing and planting of varieties much of this could be absorbed by various fruit growing areas of the United States.

There is always a market for a good quality product. Fruit and fruit products will continue to contribute to both the life and happiness of people wherever they are. Fruits form a considerable part of all diets, in many countries providing all the necessary vitamins and minerals for hungry bodies. The business of supplying fruit products to the world markets provides a stimulating and profitable livelihood to a large segment of our population.

Trends

There is a gradual trend toward more consumption per capita, notably in the medium and low income groups. Fruit products are cheap, and the consumers in all brackets are more and more "diet conscious." Fruit products are replacing many agricultural products that are high in starch and fat bases. Wine is rightfully considered as a food and hopefully used so.

Fruit products are being consumed in most areas year-round. In the past, many parts of the country had certain kinds of fruit only "in season." Many families consider fruit necessary at least once a day, whereas a few years ago it was eaten only on holidays and special occasions.

Through research and promotion, fruit products will take on new forms and different methods of serving. As a result of new methods in processing, fruit products will be one of the top grocery items in all parts of the world—and why not?

The changes that have occurred in fruit production during recent years have far-reaching implications for employment. So rapidly has the production field changed in recent years, that it might be said to be a new industry. The changes in production, technology, locations, varieties and operations have created new and necessary types of job opportunities. Basically, the modern farmer is a specialist. He must have complete training in his chosen field—and this trend is now a reality. It is important that young men arm themselves with agricultural backgrounds. Vocational agriculture, 4-H and an agricultural college training will go far in helping them be successful in the business of fruit production.

Chapter

II

OPPORTUNITIES IN
FRUIT PRODUCTION

Careers in agriculture and related industries offer employment for some 40 per cent of all jobs in the United States. The fruit industries especially offer opportunities due to the shortage of properly trained men. Ample training in agriculture, the most basic industry in the world, is a must. One of the fields in agriculture offering employment for the young man is producing crops, notably fruit which includes grapes, nuts and bushberries.

Opportunities

The various fields of the fruit industry offer opportunities which are numerous and profitable as well as challenging. Perhaps no other industry in the past 10 years has gone through such rapid changes toward mechanization, efficiency and marketing.

The next century will see most of these changes perfected to meet the demands of the farmer who is conscious of mechanization. However, in fruit production, as well as other agriculture positions, one must

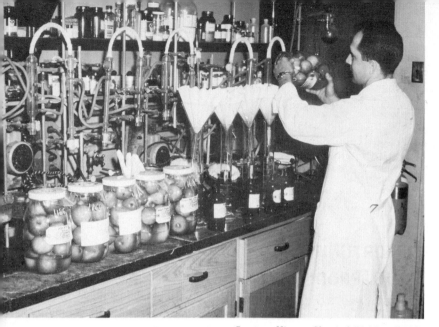

Fig. 2.1—Analyzing pesticide residues in raw agricultural commodities—apples, in this case. This person is typical of the host of persons working in fields closely related to agriculture.

apply all his ingenuity, skill and energy to do the best job he can. "A good way to succeed in life is to act on the advice you give others."

Commercial fruit grower

What can give a man more personal satisfaction and pleasure than to plan, work and harvest his own crop? Working one's own soil his own way is the goal of men throughout the world. This goal is not out of reach for anyone. It is being done by thousands of people. Whether your produce goes to fresh, processed or dried fruit markets there is the pride of knowing you are fulfilling one of the most enviable positions in the world. Getting started in fruit farming is not easy if capital is limited, but with perseverance and determination it can be done.

Diversified farmer

An increasing number of farmers raising livestock and other crops are planting part of their farms to small acreages of various types of fruits. They find much pleasure and often impressive profits in selling a few lugs of fruit to the local market. A number of young people on the farm sell produce at roadside stands and often realize an income of their own.

Part-time fruit farmer—home orchard

As our cities keep spreading to the suburban areas

Fig. 2.2—Considerable capital is necessary in order to become a successful commercial grower. New mechanical equipment like this harvester would not be practical on too small an acreage. Partnership or tenancy may be a desirable way of becoming established as a fruit grower.

it is natural that a person try his luck at a little farming at home. It offers welcome relief from the repetitious task of office or factory work. Many persons wish to retire to a little farm, and here is an opportunity to begin. With new varieties being developed to fit more climatic areas, and with an increase in the desire for urban living, this trend will continue.

Nurseryman

Nursery owners need men trained primarily in the art of caring for young plants. Budding and grafting are perhaps the most fascinating jobs in fruit culture. The ability to change nature's habits to fit our needs indeed is one of interest and skill. The fruit grower depends on reliable nurserymen for his supply of trees and often other supplies.

Ornamental horticulturist

Generally we find large nursery outlets employing pomologists to advise them on fruit culture products and to recommend fruit trees to use in landscaping many homes. A person with a background in the fruit industry could work in as a consultant while working at another job.

Fieldman—canneries and processing plants

The fieldman is one of the key personnel in the success or failure of the processing business. He must have ability to select and direct the flow of good raw fruit when it is needed. Often he is called upon to advise growers on various operations and management problems. He is indeed necessary, and companies, associations, cooperatives and corporations are constantly on the alert for the man to do the job.

Fig. 2.3—Extension agent observing application of experimental spray program. This desirable position is another opportunity to work in areas related to agriculture.

Extension service worker

Throughout the United States there is considerable employment with land grant colleges for the college graduate in fruit production. Many farmers regard the extension specialist as their final decision-maker. Perhaps no agricultural position is more respected throughout the United States than the extension specialist, often referred to as the farm advisor, who is trained to fill this important position. This is one good reason the United States is far ahead of other countries in its production of agricultural goods. If you elect to join this team, you have selected a field of dedicated tradition.

Agricultural educator

In step with the agricultural extension service you find the excitement of working primarily with young people should you decide to become a teacher of agriculture. The Smith-Hughes Law established one of the most successful methods of education known throughout the world. The Future Farmers of America has

Fig. 2.4—Teacher of agriculture demonstrating grafting to his students. Teaching is an important and gratifying way to become associated with agriculture in other than the production phase.

become a legend throughout the United States as well as many foreign countries. Many countries send their top leaders to study the vocational agriculture programs here in the United States. Nearly every state is clamoring for young men with agricultural backgrounds to enter this field. The need is critical and the position rewarding in many more ways than the salary. You will find every agriculture instructor ready to offer you advice, share his secrets of doing a good job and help you when needed.

Agricultural inspector—county, state, federal

More and more we find the quality of agricultural products being watched more closely. New pest control programs, sanitation and quality standards—all require inspection. Many counties have men that check out county shipments. Most states have border check points and federal inspection for interstate and foreign shipments. This does not always require a college degree but a background and adequate knowledge of a specific field are musts.

Fertilizer specialist

The fertilizer salesman is regarded by the farmer as a key man. His background and knowledge of the soil are a fascination and mystery to many farmers. This job is one of great responsibility and constant research. The trend to routine application of many nutrients is becoming increasingly important. The farmer depends on this specialist to make proper decisions so he will be a more successful and profitable farmer.

Agricultural chemist

In close accord with the fertilizer representative is the man who advises you on caring for the top of your plants as well as the bottom. Soil chemicals are also becoming more important in many sections of the country. Many chemicals are strange to the farmer, so it is necessary that the chemical specialist prepare thoroughly so the farmer can continue to rely on his advice. A man trained to use agricultural chemicals will find a position in many agricultural industries.

Orchard and vineyard manager

With "bigness" becoming a necessity in many parts of the United States, the demand for reliable farm managers is becoming critical. Diversified train-

Fig. 2.5—Fertilizer specialist checking the final plans. Farmers find reassurance when checking their proposed applications with the experienced specialist.

ing in a number of the fields of the agricultural industry is important. Next to owning the land, you will find the greatest satisfaction in "borrowing" the ground and growing the crops. Opportunities in management

Courtesy, Niagara Chemical Division, F.M.C.

Fig. 2.6—Not a monster from outer space, but merely an artist's conception of that destructive foe of our nation's fruit crops —the mite. The agricultural chemical industry offers great opportunity for many college graduates in agriculture.

Fig. 2.7—Fruit buyer examining fruit in the field. Much fruit is contracted prior to harvest. Quality of fruit is important in determining price.

take on many forms, and if properly prepared, you will find all segments of the industry wanting your talents.

Equipment and service contractor

Growers are relying more on equipment rentals to help them over peak periods. The high cost of having expensive equipment sitting idle for weeks or months is costly. Equipment rental and service performs a welcome relief.

Buyer-seller

With the tremendous local, state, interstate and foreign markets vying for high quality fruit products, it has become part of the industry to train people in this important segment. The demand is increasing, and it can take one to many ports of the world, and will, as different phases of the industry expand.

Other opportunities

Many additional opportunities exist including foreign service, agricultural journalism, research, farm appraisal, serving as an agricultural analyst or consultant and others, that give students ample reason for selecting a field in the production of fruit as a vocation, sideline or hobby.

Chapter

III

HOW PLANTS GROW

No one who has put a seed into the ground can help but watch with amazement and mystery the result of this simple act.

Any person who witnesses this miracle—who has seen a seemingly lifeless seed sprout, grow into a plant, mature and produce fruit, cannot help but wonder how it all happens. You will be a smarter farmer when you satisfy your curiosity about how a plant grows and produces.

Have you ever wondered about the differences that class a plant as such and an animal as such? Is there a tremendous difference between you and a plant? Certainly there is—let's look at a few of these differences.

You have a stomach to digest your food; a tree has leaves to manufacture its food. You have lungs to give clean air to your system; a tree has stomata on the bottom of its leaves to allow entry of air for its system.

In some other ways, there are similarities between the two classifications. Some plants can also move about (for example, the tumbling weed or floating algae), and circulating systems are found in plants as well as animals.

We can be glad for the small differences though, because plants make their own food, and we cannot. We must use them as our sole supply—directly as with fruit and vegetables or indirectly as the case of animal products that originally come from plants in the form of grass. Maybe it would be a good idea to study plants a little more—there is not so much difference after all!

Seed

For the most part, all fruit plants start from seed. Regardless of its size, a seed carries within its protective walls a miniature plant called the embryo. Around this tiny plant is usually a supply of food to start the plant roots down into the soil and the stem up towards the light.

The reserve food is important in many parts of the

Fig. 3.1—It is not necessary to plant many acres to observe and accumulate background into plant behavior. These three plants originated from the same source and were treated equally.

fruit industry. The almond, walnut, pecan, peanut and grain kernels are examples of the embryo's reserve food that we use as food.

Agriculture is the science of making things grow. An understanding of *how plants grow* will help you to produce good crops consistently. It is important that you understand how a fruit plant grows. All through the year you have to change well laid plans because of changes in weather, stages of growth, insect patterns and perhaps even markets. By knowing what to do, when and how, one can avoid unnecessary work, and time his decisions more intelligently.

Plant science books list over 350,000 different kinds of plants grown throughout the world and new ones being discovered in remote places. However we will pay attention primarily to the plant as it deals with factors relating to fruit trees and vines. The plant starts its life in a seed, so let's begin with it.

Seed comes to life

A combination of conditions must be present if a seed is to come to life (germinate) and fulfill nature's pattern (mature and produce). Many seeds need only to be placed in the damp warm soil to start the germination process. Some take weeks, months and even years. A number of fruit seeds appear to go through certain internal changes, after being placed in the soil, before sprouting. Many orchard farmers, for example, soak black walnut seeds in water for a week to soak up the tough shell so the sprouts can push through more easily. Some seeds will not germinate until they have been through a searing fire, others must be subjected to freezing temperature and some will not germinate until they have passed through the intestinal tract of a bird. However many of these are exceptions to the general rule. For the sake of fruit growing the following conditions are important for strong sturdy plants.

TEMPERATURE

Nearly all deciduous and evergreen seeds germinate successfully when the soil temperature is around 50°F. True, some will start under cooler conditions and some higher but we find 60°F. will start almost all fruit seeds in growth.

Most orchard trees are not started from seeds directly in the field. Some are planted for rootstock and a considerable number are planted by plant breeders seeking new varieties with some superior characteristics. Grapes are propagated vegetatively.

Mature, dry seeds of nearly all deciduous orchard varieties must go through a chilled condition before they will germinate. Stratification is the term nurserymen use when preparing seeds for chilling. The seeds can be mixed or laid in alternating layers with peat moss, sand, sawdust or other similar material, then placed in a shady, rather cool place. Moisture must be available as it is as important as chilling. Chandler, in *Deciduous Orchards,* refers to chilling as "after ripening" and goes on to say that freezing is not necessary. In many parts of the United States most seeds are frozen during the winter, but tests show many seeds germinate more evenly and with higher percentage if kept slightly above freezing. The best chilling temperature may be between 33° to 45°F. Very often the seeds from fruit that has been in cold storage for some time receive enough cold temperature to germinate. Several pome fruits, such as apple and pear, need only about six weeks of chilling. Drupes, such as plum and cherry, need close to 10 or 12 weeks. If the seeds are kept longer than the minimum time there is no damage done as long as the seeds are kept at 45°F.

or lower. Some seeds will begin sprouting above 45°F.
after the rest period is broken. Also, if seeds are allowed to dry out after their rest is broken, a high
percentage of them will not germinate.

MOISTURE

While the seed is in wet soil, it is continually
absorbing moisture. The cells are growing rapidly and
the available moisture *must* be continuous. When a
seed is growing in this manner, sudden changes in
temperature of 10° to 15° higher or lower can cause
serious setback or even death of the plant. However,
when dry, the seed can withstand very high or low
temperatures. If you plan to store seeds, they must be
kept dry and should be made so as soon as possible—
let's say promptly!

It may be of interest to compare seeds in other
fields as an illustration of the various adaptations seeds
have developed. A "hardseed" is the term used to
describe seeds that fail to germinate due to a sort of
waterproof seed coat. Several legumes, such as alfalfa
and clover, are examples. The coat can prevent the
seed from absorbing water—consequently no germination takes place. Scarification is the term used in
scratching seeds with sandpaper or other means to
allow water penetration.

OXYGEN—AIR

Just as surely as we need oxygen to start our life,
so also does a seed to germinate. A number of plant
scientists, as well as authors, have reported findings
that show that seeds planted relatively shallow, with
ample moisture, sprout stronger and more quickly than
seeds planted deep. This is perhaps because of the air
content and may also be associated with coolness of the

soil at greater depths. Some seeds planted in packed, or in water-logged soils, may never germinate because of the lack of oxygen.

Again, as in the case of moisture, some seeds develop what is known as a "gas proof" seal around the embryo. This prevents a sufficient amount of gasses (oxygen) from entering, therefore preventing germination. A number of plants develop two seeds in a case; one will not have a complete gas proof seal while the other has, resulting in one seed germinating one year and the other a year or more later—"a means of Mother Nature guaranteeing the survival of the species." Some seeds need less oxygen than others—for example, cattail, rice seeds and other water plants will germinate under water with very little oxygen.

Light

Light has an effect on some kinds of seeds but does not have any appreciable effect on fruit seeds. For example, tobacco seeds favor light, onions prefer darkness, and corn and beans germinate in either darkness or light.

Roots

The root system of fruit trees is usually considered that portion which is found underground. The roots are responsible for a number of major functions.

1.   Physical support.
2.   Storage of food materials.
3.   Providing chemical elements used by the plant.
4.   Absorption of water.

Following the life of a root can provide valuable information to the orchardist, for if the roots suffer from lack of water, nutrients, or too much water and nutrients, the orchard man must know.

As the seed is forced open by the action of the embryo, the miniature root begins to branch out into the soil. The young root, tender, and usually white, moves freely in moisture and continually sends out smaller side branches known as root hairs, seeking out chemical substances and moisture needed by the plant for survival. These small roots actually absorb these nutrients along with the water that is necessary to carry substances to different parts of the plant. It may be of interest to note that roots will not penetrate deeply into dry soil. Root hairs follow moisture but do not penetrate dry soil even if water is below. This then explains why orchards should be irrigated thoroughly so roots may penetrate subsoil and grow properly.

As roots continue to grow they take on special functions, such as anchoring the plant and continuing its absorption of chemicals and water. As they grow, they develop a covering similar to bark, but the tiny feeder root tips remain white. The type of root system, depth of penetration, and its size are influenced by heredity, soil texture and profile, fertility, water supply location and competition. Heredity is of considerable importance. For example, most apple trees do not have a good tap root but rather a branched lateral root system. The walnut will ordinarily develop a definite tap root, with a few side laterals, that will penetrate to great depths. As the main primary root develops, it produces laterals known as secondary roots. These perhaps produce more root hairs than the primary.

Drip line

The majority of feeder roots are located between the drip line and the trunk of the tree. The drip line is defined as the outside edge of the limbs around a tree.

Here the roots are assured of moisture dropping off the foliage from rain or condensed dew. Avoiding deep cultivation is a good practice in this area. Cutting off too many roots can have a damaging effect. It should be remembered that nutrients are absorbed through root tips. These tips live only a few days but others are starting to grow. A plant wilts temporarily when transplanted because many of the whisker-like root hairs have been destroyed. When replacements have grown, the plant will recover its turgidity and start growing.

The Stem or Trunk

Soon after the tiny root starts exploring the soil, there emerges from the embryo an equally tiny part of a plant, the stem, or as it is known in trees, the trunk. The trunk is defined as that portion of a plant which connects the roots or underground portion with the limbs, leaves and flowers. Man changes the form of most fruit trees that otherwise might grow straight and tall like the pine tree. He also changes the form of grapes that might send out long climbing canes. The trunk of the orchard tree is branched at a lower, convenient level by cutting or pinching off the top or terminal bud from a young tree. Regardless of the many variations in form and size, all trunks perform similar functions. They provide the physical support for the aboveground structure of the plant. A healthy trunk will transmit water and minerals from the roots to the limbs, leaves, buds, canes and flowers. It also transmits nutrients from the leaves to the roots for storage or growth. A healthy, well cared for trunk is very efficient as the plant adjusts its uptake of nutrients and water to meet the changes of its environment.

The primary branches, also known in some areas as the head, are where the first branching takes place. These scaffold branches further branch into secondaries and later produce side branches known as laterals. From these laterals develop the majority of our produce. You will note that the centers of the branches on the trunk always remain the same distance from the ground and each other. When you carve your girlfriend's initials in the bark of a tree, and receive a swift kick in the pants from someone for doing it, you may reminisce in future years, and upon returning to the tree you will find the initials still there—much wider but the same distance from the ground. Perhaps the initials don't have the romantic meaning they had when you carved them!

Leaves

Leaves are modified stems and under proper conditions manufacture food. Regardless of size or structure they consist of essentially similar layers of cells. When the leaves are exposed to sunlight, the plant gets down to work as a complete unit. Light strikes the leaves and through a complicated, mysterious process the green matter in the leaves known as chlorophyll, carbon dioxide from the air and water from the soil are converted to food for use by the entire plant. The top side of most leaves does the work of converting the elements to food. The bottom then allows entry of carbon dioxide and expels oxygen, excess water vapor and CO_2 not used during the daylight hours, through small cells that can open and close, called stomata.

Many leaves are covered with a wax-like substance, not readily seen. Closer examination will reveal the bottom side of the leaf is waxier than the top. This material aids the leaf in rejecting excess water from rain or dew. This substance is also the cause of problems in spraying. A spreader or wetting agent is added to some water sprays so insecticides will stick to the leaf.

Fig. 3.2—All parts of the plant must be healthy and in balance. Plants cannot manufacture food properly when leaves suffer as the two with obvious injury.

Scientists know there is a definite relationship in the numbers of leaves necessary to feed one fruit to maturity—around 35 in peaches. Healthy leaves in large numbers are a pretty good assurance your tree has been taken care of.

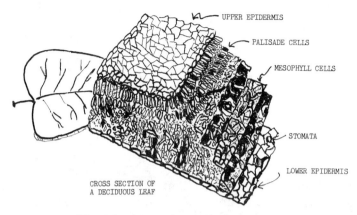

UPPER EPIDERMIS

PALISADE CELLS

MESOPHYLL CELLS

STOMATA

LOWER EPIDERMIS

CROSS SECTION OF
A DECIDUOUS LEAF

Fig. 3.3—Cross section of typical leaf.

Flowers

All fruits come from flowers—yet all flowers do not produce fruit. It may be of interest to know that every plant in your garden, with a few exceptions, will produce flowers.

The flower's primary function is to aid in the reproduction of the plant. Some flowers contain both male and female organs, and others have separate male and female flowers on the same plant, while some have male flowers on one plant and female on still another. Consequently they must be planted relatively close together to produce seeds or fruit.

The male part is known as the stamen and it produces the pollen.

The female part is known as the pistil and it produces ovules.

When the pollen is brought into contact with the tip of the stigma (top of the pistil), a chemical reaction takes place that converts the ovule into a fertile seed.

The following material about a flower may seem un-

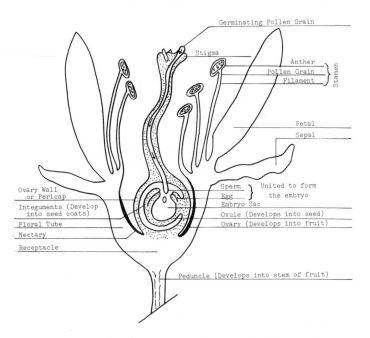

Fig. 3.4—Reproductive parts of a flower and their functions:

I. Female parts.
  A. Pistil—Central organ of the flower, consisting of ovary, style and stigma.
    1. Ovary—Enlarged basal portion of pistil which becomes the fruit.
      a. Ovule—Portion of ovary which produces seed.
      b. Egg—Actual part of ovule which unites with sperm cell to produce embryo of seed.
    2. Style—Slender column of tissue which arises from the top of the ovary and through which the pollen tube grows.
    3. Stigma—Expanded tip of style to which pollen adheres.
II. Male parts.
  A. Stamen—Flower structure, consisting of anther and filament.
    1. Anther—Pollen-bearing tip of stamen.
    2. Filament—Stalk of stamen bearing the anther at its upper tip.
    3. Pollen grain—Released from anther at proper time. Travels to stigma and releases sperm cells which travel to unite with egg through the style in the forming pollen tube. After fertilization occurs, special hormones (Auxins) are produced. The embryo quickly grows at a fast pace to form the fruit.

important. If you are to understand fruit set and further development of the fruit you will be wise to fully understand this complicated organ and its relationship to successful fruit production. Many of our management operations such as pest control and thinning are critical and necessary at this time.

Kinds of flowers

The *complete flower* contains both male and female parts, including the receptacle, sepals, petals, stamen and pistil. The sepals are called the calyx and the pistil the corolla. The stamen, known as the male part, is made up of a stalk referred to as filament and anther. The anther is at the end of the filament and is that portion of the stamen where the important pollen grains are produced.

The pistil, or female part of the plant, consists of three main parts. First from the bottom of the flower we find the ovary, which is the basal part of the pistil, then the style which is above the ovary and holds up the stigma, the top of the female portion that accepts the pollen grain.

The *incomplete or imperfect flower* has either male or female parts but not both on the same flower. When imperfect, it is called *dioecious*—a *monoecious* plant is one that has stamens and pistil-bearing flowers on the same plant. A female or pistillate flower can produce fruit but does not provide pollen for pollination.

A male flower does not develop into a fruit but is capable of producing pollen for another flower. For the most part, this type needs help from insects to complete its life cycle.

A bit of romance

The many bright colors and captivating scents attract some insects for help in pollination and reject others. Some flowers come out only in the evening or at night to attract night moving insects. However most fruit trees show their true colors during the day, the time bees are active, thereby aiding nature's romance.

Chapter

IV

FRUIT TREES, VINES AND
THEIR ENVIRONMENT

Many parts of the United States' fruit growing regions have problems with environmental factors that another area does not. Often these differences are several hundred miles away and, just as often, they may be but a few miles or even several hundred yards away.

For example, the western mountain ranges of the Pacific slope not only show variations of temperature, humidity and wind from north to south but also specific changes from east to west. Just to give the grower more problems to consider, we find environmental differences up and down.

Also, the great San Joaquin Valley of California has ample cold weather in the winter to break the rest period needed by most deciduous trees, as well as the high dry temperature in the summer to ripen the fruit to colored perfection. Yet a few miles toward the ocean, over the mountain pass, a fog belt often keeps back the layer of cold air and many deciduous fruits suffer from lack of the chilling requirement, resulting in poor fruit crops or none. However, this lack of chilling condition is desirable for citrus and avocado. The rolling

Fig. 4.1—Severely thinned peach tree. This peach tree had to be thinned severely to balance fruit set with leaves. There was poor leaf development as a result of lack of winter chill.

fog also has an air conditioning effect, holding temperature even, and causing some stone fruit and grapes to not always ripen satisfactorily as to color, texture, taste and quality.

In the southern part of this famous valley we find oranges growing side by side with trees that need lengthy periods of cold weather. Then to confuse our theories, in several areas of the San Joaquin Valley we find farmers interplanting deciduous orchards with citrus, especially in several thermal areas. However, it is obvious some environmental factors have to be changed by man. He must either apply heat to protect the crops that might freeze or apply cold to those that need it, and if necessary, plan and develop a proper wind break. So application of heat to protect crops from the frost is being done, as well as adding cold environment in greenhouse conditions in order to get plants to produce as they should.

We can either change the climate to suit the plants or grow plants that suit the climate. We do both to some extent, as mentioned before, but the fruit grower must know ahead of his venture which he shall choose.

Limiting Factors

Most pomologists consider four environmental factors essential for growing fruit. If one of the four is missing or is supplied inadequately or too much, it creates a problem. This is known as the "limiting" factor. Generally, limiting factor refers to shortage of a factor, however, an excess of any one can limit the plant's function. In some cases this can be more damaging than not enough. Taking all elements into consideration, a successful orchardist moves in accordance with the environmental forces that follow:

1. Temperature (seasonal—winter, spring, summer), also wind.
2. Soil (also nutrients).
3. Moisture (as related to soil and air).
4. Light (duration and intensity).

Temperature

Fruit trees and vines, when subjected to temperature changes, cannot "turn up the heat" if it's too cold or "expose a bare limb" if it's too hot. Since they cannot adjust the temperature directly, they can, through their processes, react to it.

All plants have their own temperature demands, winter and summer.

Winter Chilling, Rest Period and Dormancy

The above three terms are often used interchangeably. Winter chilling usually refers to conditions of the

Fig. 4.2—Delayed foliation on peaches. Lack of proper winter chill resulted in poor fruit set and straggly leaf development. Note blossom and fruit on same branch.

rest period and dormancy. However, much confusion lies with horticulturists concerning the identification of rest and dormancy—two terms of utmost importance to fruit growing.

Winter chilling: You have heard a good deal about the chilling requirement of deciduous trees. Under natural conditions chilling temperatures below 45°F. break the rest of tree buds. Following winters of insufficient chilling, deciduous trees fail to foliate normally, and the bloom may be delayed, much prolonged, and fruit set low. Though some delay in time of bloom and a moderate prolongation of the bloom period are highly desirable, extreme conditions result in difficulty in applying normal cultural operations, such as spray programs. Poor tree vigor, reduced fruit set and crop as well as bad harvest timing also result.

A special case of chilling requirement is that of the olive, where winter chilling is required to initiate blossom bud differentiation. The olive differentiates its flowers the same year they bloom rather than the preceding year. Insufficient chilling results in lack of bloom.

There are several means of experimentally breaking the rest of deciduous fruit tree buds. One or two of these may be utilized by growers, normally not as substitutes for winter chilling, but as supplements to overcome some of the more serious reactions to insufficient winter chilling. Oil sprays applied at the proper time may advance and shorten the bloom of pears, and are often applied for this purpose following warm winters. In local areas of Southern California dinitro sprays are recommended for apricots to aid in overcoming the ill effects of insufficient chilling. Unfortunately, peaches are injured by dinitro sprays applied for such purposes. The gibberellins are being investigated as aids in overcoming insufficient chilling reactions. Much still needs to be done before we can

Fig. 4.3—Peach tree injured by spray. What may help one type of fruit tree may cause injury to another. Dinitro drift caused this harmul effect on nearby peach tree.

control the reaction of the tree following warm winters. Even the methods now used must be applied at proper times to be effective. The grower needs to understand the use of oil and dinitro sprays to obtain maximum effect from their use.

Rest period: The rest period is usually spoken of when a plant is in a period of non-growth, primarily in winter months. The rest period in deciduous fruit trees and vines is controlled by internal conditions of the plants. We are more concerned with the buds in relationship to rest period than other parts of the plant although seeds and rest are of importance to the propagator.

Buds on fruit trees and vines begin forming soon after shoot growth begins in the spring. The buds to be used for next year's leaves, flowers or branches reach their desired maturity, perhaps in midsummer or later. They then stop growing and just sort of wait until next year. They now are in a period of rest. They will come out of rest only by unusual circumstances; for example, late summer pruning, or if a tree loses its leaves because of disease or pests. Some scientists call this "by-passing" the rest period. In other words, if summer pruning is done and bud growth flourishes, the bud had not yet gone into a rest period. Both internal and external conditions (temperature) must be right for renewed growth. Under normal management conditions the buds maintain their health by a minimum amount of respiration and hormone action. They also remain the same size. With winter cold beginning, activity in the plant slows down. Leaf petioles have developed an abscission (cut-off supply of nutrients to leaves) layer, and tissues harden. The leaves are falling, and the tree is approaching a state of dormancy.

Dormancy: Dormancy is that period when a plant

AMOUNT OF WINTER CHILLING NEEDED
TO BREAK REST*

Species	Approx. No. of Hours Under 45° F.
Almond	200- 500
Apricot	700-1,000
Japanese plum	700-1,000
European plum (prune)	800-1,100
Peach	800-1,200
Sweet cherry	1,100-1,300
Pear	1,200-1,500
Apple	1,200-1,500
Grape**	200

*These figures should only serve as a rough guide, as within species there are marked variations between varieties in chilling requirements. For example, in European plums (prunes), sugar prune is at the lower end of the chilling requirement and French prune is at the higher end.

Another consideration is the distribution of hours below 45°F. Periods of a few days to a week or more of mild weather will offset or reduce the effectiveness of accompanying periods of good chilling weather. Also, December and January are usually the most critical months. If each of these has about 400 hours of temperatures below 45°F., evenly distributed, no mild winter troubles are likely.

**Some grapes in tropic areas that do not go into a rest period produce less crop and poor quality.

Fig. 4.4—This grape vine is in full dormancy. Even favorable weather will not start any growth at this stage.

will not grow even if external conditions are favorable.

Now we can say the forces of rest and dormancy are both preventing the buds from growth—obviously overlapping.

In many parts of the United States and world we find early winter temperatures rising high enough for several weeks to seem favorable for growth. Yet we find our buds showing no signs of life. If the tree were not in a state of dormancy these buds would begin to grow and then be killed by the later winter frosts. Mother Nature has developed a mysterious system to prevent their growth. Both external and internal conditions of the tree must be satisfied before the buds will come to life with the first signs of spring. Often we find the rest periods of buds are satisfied but the tree is still in a dormant state and allows no growth until that certain number of hours below 45°F. has been accumulated.

Injury by Freezing

Injury to fruit trees and vines as a result of cold winter weather is inherited. However, local and temporary conditions can be important factors and must be understood for proper management decisions.

The question of "how does freezing temperature damage plants" has been discussed at length by many scientists. Most seem to agree that water freezing within cell structures and in surrounding tissues causes the damage.

Water exists in deciduous tissue in a pure state, or reasonably pure, around the cells. Being nearly pure water, it freezes at 32°F. With freezing of water there is some expansion resulting in cell damage—cells may be punctured or ruptured by ice crystals.

Water exists in other forms in the cell protoplasm.

Fig. 4.5—Freezing damage to fruit tree. Extreme winter freezing destroyed nearly all of the fruit and leaf buds on this tree.

This water is combined with sugars and salts within the cell vacuole, and is referred to as "bound" water. This "bound" water can stand much lower freezing temperatures. The less free water we have then in the plant, and the more "bound" water, the greater resistance to cold temperatures.

Another serious form of cold damage results from high, dry winds. The moisture is drawn from the tissue faster than the plant can replace it, resulting in what Christopher calls "desiccation of the tissue." Injury, in many cases, can be held at a minimum by providing available moisture in the late summer or fall through irrigation.

Experiments have shown that speed of freezing also influences damage. Pomologists have noted that a quick temperature drop from 32°F. to 25°F. can often cause more damage than the same degree drop over a longer period of time. It should be mentioned that working with frozen plants and branches, especially pruning, should be avoided, as a slight disturbance or jarring of the tree could result in ice forming instantly throughout the plant's tissue.

Most common types of freezing are typical of certain areas of the United States.

Many have heard and perhaps wondered about the loud, clear "BANG" heard in the midwestern and eastern states on a cold night after a period of warm weather. This noise is a result of the splitting of the bark caused by uneven stress of the cells.

The stress is set up when the outer layer of bark becomes frozen. The tissue inside cannot control the pressure, consequently there is a rupture of the bark and it pops open causing the bark to split up and down the tree. Generally this is not too serious as healing takes place rapidly during the spring thaw. Occasionally the split has to be treated with braces or tree seal compounds, and in some extreme cases, removed later in the summer.

The drying out injury is quite serious in many of the northern great plain states. Perhaps the most serious injury of all is the killing of fruit buds. Leaf buds are not so easily injured from freezing as fruit buds or blossoms. Freezing damage in general depends upon the stage of bud development. A nectarine bud in the midwinter dormant stage can stand temperatures ranging from 10° to 15°F. However, when the bud is beginning to grow and is in what is known as the pink bud stage, it will be injured at 25° to 27°F. The open bud will also freeze at this temperature and even at 28° and 29°F. The apple may withstand temperatures of 30° below zero in dormant state. American grapes can stand more severe winter cold than the European type.

It should be kept in mind that a continuous killing temperature will cause more damage than a brief period of the same temperature.

Winter Sun Scald

A combination of heat and cold causes the damage referred to as winter sun scald in many of the colder regions of the United States.

During a cold spell, say, zero degrees F., with the sun shining directly on the unshaded trunk or limbs, damage from sun and cold results. The sun warms up the frozen bark and inside tissues, often to the melting point of ice. After a while, the sun goes down and the bark very quickly returns to the temperature of the air with splitting, tearing and similar damage resulting. Sun scald usually does not occur if there is air, movement enough to carry away the heat generated by the direct rays hitting the bark.

Frozen "Rules of Thumb"

1. Large pruning wounds made before a severe cold spell leave surrounding tissue quite tender and may kill cells around the edge of cut.

2. Occasionally fall application of potassium or nitrogen results in freezing of parts of a plant. These fertilizers seem to obstruct the normal changes that take place in preparing the protoplasm for hardiness.

3. A large fresh wound or prune cut may cause death to bark and tissue completely around the trunk or limbs.

4. Do not cut away frozen parts until late summer or even next year. Trees and vines recover better and faster if left alone for a considerable length of time. Pulling off frozen shoots on grapes is discussed later.

5. A heavy crop tends to lower cold resistance.

6. Plants with small leaf surface are more susceptible to cold damage than those with full, healthy leaf surface.

7. Trees and vines on good soil with adequate moisture and nutrients will show a higher recovery percentage.

8. Parts nearest the foliage tend to be more resistant to cold.

9. Plants growing on soils that are poorly drained, such as clay, tend to be more subject to freezing damage.

10. Winter injury occurs when a tree or vine is dormant or not growing. Frost damage occurs when parts of the vine or tree are growing. This is the case in autumn or spring. Often much can be done to control frost, but very little in case of freezing.

11. White frost occurs when humidity is high and moisture has accumulated on foliage, limbs, etc. The "dew" has frozen, turning white.

12. Black frost occurs when humidity is low and the frozen foliage turns black.

13. Black frost may occur at temperatures higher than white frost because the moisture or dew gives a small amount of protection.

14. Roots can be damaged by severe temperatures but proper management eliminates most. There seems to be a relationship between damage of roots and fruit set.

Injury from Frost

As mentioned in Rule of Thumb No. 10, frost damage can be largely controlled, but freezing cannot.

Frost is usually associated with growing parts of the plant and its crop, fall or spring, while freezing takes place more or less when the plant is in a state of dormancy or no apparent growth, usually in winter in deciduous trees. Frosts cause some damage in the fall but the greatest economic loss is the harm done from those that occur in the spring after growth has started.

Fig. 4.6—Helicopter, a modern implement. Picture shows helicopter applying sprays to fruit trees. When temperatures fall to freezing conditions, the helicopter is put to use keeping the air circulating to aid in frost protection.

Frosts occur when the temperature is below 32°F., depending upon the stage of growth. It is relatively easy to determine frost damage to blossoms. Within a day or two the pistil of the flower turns dark. If fruit is damaged, the seed of the young fruit turns brown and soon falls to the ground. Young fruit less than one-half inch in diameter is injured more severely by frosts than during the time of opening flowers. It should be noted that the seeds or stone of the fruit causes the trouble and not the flesh. This results in the fruit falling. Some success has been achieved using sprays such as 2, 4, 5-T in keeping apricots on the tree. Damage to leaves can be seen easily 3 to 4 hours after a damaging frost. Shoot damage symptoms may not show up for several days.

Keep in mind that freezing of flowers varies among

varieties. For example, most apple blossoms will freeze more quickly than peach blossoms; yet there is more damage to peach blossoms because the peach blooms earlier.

ABOVE NORMAL TEMPERATURE

Burning of grass, leaves or brush near plants should be avoided. Bark can be killed or damaged easily from fire. Wood is also damaged from direct fire as well as other sources of heat. The appearance of the damage is the same as that of winter injury. However, winter injury will usually be on the top of limbs while fire damage will be located on the undersides of branches and the trunk next to the fire.

A saggy, peeling bark could indicate summer sun scald. Generally, this is the result of a tree producing an inadequate amount of foliage exposing bare limb areas to the sun, particularly in hot areas. Lack of adequate leaf surface could be from inadequate winter chilling, resulting in delayed foliation. However, under proper management conditions many trees can stand temperatures around 135°F. or slightly higher.

Chapter

V

ESTABLISHING THE
ORCHARD AND VINEYARD

The key to successful fruit growing is the variety selected; however, the variety must fit the location, and a proper site must be picked that offers all of the essentials necessary for good plant growth.

Activities Which Involve Approved Practices

1. Selecting the location.
2. Selecting variety of fruit to grow.
3. Selecting rootstocks if necessary.
4. Recognizing pollination effect.
5. Purchasing trees and vines.
6. Caring for trees and vines.
7. Cold storage.
8. Deciding when to plant.
9. Deciding plot plan and distances—orchard.
10. Deciding plot plan and distances—vines.
11. Preparing ground for planting.
12. Planting trees and vines.
13. Intercropping consideration.

1. Selecting the Location

A landmark like a valley usually is referred to as an orchard or vineyard location. The site is more exacting, such as a farm near a body of water or a landmark with certain elevations, topography and as many situations as possible, that exist favorable to fruit tree production. The three factors which determine the distribution of fruit growing are soil, water and climate.

Choose most suitable soil

In general, trees and vines require a deep, fertile soil, which may range in texture from sand to clay loams. The most successful soils fall into the sandy loam to loamy clay classification.

Fig. 5.1—A thorough checking of soils is important—so important that the president and vice-president of Pacific Agrilands, a California farm management company, are the observers. This backhoe will dig a hole 8 to 9 feet deep.

The ideal soil is deep, fertile, easily worked, well drained, not too heavy and free from alkali, salts and excess acid.

The best soil for a tree such as the apricot is also the best for the pear, almond, prune, plum, peach, etc.; it is also best for the grape. It is difficult to make an ideal soil from one that is lacking in any of these factors.

Fruits differ somewhat in their ability to adapt to various soil textures, and within a given planting area soil texture may determine the tree crop to be grown.

Orchards must be planted in deep (over 4-foot), well drained soil. Poor subsoils of any kind result in unsatisfactory growth. The most suitable soil is sandy loam with good organic matter content, moisture holding capacity and a pH of 5.8 to 6.6.

Supply good agricultural water

The more accurately the orchardist can regulate his water supply the more successful he will be. Securing a good agricultural water supply for satisfactory growth of plants, and in many cases, for spraying, is a must. Plants must not suffer from either drought or excess water.

Plant variety adapted to climate

Climatic factors as well as the internal or physiological factors of the trees and vines themselves largely determine the areas to grow them. The entire United States is well favored with areas of climates, soils and water for fruit production of some sort, and we have many situations to choose from. Climate conditions in detail have been discussed previously.

Fig. 5.2—A good supply of agriculture water.

Secure professional advice

The job of finding the "right" place for you may well require much time and effort. Read available circulars. Discuss the county picture with the farm advisor. Talk with growers, marketing people, real estate agents. Above all, look at enough places to obtain a basis for comparison. Consider securing professional advice, if you are totally unfamiliar with soils and trees, or if the investment is considerable. When you find the parcel you are interested in, make soil tests and check depth of soil and profile with a soil probe, or better yet, a backhoe. Evaluate at that time what has to be done as to ripping, draining, fertilizing, fumigating, irrigating or other.

2. Selecting Variety of Fruit to Grow

The grower must select fruit varieties that will bring him satisfactory monetary returns. Before too much planning takes place on an orchard or vineyard venture, the selection of a suitable fruit variety is a must.

Choose variety that brings high returns

The difficulty of making the proper choice varies from species to species. For many fruits there is a very extended list, often running into hundreds of varieties from which to choose. Canning clingstone peaches is an example.

There are approximately 25 to 30 relatively important clingstone peach varieties grown in California today. About a dozen of these enjoy a bulk of the acreage planted. The canning clingstone peach has rather rigid requirements, In some instances fruits are mixed in the cannery as they are delivered from various districts or orchards. To make a uniform product they must all be very close in their physical characteristics after processing. Varieties grown must meet these requirements.

Spread labor load

The clingstone peach industry is built upon a single price. Therefore it makes no difference to the grower whether he plants Carolyn, Loadel or Halford, to name some of the more important varieties. These varieties, although all capable of producing very excellent commercial tonnage, do differ somewhat in their average production over a period of years. On this basis of a single price each year one might expect the grower to choose the heaviest producing variety or varieties. However, this is not the case. A grower with more than a few acres of canning clingstone peaches will choose from two or three to a half dozen different varieties. The object of doing this is to spread his labor load over

Courtesy, *Union Carbide Co.*

Fig. 5.3—The proper variety of peach in a desirable location is necessary in order to produce quality fruit like these peaches.

a reasonable period. Thus he may select an early, an early-mid, mid-season, a late-mid, and a very late variety in establishing an orchard planting of any size. This then will give him a harvest period of approximately 7 or 8 weeks as compared to that of about

8 to 10 days for a single variety. In addition there will be no slack times between first and second harvest of a given variety. Thus he is able to attract and hold for a rather long period a better harvest crew. However, some areas of the United States do not have the long harvest period, and may select fewer varieties.

Choose varieties that have advantageous market characteristics

If we turn to freestone peaches, we find a multitude of varieties to choose from. Those that ripen very early will be selected by growers in the earliest maturing districts, to be grown for shipping. In later districts the grower may select a variety which has proved over the years to be reasonably profitable or to have a multiple outlet, such as Fay Elberta, for shipping or canning. Because of the relatively short life of the peach tree he may decide to take a flyer on some more recent introduction. This may prove to be a dud, but on the other hand, it may prove to have advantageous market characteristics which will bring a premium and good profits.

Choose dependable varieties

Many varieties of peaches, nectarines, almonds and plums are being introduced to commercial culture today. Even for the most promising of these, it will take many years to prove the final worth to the fruit industry. Something that looks promising today may prove to be unmarketable in a few years either through the appearance of serious faults, low production or the advent of still better varieties. To turn to the other extreme we might cite the pear and apricot industries. In both of these many varieties are available, but 85 per cent of the pears are planted to a single variety, the Bartlett, and some 95 per cent of apricots are divided between two varieties, Royal or Blenheim and Tilton. These have proven their acceptance and usefulness in multiple outlets over many years, and it would be very difficult to replace them. Another example of an industry dependent primarily upon a single variety is the prune, which has approximately 85 to 90 per cent of its total production coming from one variety, French.

The job of selecting the right variety for a specific area will require time and effort. Prospective growers should talk with producers and marketing people.

Fig. 5.4—Oak-root fungus. The use of resistant rootstock or fumigation would limit this type of injury.

3. Selecting Rootstocks If Necessary

Another decision a grower must make before he plants is the choice of the rootstock. Most varieties of fruit trees are grafted or budded on seedling plants because planting a fruit seed does not give the same fruit you started with. Grape rootstocks are easily propagated vegetatively. Fruit varieties are maintained genetically identical by vegetative propagation.

Many contradictions occur and reoccur due to wide variety of climate, soil and other circumstances. Plants in one part of the country may not respond as do similar plants in another area. However, there are some clear-cut findings for most areas, which should be followed closely. Most fruit varieties other than vines cannot be grown from cuttings, although there are a few exceptions, but must be budded or grafted upon a rootstock. If we consider only congenial combinations, choices still enter into the picture, depending upon soil structure, the prevalence of water-logged soils and soil-borne diseases. For example, Japanese plum varieties grow approximately equally well on peach seedlings, on Myrobalan seedlings, or Mariana 2624 rootstocks, the latter being a vegetatively produced hybrid stock. Peach rootstocks are extremely susceptible to damage in wet or heavily saturated soils. Therefore, under these conditions either the Myrobalan or Marianna rootstock would be preferred, as they are quite resistant to these unfavorable conditions. On the other hand, there have been developed peach rootstocks which are either resistant or nearly immune to the ravages of certain nematodes. Therefore, one of these might be preferable to, say, Myrobalan rootstock, which is variable in its reaction to nematode damage. If oak root fungus is known to be present in the soil the use of Marianna 2624 would be indicated as the preferred stock. It is highly resistant to the inroads of this

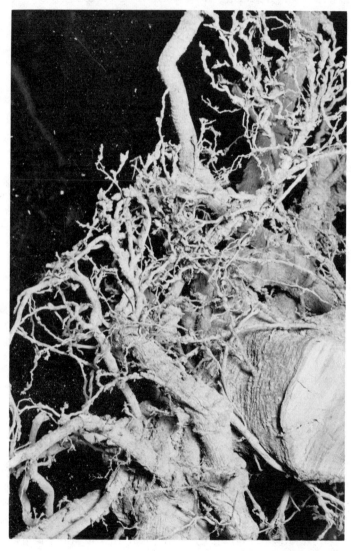

Fig 5.5—Nematode-infected peach root. Resistant rootstock would prevent the loss of this tree.

Fig. 5.6—Two-year-old Montmorency cherry trees in Oceana County, Michigan. The row on the left is growing in soil treated with Dowfume at 12 gallons per acre. The row on the right is growing in unfumigated soil.

devasting soil-borne disease, whereas both Myrobalan and peach rootstocks are susceptible.

The number of kinds of rootstocks for various fruit species differ. Though the peach may be grown upon apricot and almond rootstocks, it generally does not do well on these, and peach rootstocks are used almost 100 per cent in our commercial orchards. The peach will not grow well upon many of the plum rootstocks. Apricot, on the other hand, will grow well on peach, Myrobalan, plum, and Marianna 2624 rootstocks.

Do not replant same rootstock

Another example where the proper choice of a rootstock is important is in so-called replant situations. Some trees and vines do poorly when planted back upon land which had previously been in the same fruit crop. The most striking example of this is in the case of peaches. In this case, unfortunately, we have no suitable choice of rootstock except peach. On the other hand, we know that replanted trees in walnut orchards do much better in their early years if planted upon the Paradox rootstock than if replanted upon the more common Black Walnut rootstock.

Dwarf by use of rootstock

Sometimes rootstocks can be chosen to impart special characteristics to the growth and development of the tree. A good example of this occurs in the culture of pears. The pear is compatible, under certain conditions, with quince. However, when grown upon the quince rootstock the trees are dwarfed considerably. Therefore, a dwarfed orchard may be developed by using this root, and several orchards have been so grown. Extreme examples of the use of special rootstocks for dwarfing are known in the case of the apple and these trees are used often in landscaping around home patios.

Study characteristics of rootstocks

1. Certain varieties in all trees and vines are more resistant to certain diseases, nematodes, or even insects, than other varieties.

2. The type of rooting system of each variety varies and it is now impossible to select a rootstock that will give the best results on any given soil condition. The shallow rooted varieties are recommended for the heavy, wet soils (usually clays). The deep rooting varieties may be used in a sandy soil. Nematodes are a serious problem in sandy soil so be sure to check for their presence. Oak root fungus (Armillaria) can be a serious problem in many areas, and when it is present, you should use a resistant variety if available, or else fumigate.

3. Varieties are adapted to certain climates and do not do well in another climate. The variety which does well in one area should always be recommended first, providing all other factors are equal.

4. Certain rootstock varieties have a dwarfing effect upon certain varieties. The size of the matured

Fig. 5.7—This plum rootstock was top-worked with two different varieties. The three limbs showing overgrowth at the graft union are considered uncongenial, while the other limb is quite compatible.

plant can, to a degree, be controlled by the proper selection of the rootstock.

5. The age at which the tree or vine reaches maturity as well as the length of time it will stay in heavy production is often determined by the type of rootstock used.

6. Often the blooming time can be controlled (delayed or early bloom) by selecting a stock which requires a higher (or lower) soil temperature to break its dormant period.

7. The quality of fruit produced is also a limiting factor. Some of the rootstocks which produce the most vigorous, disease-resistant, heaviest producing trees cannot be used because they produce a low-quality or off-character product. Check carefully in selecting rootstock for table grapes.

8. Certain varieties are incompatible or uncon-

genial and may produce a bud or graft union which is weak and will allow the tree to break off in a wind. Certain other bud unions may produce heavily for years and then create a blocked passage years later, as has occurred in the citrus industry with sour root and sweet top.

9. Experiments are constantly being run on rootstocks, and a variety that is being recommended this year may be obsolete next year, or a variety that is being recommended may suddenly develop a serious problem.

10. Local conditions should be studied along with individual farm problems before any recommendations are made.

CHERRY ROOTSTOCK

Mazzard: Sixty-five per cent of the cherries in California are grafted on Mazzard. Mazzard root system is stock, and spreading in habit, with a large number of fibrous roots. The shallow rooting habit of Mazzard makes it sensitive to drought and deep cultivation. It will tolerate excess soil moisture and heavy soils.

Mahaleb: Thirty per cent of the cherries in California are on Mahaleb. It has a tendency to dwarf the sweet cherry but not to the extent that Stockton Morello does. The roots are slender and much more deeply penetrating. It cannot withstand excess soil moisture and is more adaptable to open, sandy-type soils.

Morello: Five per cent of the cherries in California are Morello. It has a tendency to be shallow-rooted, but is not easily injured by deep cultivation.

Apple Rootstock

French root: A mixture of apple seedlings was imported from France and, over a period, the parentage has mixed, and the result has become known as the French root. It is best adapted to deep loam soil.

Others: Delicious, Rome Beauty, Winesap, Yellow Newtown, Black Twig, Winter Banana and Stayman Winesap all are being used by nurserymen in the Pacific Northwest. The first three are said to be preferable from the standpoint of uniformity and vigor in the nursery. Practically all of the apple trees offered by California nurserymen are on seedling of American origin, mostly from Oregon and Washington. Experiments with seedling at various stations indicate that varieties differ in suitability as rootstock for any one variety. This leads to the conclusion that there isn't a completely satifactory apple rootstock at the present time.

Malling IX (Paradise strain): Dwarfing rootstock is used in home gardens where dwarfing is desired.

No known variety is completely resistant to wooly apple aphid.

Pear Rootstock

French pear: (Usual rootstock for California pears.) Vigorous stock unites well with all pear varieties. Grows in large variety of soils. Tolerates wet, heavy soils. (Not a water-logged soil). Resistant to oak root fungus. Susceptible to pear root aphid and fire blight. May send up sucker to become infected with fire blight. A serious problem.

Japanese pear: Has been an unsatisfactory rootstock because of black-end trouble (hardening and rounding out of the blossom end, or development of black spots in that region of the fruit).

Old Home: Resistant to pear decline. However, infected with vein yellow virus. Bartletts show up with measles.

Quince Rootstock

Hardy (Beurre hardy): Must first be grafted on the quince, then *Bartlett* grafted on the hardy. Bartlett worked directly on quince are usually dwarfish, weak at the union and tend to break off at that point.

Others: There are several other oriental species which for various reasons haven't shown much promise.

Peach and Nectarine Rootstocks

Lovell: Seedling more vigorous than the Muir or Elberta. The only other freestones used for drying whose seeds are available in large quantities.

Germination may be low in some cases. All commercial varieties of peach and nectarine are compatible.

Elberta: Nurserymen cannot work this variety so easily as Lovell.

S-37: Considered a leading stock in many areas. Outstanding resistance in nematode areas.

Nemguard: New peach rootstock. Considered completely resistant to root-knot nematode.

Shalil: Moderately resistant to nematode. May be that certain varieties do not grow so well on Shalil as on Lovell in nematode-free soil.

Apricot: Union is not always successful.

Plum: Hasn't proven satisfactory.

Apricot Rootstock

Replants in an old established orchard. Grows more vigorous. Not subject to nematode damage. Will tolerate a relatively high alkali soil content.

Some trouble with bud union when budding apricot on apricot. Will not stand excessive soil moisture. Pocket gophers seem to prefer apricot roots. Some resistance to bacteria canker.

Peach: Will not tolerate excessive soil moisture. Susceptible to oak root fungus to certain degree.

More susceptible to Pacific peach twig borer than when grown on apricot.

More susceptible to crown gall attack than either apricot or plum. May not grow as vigorous as apricot on apricot.

Plum—(Myrobalan—Mariana): Will tolerate heavy damp soils. Small percentage make poor unions with apricot. This may result in a poorer grower or cause tree to break off at bud union. More susceptible to bacteria canker than either peach or apricot. Oak root rot spreads more slowly. More susceptible to Pacific peach twig borer than apricot or peach.

Plum and Prune Rootstock

Myrobalan plum: (Fifty to seventy-five per cent of plums are on Myrobalan.) A top-notch rootstock for either plum or prune. Is not injured by root-knot nematodes. Is not so resistant to oak root fungus as Marianna 2624. Adapted to wet heavy soil (not waterlogged soils).

Peach: Nearly all prune and plum varieties do well on it.

Marianna Plum 2624: Appears to withstand oak

root fungus better than any plum root tested so far, but it will take a number of years for all tests to be brought to a conclusion.

Apricot: Many varieties do well on this in nematode-infested soils.

WALNUT ROOTSTOCK

Northern California black walnut seedling: Resistant to oak root fungus.
Susceptible to crown-rot disease.
Very vigorous grower and main rootstock used.

English walnut: Susceptible to oak-root fungus. Resistant to crown rot.

Persian walnut: Sometimes used where crown rot is a problem and oak rot isn't present.

Paradox walnut (English cross on black): Resistant to crown gall, excessive water, and somewhat to nematodes. Now can be used in quantity because it can be grown from cutting as well as seeds. Fast growing and strong.

OLIVE ROOTSTOCK

The relative success of an olive variety on its own roots as compared to the same variety growing on a seedling stock has not been determined. Thousands of *Mission* and *Manzanillo* trees grown from cuttings are excellent producers, but for some varieties, such as the *Sevillano*, seedling rootstocks are commonly used. The small-fruited *Redding* olive has been selected as stock since the seeds are practically 100 per cent viable and the seedlings vigorous in growth.

The olive has been successfully grafted on the common *lilac*, on the *ash tree* and on the *California wild olive.* The California wild olive has possible value as dwarfing stock for vigorous olives such as the *Mission*.

GRAPE ROOTSTOCKS

Do not use a rootstock if it isn't necessary. Use plants on their own roots when possible or perhaps unrooted cuttings. Rootstocks should be disbudded completely except top bud before planting.

When selecting a grape rootstock it may be necessary to select one that is resistant only partly to several conditions. Usually, however, select one recommended for the major problem.

St. George: Used to advantage in the dry, non-irrigated hillsides of coastal areas. It is highly resistant to phylloxera, produces vigorous growing vines, cuttings root readily and it is grafted or budded easily. However, it is not resistant to nematodes or oak-root fungus; and with light bearing varieties, it can result in even less production.

AXR: A hybrid, performs satisfactorily under irrigation, in deep, heavy soils. Also resistant to phylloxera but susceptible to nematodes. It produces vigorous vines of high quality fruit; cuttings root quite well and bud and graft easily.

1613: A hybrid that can be used in most all soils (except light sand) and specifically where root-knot nematodes are entrenched; moderately resistant to phylloxera; does not sucker excessively.

Dogridge: A vigorous stock native to Texas used in lighter, less fertile sandy soils. It is resistant to nematodes and moderately so to phylloxera. The cuttings root with difficulty but bud and graft readily. Suckering is usually a problem.

Salt Creek: Very similar to Dogridge in use except less vigorous and only moderately resistant to nematodes. Its use is broader, however, because of its less vigor.

Harmony: A cross between 1613 and Dogridge (U.S.D.A.). Adaptive to all except very sandy. Vines grafted to it are more vigorous than 1613 but less than Dogridge or Salt Creek. It displays more resistance to root-knot, nematodes and phylloxera than 1613 but is not completely immune to any of them. It roots, buds and grafts easily.

4. Recognizing Pollination Effect

Pollination is the physical transfer of pollen (male element) from the anther to the surface of the pistil (female element). If conditions are favorable there is a union of male and female cell resulting in the formation of an embryo (beginning of tiny fruit); this is fertilization.

Learn characteristics of your variety

Most fruit species are self-fruitful, that is, the flower is capable of producing fruit if pollen is from the same plant, variety or flower. Self-unfruitful, then, is the opposite; fruit will not be produced if the flower is pollinated only by pollen from its own plant.

Use of bees

The several thousand bees in a colony are divided into three types: the workers, male drones and usually a single adult queen.

The queen may lay 1,500 eggs per day during her busy season. The hive will average around 50,000 worker bees. It takes around 550 worker bees to produce a pound of honey. The bees fly roughly 35,000 miles, which is more than once around the world to gather material for this pound of honey.

The average worker bee lives six weeks, using half of this time gathering pollen and nectar and the other half doing housework within the hive.

As over 50 of our crops depend upon the pollination service of honey bees, they become an important part of our agricultural tools. It is conservatively estimated that crops valued at over $200 million in California alone require insect pollination—mainly the result of honey bees.

It is an accepted profitable practice to have colonies of honey bees in almond, plum and prune orchards, cherry and avocado groves as well as field and seed crops. The grower will pay $3.00 for each hive put in his orchard or field and doesn't even get the honey.

5. Purchasing Trees and Vines

Order early

Trees should be ordered nine months before planting time. Early ordering will insure good June budded trees, punctual delivery of the better grade of stock and assurance of an ample number of trees. It is important to obtain larger, better grade plants of a given age. Growers should be prepared to pay a deposit upon verification of order. One-year whips are in great demand for the following reasons:

1. Trees have proven more vigorous.
2. Trees cost less than two-year-olds.
3. They withstand transplanting and handling with less setback.
4. Trees cost less to plant because they are small.
5. Growth starts earlier on young trees.

6. Orchardist has opportunity to select young limbs for primary scaffold branches early.

Vines must be ordered early. Often a nursery will require over two years to prepare an order, as in the case of some root stocks and growing of live plants in pots. Most varieties to be planted on their own root can be obtained with less advance notice.

Order large quantities

A number of reliable nurseries also give discounts for ordering trees and vines early as well as for ordering by large numbers.

Tree sizes

Trees for transplanting are usually ordered by the trunk diameter. For example, peach trees range in size from 5/16 inch to 11/16 inch in diameter. Medium size trees are best, as previously stated, because after several years there is no difference in size of the medium and larger trees planted. Grapes in most areas also have trunk size requirements.

Check trees and vines

When the plants are delivered, check them thoroughly. Look for dried out roots, diseases, mechanical injuries and any unusual twisting or bending of the main roots. Most states have laws that enforce inspection when plants are transported from county to county. Deciduous trees, berry plants and some vines are sold as "bare-root," that is, they have no soil around the roots. Citrus and other evergreen plants are sold as "balled" or in cans, and have undisturbed soil about the roots.

6. Caring for Trees and Vines

After arrival—"heeling in"

If plants cannot be planted the day they are delivered, they should be heeled in immediately.

The least exposure to the sun and dry air may injure the "bare root" orders enough to retard growth seriously or prevent it entirely. Heeling in is placing roots in moist soil or organic matter until ready for permanent planting. Cuttings or rootings of grapes

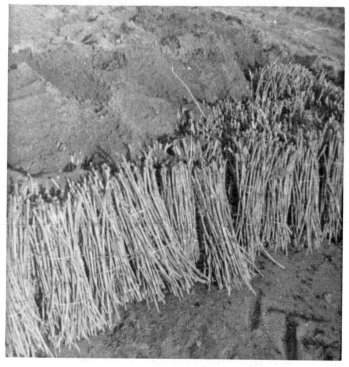

Fig. 5.8—Grape cuttings upside down ready to be covered with 8 to 10 inches of sand. After callousing, the cuttings can be planted in vineyard or nursery.

can be buried completely under 6 to 10 inches of moist, sandy, well drained soil or organic matter for several weeks.

Cover roots

Cut the bundle ties on trees and shift the soil or other material in and around the roots until they are completely covered. Piling sand too high on trunk may encourage the development of crown rot at the base of the trunk. Soaking the soil after heeling in insures enough moisture for the roots and firms the soil around them. The trench should have adequate drainage to avoid water damage.

7. Cold Storage

If weather is unsatisfactory, some growers put bare-rooted plants in cold storage for planting later in the spring. However, too late spring planting results in poorer growth. Plants which have been in cold storage must be watered as soon as they are planted. While in cold storage they should be protected from drying out with shavings, peat moss or sawdust. Under moist conditions plants can be held at 32° to 38°F.

Fully dormant plants in storage give good results; however if they are placed in storage after growth starts, the results are unsatisfactory; too long storage is not advisable.

8. Deciding When to Plant

A decision concerning the best time to plant should be based upon the local climate, type of plant and condition of the soil, also availability of water. Many areas of California prefer February plantings; the colder midwest and south have satisfactory growth with fall plantings.

Fig. 5.9—Trees waiting to grow. These trees have been graded, bunched and heeled in.

Fall plantings take more care such as rodent and animal control and preventing winter freezing and drying. However, roots do grow slightly during fall periods and give the plant an early spring start. Spring plantings take less care but are usually slower to start growth in California. Bare-rooted stock should be planted in February or March.

9. Deciding Plot Plan and Distances—Orchard

Space fruit trees in orchard according to their size when full grown

Keep in mind a fertile soil calls for regular distances such as 20' × 20', and a less fertile soil calls for planting trees more closely because they will be smaller, and more trees will be needed for good production.

Follow a planting plan

A planting plan or blueprint must be made before planting for a number of reasons.

1. Aids grower in determining number of trees to order.

2. Becomes a record of varieties and in some cases replacements.

3. Aids in planning irrigation valves, equipment use.

4. Determines turning area (headlands) at ends of rows for equipment.

There are a number of good plans for an orchard.

SQUARE SYSTEM

A few years ago the square system, trees planted an equal distance apart, was used often. This system

ORCHARD LAYOUT - STAKE METHOD

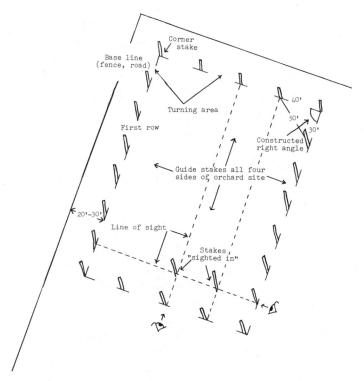

Fig. 5.10—An approved practice is to lay out the orchard properly prior to planting.

is easily worked from both directions, but has less trees per acre.

RECTANGULAR SYSTEM

Many new orchards are being prepared for future machines that will aid in cutting down the labor problems. The trees are placed closer together in the row,

Methods of laying out orchards can all be based upon the square system. Get a piece of annealed 1/8" wire and solder gobs of solder the distance that you want the trees to be planted. Measure out the distance that you want the first row of trees to be from a fence, road, ditch or similar boundary; stretch wire and place pointed lathe at every gob of solder. Square the corners by the 3-4-5 method. Stretch the wire and stake the side line. Using the side lines as guides for the ends of the wire, place a lathe at every point.

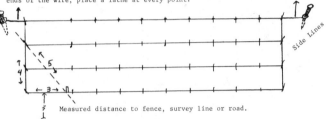

Measured distance to fence, survey line or road.

Fig. 5.11—The square system.

To lay out the Quincunx system, simply lay off the base and side lines as in the square system; but the distances down the side lines will be just one-half that of the square system. Move wire one-half distance of planting on every other row, thus:

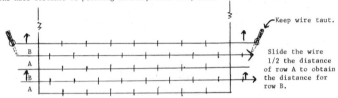

Keep wire taut.

Slide the wire 1/2 the distance of row A to obtain the distance for row B.

Fig. 5.12—The quincunx system.

To lay out the Triangular system, do the same as for the Quincunx, but with the distances down the side lines to be:

A Trees Set			B Side Line Stakes Should Be			
10 feet apart	"	"	8 feet, 8 inches			
12	"	"	10	" ,	4-2/5	"
14	"	"	12	" ,	7/8	"
16	"	"	13	" ,	10½	"
18	"	"	15	" ,	7	"
20	"	"	17	" ,	4	"
21	"	"	18	" ,	2½	"
22	"	"	19	" ,	7/8	"
24	"	"	20	" ,	9½	"

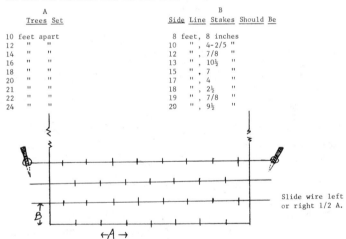

Slide wire left or right 1/2 A.

Fig. 5.13—The triangular system.

but the rows are farther apart to facilitate spraying, pruning and harvesting by machines.

Hexagonal or Triangular System

All trees are an equal distance apart in all directions if your plan calls for this system.

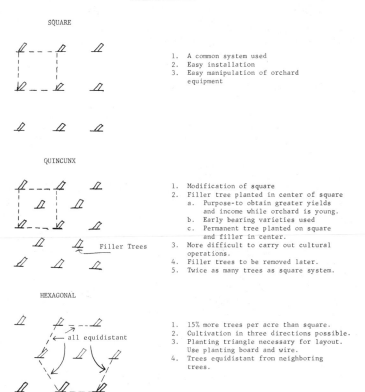

PLANTING SYSTEMS

SQUARE

1. A common system used
2. Easy installation
3. Easy manipulation of orchard equipment

QUINCUNX

1. Modification of square
2. Filler tree planted in center of square
   a. Purpose-to obtain greater yields and income while orchard is young.
   b. Early bearing varieties used
   c. Permanent tree planted on square and filler in center.
3. More difficult to carry out cultural operations.
4. Filler trees to be removed later.
5. Twice as many trees as square system.

Filler Trees

HEXAGONAL

all equidistant

1. 15% more trees per acre than square.
2. Cultivation in three directions possible.
3. Planting triangle necessary for layout. Use planting board and wire.
4. Trees equidistant from neighboring trees.

Fig. 5.14—Comparison of planting systems.

Plants per acre are determined by:

Square feet in acre (43,560)

Tree row distance across times tree row distance side
25 feet   25 feet
43,560 ÷ 625 = 69 (70) trees per acre

Plan a turning area

It is important to plan how much room you will
need to turn at the end of the field. It is becoming more
difficult and dangerous to depend on county roads, so
one should plan to use his own land. Make allowances
for large equipment as used in mechanization.

TYPICAL PLANTING DISTANCES AND PLANTS PER ACRE

Kinds Planted	No. of Plants per Acre	Planting Distance
		(feet)
Peach, plum, nectarine, pear, sweet cherry	134.0	18 × 18
Peach, plum, nectarine, pear, sweet cherry	109.0	20 × 20
Apricot, peach, plum, nectarine, pear	91.0	20 × 24
Apricot, peach, plum, nectarine, pear	90.0	22 × 22
Apricot, olive, apple, prune, fig	76.0	24 × 24
Apricot, almond, olive, prune, sweet cherry, fig, apple	70.0	25 × 25
Apple, almond, olive, sweet cherry, fig	48.0	30 × 30
Apple, walnut, olive, sweet cherry	27.2	40 × 40
Apple, walnut	17.4	50 × 50
Walnut	12.1	60 × 60
Grape	565.0	7 × 11
Grape	453.0	8 × 12

10. Deciding Plot Plan and Distances—Vines

Planting distances for vinefera (European type) grapes should be evaluated carefully. As with trees, grapes on good soils should be spaced farther apart than those to be planted in poorer soils. Also important in some areas is temperature, variety, type cultivation planned and moisture supply. Not to be ignored is spacing between rows to facilitate the use of larger equipment such as mechanical harvesters when grapes are on wire. Eleven feet between rows is the minimum distance in good soils and 12 feet should be considered adequate for maximum. Some head pruned grapes are 8′ × 10′ or 10′ × 10′.

It should be understood that the increased number of vines per acre, as a result of closer planting, is not a criteria for increased tonnage or income throughout the life of the vineyard. This may be true during the first 3 to 5 years, but thereafter added expense of trimming, pruning, dusting and other cultural practices can take away quickly what was perhaps gained for only a few years.

The distance between plants in the row varies from 6· to 10 feet. In the large, hot grape growing regions of California the distance is usually 7 or 8 feet.

Grape vines of the American type vary in planting distance as to areas. The eastern areas consider proper spacing bordering on the 8′ × 9′ spacing. Some of the older vineyards are somewhat less. Washington and other western states have plantings 8′ × 8′, 8′ × 10′ and 10′ × 10′, depending upon the various conditions mentioned for vinefera grapes. Usually American grapes in California are planted similar to vinefera.

Direction of rows

Direction of rows is particularly important when

planting grapes for the purpose of making raisins. Rows running east and west allow more sun exposure on the grapes that have been picked and placed on the ground on paper or paper trays.

Sunburn is controlled more in table grapes when rows travel in a southwest-northeast direction.

As far as wine grapes are concerned, many growers plant their rows in the direction that suits the lay of the land. Such things as source of water supply, topography of land and shape of property (to avoid short rows) are taken into consideration.

11. Preparing Ground for Planting

The ground must be prepared well in advance of planting time. The condition of your proposed site must be in as good condition as the topography of the land permits. There is no substitute for well prepared land for the new plants.

The land should be level enough to be adequately and uniformly irrigated and drained. It must not be too steep for equipment. The irrigation planned determines the degree and nature of leveling.

Uniform irrigation is important. Poorly irrigated plants show stress quickly while overwatering can cause root and crown troubles.

Subsoil

Most farm lands have what is commonly called a "plow-pan," a zone of compacted soil, 4 to 12 inches thick, just below the depth of cultivation. It is caused by years of cultivating operations, equipment moving and in some cases, compaction from animals, and prevents irrigation water from penetrating to the roots properly. Since leveling the land also compacts the soil, subsoiling to a depth of about 20 inches or more will

HEADLANDS FOR ORCHARDS

HOW TO FIGURE TURNING SPACE

1. Measure distance across field. Assume it is 208' 9".

2. Divide this distance by your planting distance. Select 25'.

$$25 \overline{)\begin{array}{r} 8 \\ 208' - 9" \\ 200 \end{array}}$$

a) This means 8 trees in a row, with 8' 9" left over.

3. To obtain enough turning area, take out one tree distance and add it to remainder.
    Thus: 25' + 8' 9" = 33' 9"

4. Divide 33' 9" by 2, in order to have some turning area on each end of the orchard.
    $\frac{33' \ 9"}{2}$ = 16' 10½" = headlands. This is ample turning distance between last tree
    and fence, road ditch, etc.

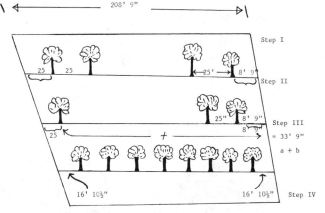

Fig. 5.15.

help break up the compaction. In case of hardpan and other soil problems, it is not uncommon for growers to rip 42 to 50 inches. Some soils may require ripping to depths of 5 to 6 feet. In specific situations growers have used a slip plow. This involves a ripper type shaft that mixes the top soil with soil down to depths of 4 to 6 feet.

If fills are made while leveling, subsoiling should be done before beginning leveling as well as afterwards.

If the fills are deeper than 12 inches, subsoiling should be done at 1-foot intervals during leveling. In some soils there may be deficiency problems if the fills are deeper than 12 inches.

Remove noxious weeds

Make sure the land is cleared of noxious weeds before planting. Dry plowing several times during the latter half of the previous growing season will sharply reduce many weeds.

Fumigate in advance

Complete any fumigating, such as for root-knot nematode or oak-root fungus, well in advance. Thirty

Fig. 5.16—Berries on the left were grown on fumigated soil. Berries on the right show disease and parasite damage.

days should elapse between planting and fumigating. Planting holes can be dug about two days before planting to allow any trapped gas to escape.

12. Planting Trees and Vines

Keep plants moist at all times

Do not allow the roots to dry out after you remove them from the heel-in trench or cold storage. Bare roots in particular dry out quickly when exposed to the sun

Fig. 5.17—Young trees soaking up some water before being planted. These roots will be in good condition.

or dry air. Keep them damp. Do not spread them over
the field near the holes to speed up planting. Take them
directly from under a protective canvas, sack or other
cover immediately before planting. Some growers like
to soak the roots in water a few minutes before planting.

Take care in planting

Bare-root plants should be planted when soil is
moist, no longer than a few days after a hole is dug.
Holes can be dug with a shovel, a mechanical post hole
digger or if need be, a backhoe. In some cases, a shank
is pulled ahead to loosen the soil before hand planting.

The hole should be large enough in diameter that
it will not cause root crowding and deep enough so that
the graft union is several inches above the ground level.
The roots should slope slightly downward in the bottom
of the hole. A hole 18 inches in diameter and 12 inches
deep is most often used for trees while a hole 16 inches
deep by 6 to 8 inches in diameter is typical for a bare-
root vine.

Planting the heat-treated (virus free) vines that
are green and growing in specially designed pots or
cylinders calls for a change in the usual planting procedure. Most pots are about 4 to 6 inches deep; cylinders are about 1 foot deep.

In the first place, the live growing plant can be
planted any time of the year. However, if planted too
late and the lower buds are not mature, they must be
covered with a few inches of soil to keep them from
freezing. The soil can be removed after danger of frost.

The hole is dug at least several inches deeper than
the thickness of the pot mixture. If the container is
plastic it must be taken off before planting, or as the
case with the cylinders or tubes, the plant is pushed out
the bottom for several inches and the side is torn open

so roots can contact soil quickly. The tube can be left in the hole. One to 2 inches of soil is spread on top of the well packed vine. Some pots are made of organic type material and are placed in the hole and covered with the plant.

Firm the soil

Roots need close contact with the soil. The best method in clay soils is to settle or firm the soil with water. In sandy or loam soils, careful packing or tamping is practiced. Adding organic matter around the roots during planting time has no particular advantage, and if done in excess, can be harmful. Adding water in any situation helps bring roots in closer contact with available soil elements more quickly.

Use of planting board helps keep straight row

Place planting board "V" at stake where tree is to be planted. Drive stakes at the ends of the board. Remove planting board and dig the hole as close to center of stakes as possible. After a satisfactory hole is dug, insert tree in the hole and carefully replace the planting board. The most heavily branched side of the tree should be placed into prevailing wind or northerly direction.

Pack gently

Place several shovelfuls of surface soil around roots and pack gently, eliminating air pockets but not injuring roots. The plant can be pulled up slightly to allow roots a downward start. Complete filling the hole and, depending on soil and condition, water or tamp. Remove planting board and leave the soil in proper condition for further care.

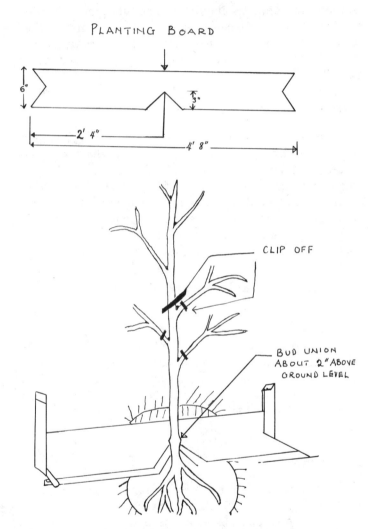

Fig. 5.18—Planting board. Use of a planting board insures that trees will be spaced accurately in a straight line and at the proper depth.

Fig. 5.19—Successful intercrop operation. These young walnuts will take a long time to grow, and the soil between can be utilized. The intercrop is planted well away from the trees.

Supports for plants

Usually trees, with the exception of walnut, do not use support such as stakes and similar type training when planted, or soon after. Grapes need supports for training. Supports will be covered when applicable.

13. Intercropping Consideration

A grower must bear in mind, when considering intercrops, that the plants are the first consideration. Intercrops should be grown only where there is plenty of good water.

Choose intercrops which do not interfere with normal irrigation and other management practices. Do not plant crops which harbor detrimental insects, nematodes, diseases, viruses or weeds. For example, tomatoes and cotton should be used sparingly as orchard intercrops because they may increase Verticillium wilt in the soil.

The first few years after the young trees are planted, beans, melons, strawberries, forage crops and others are often grown between the young trees. While this may be necessary financially, intercrops compete with the new trees for plant foods, moisture, space and cultural operations. Tree growth may slow down considerably; in some cases, trees lose one year's growth in three years of intercropping. For the most part intercrops are not grown between the 11' x 12' spacing of grapes. However beans, melons and some winter grains have been grown successfully for the first year.

Chapter

VI

PROPAGATION

Propagating, or growing, your own trees and vines can be most rewarding. However, the method selected and practice used will determine the extent of the reward. Many commercial growers depend upon nurseries for their supplies.

Activities Which Involve Approved Practices

1. Selecting propagation practices to fit needs.
2. Learning propagation terms.
3. Preparing for the grafting operation.
4. Grafting.
5. Matching cambium and stock.
6. Selecting best methods of grafting.
7. Top-working trees and vines.
8. Saving trees with bridge grafts.
9. Inarching trees.
10. Budding.

1. Selecting Propagation Practices to Fit Needs

Do not grow plants from seeds

As a rule, the use of seeds as a source of fruit

varieties, although simple and economical, is not satisfactory; the seedlings produced are usually different from the parents, especially in size, shape and quality of the fruit. In addition, the various seedlings are likely to differ from one another. This great variation, although undesirable to the plant propagator, is a valuable aid to the breeder who is trying to produce different plants. Fruit varieties that would come reasonably true from seed could be obtained by selection and breeding over several plant generations, but since each generation requires a number of years, the time necessary would be prohibitive.

Use seedlings as rootstocks

Many seedlings are used as root or understock for grafting and budding because of certain advantages in soil or vegetative propagation behavior.

Vegetative propagation is a means of producing the desired trees or vines from other parts of the plant than the seed. Vegetative propagation is the main source of grape plants.

Grow roots on part of the plant

The fruit-plant propagator must therefore use a vegetative method—that is, he must root some part of the parent plant, such as stem or root (by cuttings, layering or similar processes), or must place a part of one plant on another in such a way that it will grow (grafting or budding). Since, in vegetative propagation, a portion of the parent plant is simply growing in a different location, a plant so propagated will ordinarily be identical with the parent.

Rooting not an expensive operation

Placing a piece of branch or cane—a section a few

inches to 24″ long—in soil or in sand so that it will form roots and new branches is not difficult or expensive. This method—propagation by cuttings—is used for the quince, fig, pomegranate, grape, olive, currant, gooseberry and certain other fruits.

Expense may be necessary

Unfortunately, some of the principal tree fruits (for example, pears, apples, cherries, peaches, apricots, almonds, walnuts and most plums) are so difficult to propagate by cuttings or similar methods that these procedures cannot be followed economically under ordinary circumstances.

However, some trees must be propagated in this manner in spite of the added expense. Pears, for example, are being rooted vegetatively as a means of controlling the serious movement of the disease "Pear Decline."

Choose proper seed for tree rootstock

Many plants are propagated by first growing seedlings and then budding or grafting the desired variety upon them. The plants upon which fruit varieties are budded or grafted are called rootstocks. Seedlings are usually uniform enough for this purpose, but vegetatively propagated plants are sometimes used to secure such benefits as disease resistance and uniform vigor.

All varieties not on own roots

Many additional varieties would be propagated on their own roots by cuttings or similar methods if this procedure were possible or economical. Sometimes, however, it would not be desirable. For example, certain rootstocks now available are more resistant to

GRAFT   LOCATIONS

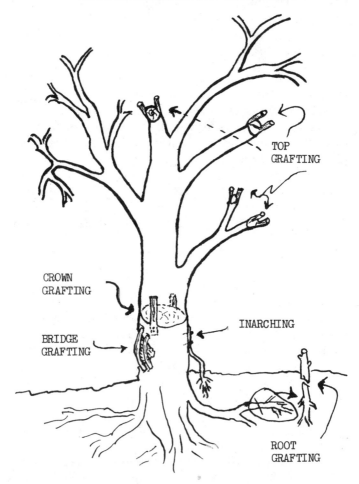

Fig. 6.1—Pictorial view of graft locations.

nematodes, diseases or adverse soil conditions than are the varieties on their own roots.

2. Learning Propagation Terms

Propagators use a number of terms that one should learn in order to understand the full meaning of propagation.

Grafting: Successful grafting involves the placing of the part of a plant, usually a twig, or short section of a shoot, upon a prepared stock. The different kinds of grafting are named according to the part of the plant on which the vegetative portion (scion) is placed.

Based on the position, there are five classes of grafting possible: root grafting, crown grafting, top grafting, bridge grafting and inarching.

As a rule, closely related plants may be grafted one upon the other. Since there are many exceptions, however, a table has been included to show the combinations possible among common deciduous fruit tree species.

Horticultural or pomological variety: An individual or group of individuals that are different from the rest of the species and whose differences can be reproduced vegetatively.

Clone or clon: A group of plants composed of individuals reproduced vegetatively from a single plant.

Cereal and vegetable variety: An individual or group of individuals that are different from the rest of the species and whose differences can be reproduced (but not identically) by seed. Seed propagated varieties change in time.

Stock: The plant or plant part upon which the scion variety is budded or grafted.

GRAFTING AFFINITIES OF SOME COMMON DECIDUOUS FRUIT TREE SPECIES

Scion	Almond	Apple	Apricot	Mahaleb Cherry	Mazzard Cherry	Stockton Morello Cherry	Peach	Pear	Myrobalan Plum	Quince	English Walnut	Northern California Black Walnut
												Stock
Almond	SC	S̄C̄	US	—	—	—	SC	ŪS	PS	—	—	—
Apple	ŪS	S̄C̄	S̄C̄	—	—	—	S̄C̄	—	S̄C̄	ŪS	—	—
Apricot	P̄S̄	—	P̄S̄	S̄C̄	S̄C̄	S̄*	S̄C̄	—	ŪS	—	—	—
Cherry	—	—	—	S̄C̄	S̄C̄	S̄*	—	—	—	—	—	—
Peach and nectarine	P̄S̄	—	P̄S̄	—	—	—	S̄C̄	—	ŪS	—	—	—
Pear	—	ŪS	—	—	—	—	—	S̄C̄	—	S̄C†	—	—
Plum (Japanese and European)++	S̄*	—	S̄*	—	—	—	S̄C*	ŪS	SC	S̄C̄	—	—
Quince	—	ŪS	—	—	—	—	—	ŪS	—	S̄C̄	—	—
English walnut	—	—	—	—	—	—	—	—	—	—	S̄C̄	S̄C̄

Courtesy, University of California

— indicates grafts that will not grow, or where growth is very weak and short-lived.

S̄ indicates satisfactory grafting affinity; SC indicates satisfactory and most commonly used in California.

ŪS indicates grafts that will grow for a while, but are unsatisfactory.

P̄S̄ indicates grafts that are partially satisfactory.

* A few varieties in these combinations do not make satisfactory unions.

† Some pear varieties, such as the Bartlett, do not make good unions with quince, although others, such as the Hardy, do. They are therefore double-worked with Hardy or with some other compatible variety.

++ In general, many European and Japanese plums may be grafted on European plums. Although many Japanese varieties do well on other Japanese varieties, most European varieties are not successful on Japanese. Peaches, almonds, and apricots may sometimes be grafted on Japanese and European plums with fair success, but as a rule they either fail to grow or grow unsatisfactorily.

Scion or cion: The portion of the plant which is topworked on the stock. If the scion is only a bud, then the operation is called budding.

Later on the scion in turn may be topworked (double worked) by budding or grafting to still another variety which is called the scion variety, in which case the erstwhile scion thereby becomes the intermediate stock; e.g., Jonathan apple as the fruit desired, Virginia Crab as intermediate and French Crab as rootstock.

Rootstock: Used to denote the portion of the tree or vine making up the root of the grafted or budded plant. The term "understock" is considered preferable because botanists use the term "rootstock" as synonymous with rhizome (an underground root-like stem).

Seedling stocks: Understocks or rootstocks obtained from seeds. Generally not used for fruit.

Clonal stocks: Understocks or rootstocks derived from the asexual multiplication of individuals. All fruit will be the same.

Propagation: The reproduction of plants by artificial or natural means.

3. Preparing for the Grafting Operation

Grafting must be planned well ahead of the actual performance. Although some methods can be accomplished at the same time, experience indicates that preparation is essential.

Collect scion wood

Scion wood is collected while dormant during the winter. In some cases it may be used immediately, but with certain methods it may be necessary to store the scions in a cool place in moist sphagnum moss, peat moss or sand. The scions and the moist material may be placed in a box, wrapped in waterproof paper or enclosed in a polyethylene plastic bag. Scion wood is selected usually from one-year growth and cut to length. The buds can be cut off and used in a budding operation.

Do not keep scions too wet

It is important not to have the moss too wet; it should release only a small amount of water when squeezed.

Store scions properly

The best place to store the scion wood is in a refrigerator at a temperature a little above freezing. However, a cool cellar or similar location is satisfactory if the storage period is not too long.

Select good scion wood for grafting

Shoots that are soft, with a large pith (central, soft portion of the stem, surrounded by the wood), should be discarded in favor of a more solid type of growth. Often the apical third, or even more, of each shoot must be discarded in order to eliminate undesirable scion wood. The precautions just discussed apply particularly to the English, or Persian, walnut. The danger of using flower buds is much less in grafting than in budding.

4. Grafting

Grafting is still considered a mystery by many people, yet it was practiced in early biblical times. Most plant scientists consider it as a necessary skill, and it can be mastered by those who develop the technique and understand a plant and conditions affecting it.

Reasons for grafting

1. To propagate by asexual means because some plants do not produce seeds. Example: Seedless orange, seedless grape, banana.

2. Grafted trees can increase hardiness. Some hardy stocks are "sandwiched" between rootstock and desired production variety.

3. Dwarfing trees. Some roots and stock create a stunting or dwarfing effect. Gardeners and home owners have created a demand for this type in landscaping. Some commercial growers use dwarf trees as fillers.

4. Grafting can help strengthen framework of trees. This can be done by adding branches or natural braces and using grafts to aid in repairing injured or diseased sections.

5. Grafting on rootstocks can improve growth habits resulting in more resistance to disease, insects and soil conditions.

6. Grafting can give one pleasure in having a number of varieties on a tree. It will also aid in pollination when pollinator is grafted on tree.

5. Matching Cambium and Stock

Match closely enough for nutrient exchange

It is essential that the cambium layers of both stock and scion match closely enough to allow nutrient exchange between the two, encouraging callus growth. Callus growth is necessary for intimate cell development at the point of operation.

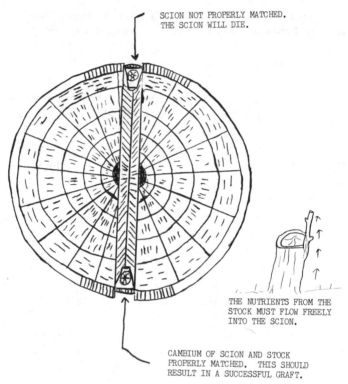

SCION NOT PROPERLY MATCHED.
THE SCION WILL DIE.

THE NUTRIENTS FROM THE
STOCK MUST FLOW FREELY
INTO THE SCION.

CAMBIUM OF SCION AND STOCK
PROPERLY MATCHED. THIS SHOULD
RESULT IN A SUCCESSFUL GRAFT.

Fig. 6.2—Matching cambiums properly.

6. Selecting Best Methods of Grafting

Root grafting

This method consists of grafting a scion 3 to 6 inches long on a whole root or a portion of a root. California nurserymen bud instead of root graft, but the root grafting method is used by some nurserymen in the Midwest mainly for the propagation of apples.

Time to Begin Operation

The rootings are dug in the fall, and the grafting is

done indoors during the winter. Since the work is carried on at a table or bench, the term "bench grafting" is sometimes used. The whip, or tongue, graft is commonly used for root grafting.

Whip, or tongue, grafting

At the base of the scion and the top of the stock, sloping cuts $1\frac{1}{2}$ to $2\frac{1}{2}$ inches long are made. The cuts should be adjusted to the size of the branches or roots being grafted; they should be longest on the pieces with the largest diameters.

STORE GRAFTS

If the work is done in winter when the nursery is too wet to cultivate, the grafts must be stored until early spring in cool, moist sand, moss or some similar material. Stored grafts will callus, and unless they are carefully handled, the partial union of the stock and scion may be destroyed. The grafts are usually planted deep enough so that only the upper bud is aboveground.

TOP-WORK YOUNG TREES

When the whip graft is used in top-working young trees, all cut surfaces should be covered with wax, except that with tape. The wax is necessary only on the tip of the scion. Tape and the stronger types of string, when used for whip grafting aboveground, must be cut, after the parts have united, to prevent constriction.

Grapes are sometimes whip grafted to phylloxera- or nematode-resistant rootstocks: the disbudded cuttings of the rootstock variety, about 12 inches long, are used.

THE LONG WHIP GRAFT

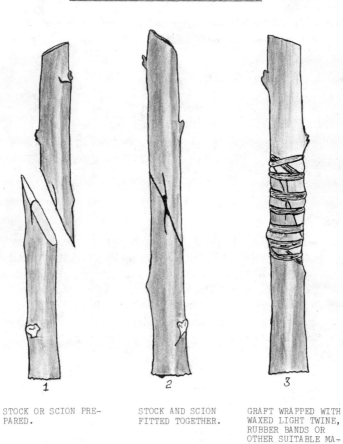

1
STOCK OR SCION PRE-
PARED.

2
STOCK AND SCION
FITTED TOGETHER.

3
GRAFT WRAPPED WITH
WAXED LIGHT TWINE,
RUBBER BANDS OR
OTHER SUITABLE MA-
TERIAL.

Fig. 6.3—The long whip graft.

Crown grafting

In this method the graft is made at or near the crown of the plant, that is, just below the surface of the ground.

CARE FOR GRAFT

After the graft union is tied and waxed, replace the soil around the base of the tree and add enough additional fine, moist soil to cover the entire scion to a depth of 1 or 2 inches. However, if walnut trees are to be planted where oak-root fungus is present, the graft union should be a foot or more above the soil surface, and the resistant northern California black walnut should be used as a rootstock. It would be difficult to place soil over a graft union this high above the ground, but without protection the grafts may be injured by the heat of the sun. A satisfactory procedure to prevent this type of injury is to whitewash the entire aboveground part of the tree, including the scion. Also the use of a tree seal material is recommended. (Persimmons are also often crown grafted in much the same manner as walnuts.)

CROWN GRAFTING OF GRAPES

Crown grafting is also practiced in changing from one grape variety to another. In this work, either the cleft graft or the notch graft is used. The graft, in some cases, is made 2 to 6 inches below the ground level and is covered with moist soil, but is not waxed. Late winter or early spring is the usual time to crown graft. The graft is also covered with fine, moist soil.

Top grafting

This is the usual method of changing from one variety of fruit to another and is an important time saver. This and top budding are generally considered together as top-working. In top grafting, scions should be placed in branches of not more than 3 or 4 inches in diameter. See Figure 6.6.

Fig. 6.4—This 10-year-old Thompson vine was cleft grafted to a wine grape variety. Sand was piled over the graft soon after the operation. The growth is six weeks old. It was up and out on the wire in late summer.

Fig. 6.5—This 12-year-old Malaga vine was notch grafted 30 inches above the ground to a vine grape variety. Graft was treated with a seal. Vineyard produced 2½ tons of grapes the next year.

WORK ON LARGE TREES

If good sized trees must be top-worked, usually the grafts are placed high where the branches are reasonably small. This procedure will be more expensive

Fig. 6.6—Top-worked walnut tree. Black walnut seeds were planted, and tree was top grafted when it was six years old.

Courtesy, California Polytechnic State University

Fig. 6.7—Agriculture class top grafting well developed, mature plum trees to a new variety. Sometimes a poor variety is ordered or the market changes. A grower can save some time by this system.

because it requires more grafts. On the other hand, trees grafted high in reasonably small branches will usually bear sooner than trees grafted close to the ground, and usually the limbs are trained where you want them. The income from this fruit will more than offset the original expense.

LEAVE SOME SMALL BRANCHES

A limited number of spurs and small branches may be left on the top-worked trees below the grafts or buds to help protect the tree from sunburn and also to manufacture some food for the roots until the grafts are large enough to take over that function.

NOT ALL OF TREE GRAFTED AT ONCE

Sometimes only part of the branches are grafted at first and the remaining ones grafted the next year.

This procedure is somewhat more expensive, but is better than cutting off the entire top at the time of grafting. This is not recommended for deciduous trees, although it can be successful. In evergreen trees, however, a few branches are often left as nurse limbs until the new tops have become well established, at which time they are completely removed.

DECIDE WHEN TO TOP GRAFT

The proper season to top graft trees or vines depends on the method used. For example, bark grafting can be done only in the early spring after the bark of the stock has begun to slip. Cleft, saw-kerf, whip and side grafting, however, may be done over a rather long period beginning in January. Even earlier grafting has been done, but is usually not advisable because of the danger that the scions may dry out.

Cleft grafting

This method of top-working trees has probably been used more than all others combined. The grafting may be done at any time during the dormant season. It may even be continued after the stock has begun to grow if the scions are kept dormant. If the work is done very early in the winter, however, there is more opportunity for the scions to dry out, especially if the waxing has not been thorough. On the other hand, most propagators believe that more scions will grow if the grafts are completed before the trees have made much growth; consequently, most cleft grafting is done in January, February and March.

DOING THE ACTUAL JOB

In cleft grafting, after the top of the tree or vine

has been sawed off, the stock branches are split down the center. Whatever type of knife is used, it is driven in 1½ to 2 inches. It is then removed and a narrow wedge is driven into the center of the cleft or the split, to hold it open while the scions are inserted. The wedge is often a part of the splitting tool.

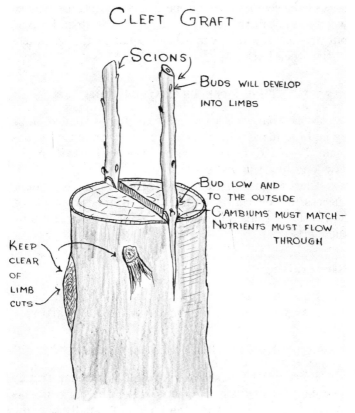

CLEFT GRAFT

SCIONS

BUDS WILL DEVELOP INTO LIMBS

BUD LOW AND TO THE OUTSIDE

CAMBIUMS MUST MATCH — NUTRIENTS MUST FLOW THROUGH

KEEP CLEAR OF LIMB CUTS

SCIONS FITTED INTO STOCK AND READY FOR WAXING

Fig. 6.8—Cleft graft with scions in proper position.

SELECT SCIONS WITH CARE

Scions 3 or 4 inches long and containing not over two or three buds are usually selected from one-year wood of the variety desired. Scions are cut wedge-shaped, with the outer edge slightly thicker than the inner. This unequal cutting insures contact between the cambium of the stock and the cambium on the outer part of the scion. Scions properly placed in thick-barked wood are not flush with the surface of the stock branch, but are set in a distance almost equal to the thickness of the stock bark.

USE MORE THAN ONE SCION

More than one scion may be placed in one stock by making more than one cleft. If more than two scions seem desirable, however, either the bark graft or the saw-kerf graft is preferred.

Cleft grafting is easily performed and may be done successfully over a rather long period. Its disadvantage, however, is that wood-decay organisms may get into the cleft.

Bark grafting

Since the stock is not split in this method, decay organisms cannot enter so easily as in cleft grafting.

BARK GRAFTING HAS DISADVANTAGES

Bark grafting is disadvantageous in that it may be done only in the early spring after the bark has begun to slip. By that time the buds are usually opening on the one-year wood that is to be used for scions, and are too easily rubbed off and unusable.

GATHER SCION WOOD EARLY

Storage of scion wood may be unnecessary in a few instances where late-leafing varieties are grafted on early-leafing varieties, the scions being taken directly from the tree and used immediately. In addition, in the olive, scion wood may be taken directly from the tree at the time of grafting. In almost all types of grafting, scion wood is gathered when it is dormant.

Various modifications of bark grafting have been described, but only three of the best will be considered in detail. If the work is carefully done, all three will give satisfactory results.

METHOD NO. 1

The bark-grafting method (No. 1) will be considered first because it is the type usually described. Although still important, it is gradually being replaced by the other two methods.

Shoulder on scion is important: The scions are usually cut as shown in figure, although slight modifications may be made, especially in the size of the shoulder. When nails are used to hold the scions in place, the only function of the shoulder is to reduce the thickness so that the stock bark will not be pushed out too far when the scions are inserted. When waxed cloth, tape or string is used to hold the scions, the shoulder perhaps helps to keep them in position. Small scions may be made with little or no shoulder, whereas large ones will require a larger shoulder than illustrated. Care should be taken, however, not to make the scions too thin, or they may be broken off after growth begins. The slit in the bark of the stock should be just long enough so that the scion can be pushed into place without splitting the bark. The scion is placed in the center of the slit.

Use nails carefully. Nails are recommended for bark grafting. As a rule, one nail is then driven through it, and one through the bark of the stock on each side of the scion. Usually an additional nail is put through the lower part of the scion. The proper size of the nails depends on the size of the scion wood, but for most deciduous fruits, except walnut, No. 20 flat-headed wire nails ⅝ or ¾ inch long are satisfactory. The large walnut scions usually require No. 19 flat-headed wire nails 1 inch long. As soon as possible after the grafting is completed, all cut surfaces, including the tops of the scions, are waxed over.

Other methods of holding scion: The scions can be held in place by waxed cloth, tape or string wrapped around the stock. These materials should be cut if they show signs of constricting the stock branch.

Method No. 2

The second method of bark grafting has been widely used, and nearly always with good results. The scions are more easily nailed in place, and there is less danger of injuring them than when the first method is used. A single slit is made in the bark of the stock, but the bark is raised on only one side of the slit. A scion cut as in Figure 6.9 is inserted under the raised bark so that one edge will rest against the undisturbed edge of the slit.

Shoulder necessary: As in the first method, a shoulder is usually necessary. The scion is held in place by two nails which pass through it and the raised flap of bark. One or two more nails are driven through the

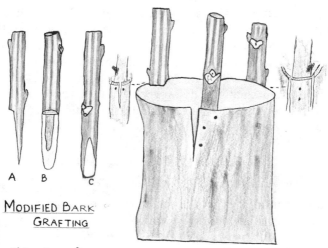

MODIFIED BARK
GRAFTING

A: Side view of SCION.
B: Side of scion that rests against wood of stock.
C: Opposite side from B.
Right: Scions in position.
Cut on scion C is not centered; bark is raised
on only one side of the slit.

Fig. 6.9—Modified bark grafts.

bark into the wood of the stock near the scion, to pull
the bark tightly into place.

METHOD No. 3

The third method of bark grafting is one in which
two slits are made in the stock, the width of the scion
apart, instead of one. These slits should be just long
enough so that the scion can be pushed into place without splitting the bark. The scions are usually cut, as
shown, without a shoulder. The strip of bark between
the two slits is raised, and the upper one third to one
half is usually removed. The scion is then inserted under the bark far enough so that only a little of the cut

surface extends above the top of the stock. Two nails hold the scion in place, the upper one driven directly into the scion, the lower one driven first through the strip of bark. The scions for this method can be prepared more rapidly than for the first two methods since there is no shoulder. However, to make the two slits the proper distance apart requires a little more time than to make a single slit.

THIRD METHOD MOST SATISFACTORY

All three methods of bark grafting have given good results, but there is considerable evidence to show that the third method, which does not require a shoulder on the scion, is the most satisfactory for the majority of grafters. In the second method, one edge of the scion rests against the undisturbed bark of the stock, whereas in the third method both edges rest against undisturbed bark. According to some, better contact of the cambiums of the stock and scion would be obtained if the bark on the edge of the scion that rests against the undisturbed bark of the stock is trimmed off just enough to expose the cambium.

The lower bud on a scion should be on the outside, only a short distance above the top of the stock.

USE RIGHT SIZE STOCK

Most bark grafting is done on moderate-sized stock. Sometimes, however, the method is adapted to small branches by making the inner surface of the scion concave (with a curved chisel), to fit around a small branch.

Saw-kerf, or notch, grafting

This method has the same advantage as the cleft

graft, in that the work can be done over a considerable period, but most notch grafting is done in January, February and March. Since the stock is not split, there is less danger from wood-decay organisms than in cleft grafting. In addition, curly-grained stock branches that cannot be split properly for cleft grafting may be notch grafted. Despite these advantages, notch grafting is less common than cleft and bark grafting because it requires considerable skill.

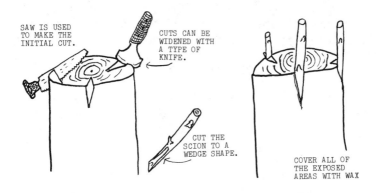

SAW KERF (NOTCH) GRAFT

Fig. 6.10—Saw-kerf grafting. A thin-bladed saw is often used to make the cuts.

Two Types of Notch Grafting

There are two types of notch grafting—deep and shallow. Nails are used to hold the scions in place in the shallow notch but are not necessary for the deep one.

First method: The one generally used, a rather deep notch extends approximately to the center of the stock. A single cut made with a fine-toothed saw is widened (to fit the scion) with the round knife. This knife has a blade that is almost the shape of a half circle; but for grafting it should be cut down to the size illustrated. The knife gives best results if one side of the blade is ground flat and the other side beveled as usual. If such a tool is not available, an ordinary grafting knife with a moderately large blade may be used. As in cleft grafting, the scions are wedge-shaped, with the outer edge slightly thicker than the inner. The cambium on this thicker, outer edge of the scion is brought into contact with cambium of the stock. The scions must be carefully but firmly driven into position, preferably with a hardwood stick about 1 inch in diameter.

Second method: The second method resembles the first, except that the notch is very shallow. The scions are usually cut with the outer edge considerably thicker than the inner and are nailed with the flat-head wire nails used in bark grafting. Again, care should be taken to match the cambiums of the stock and the scion.

Scions properly placed in thick-barked branches will not be flush with the surface of the stock branch, but will set in a distance almost equal to the thickness of the stock bark.

The lower bud on the scion should be on the outside, only a short distance above the top of the stock.

Whip, or tongue, grafting

This method, discussed under root grafting, is satisfactory for grafting over young trees or vines in which branches or young vines are the same size as the scions, or slightly larger. As in other methods of top grafting, all cut surfaces, including the scion tips, should be waxed. If tape is used instead of string, however, the wax is needed only on the scion tips. The work is usually done in late winter or in early spring.

Side grafting

This method is less commonly used than those already discussed. The graft is usually made as in Figure 6.11, but there are many possible modifications, including some that require special tools. This method is most useful for branches about 1 inch in diameter—that is, too large for satisfactory whip grafting but somewhat small for cleft, bark or saw-kerf grafting.

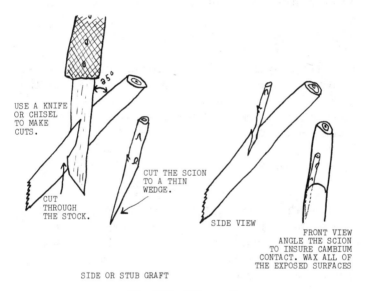

USE A KNIFE
OR CHISEL
TO MAKE
CUTS.

CUT THE SCION
TO A THIN
WEDGE.

CUT
THROUGH
THE STOCK.

SIDE VIEW

FRONT VIEW
ANGLE THE SCION
TO INSURE CAMBIUM
CONTACT. WAX ALL OF
THE EXPOSED SURFACES

SIDE OR STUB GRAFT

Fig. 6.11—Side graft.

The oblique cut in the stock is made with a chisel or a heavy knife. The scion is usually wedge-shaped, as in the cleft graft. Although the tension of the wood will usually hold the scion in place, small nails or string can be used. The stock branch is generally cut off just above the point of insertion of the scion, and all cut surfaces are waxed.

ALLOW GRAFTS TO GROW

Some workers allow side grafts to grow a year before removing the entire tops of the grafted branches, in order to save part of a year's crop while the grafts are growing, but this procedure is rarely successful.

Sometimes a side graft may be placed on the side of a rather large branch if additional branches are desired in that position.

7. Top-working Trees and Vines

The care of the tree and vine during the first few years after grafting is as important as the operation itself—a fact not commonly realized until breakage begins to occur because of heart rot, weak crotches and limbs and canes.

Use whitewash

As soon as the grafting is completed, the stock, including the scions and the waxed areas, should be thoroughly whitewashed to help prevent sunburn. However, if a water emulsion of asphalt (tree seal) is used instead of a hot wax, it must be allowed to dry before the whitewash is applied.

Use paper bags

Paper bags with holes cut in the corners to provide ventilation are sometimes placed over the grafts to protect the scions from the sun, but experiments have demonstrated that whitewash is more effective. From this time until the trees start growing, an occasional inspection and possibly some rewaxing are all that are needed.

Fig. 6.12—Care of grafts after grafting. Picture shows paper
bags covering the grafts for protection from wind, sun and
birds.

Cracks must be treated

When growth begins, however, cracks will always
appear in the wax and allow decay organisms to enter
the wood. Then the grafts must be watched carefully
and rewaxed when necessary. In those cases where
considerable rewaxing is required, it is desirable to
cover the newly waxed areas with whitewash.

Remove water sprouts

If water spouts appearing below the grafts are
allowed to grow without restriction, they will usually
choke out the grafts. This trouble may be prevented by
removing all water sprouts. A better procedure, however, is to thin them out and cut the remaining ones
back severely to keep them reasonably small. They will
then help protect the tree from sunburn and also manufacture some food for the roots until the grafts are

large enough to take over that function. The water sprouts must not be permitted to become too large.

Keep only one scion

If more than one scion is grown on a branch, probably not more than one should be retained permanently, otherwise a weak crotch is likely to be formed. The branches to be saved should be pruned as lightly as possible to encourage rapid growth, and those that will later be removed should be pruned heavily to keep them from becoming too large. The

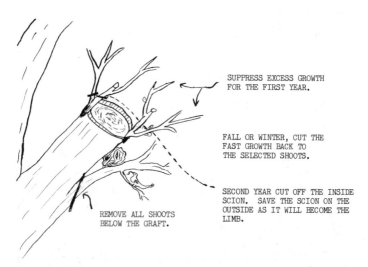

SUPPRESS EXCESS GROWTH FOR THE FIRST YEAR.

FALL OR WINTER, CUT THE FAST GROWTH BACK TO THE SELECTED SHOOTS.

SECOND YEAR CUT OFF THE INSIDE SCION. SAVE THE SCION ON THE OUTSIDE AS IT WILL BECOME THE LIMB.

REMOVE ALL SHOOTS BELOW THE GRAFT.

Fig. 6.13—Training of grafts after growing starts.

suppressed branches help to heal over the stub, and are removed when that purpose is accomplished.

If only one scion grows, the square shoulder on the opposite side of the branch will die and probably decay before healing over. More rapid healing will take place if a sloping cut is made downward and away from the side where the scion is growing. The cut surface should be thoroughly waxed.

Support fast-growing grafts

Often young grafts, especially of walnuts, need to be supported with laths or strips of wood for a few years. If grafts of stone fruits, such as apricots and plums, grow extremely fast, and the use of supports is considered uneconomical, then the best procedure is to pinch off a few inches at the ends of the grafts after they have grown about 18 inches. Later pinching back may also be desirable. This treatment slows down the growth enough to allow the succulent shoots to mature somewhat and thus keeps them from breaking or bending. Some of the shoots may be thinned out to reduce wind resistance. Grape shoots should be tied on a stake when 12 to 14 inches long.

8. Saving Trees with Bridge Grafts

Each year many trees are partly or completely girdled by rodents, blight, mechanical injury or frost. Often the tree or vine can be saved by bridging over the injured area. In the early spring, as soon as the bark will slip, scions are inserted into the live tissue above and below the wound. It is best to gather the scions while they are still dormant as mentioned previously, and store them.

Cut scions at both ends

The scions are cut wedge-shaped at both ends, but the cut on one side is only about half as long as that

Fig. 6.14—A friend in need. The old peach on the right was leaning over too far and was ready to fall. Seeds were planted on the left and right front, and seedlings then inarched. The tree has continued bearing satisfactorily.

on the opposite side. The wedge-shaped ends are then inserted under the bark so that the longest cut surface is next to the wood. Two slits are made in the bark to receive the scion, in the manner described for one of the methods of bark grafting. The scions are then nailed into place. If they are made slightly longer than the space to be bridged, they will bow out slightly, and the flat cut surfaces will rest squarely against the wood of the stock.

Wax bridge grafts

The part of the graft where the scions are inserted under the bark must be waxed over. Preferably, the exposed wood in the girdled area should be covered with wax or some of the materials used on pruning cuts, but this is often not done. Remove all buds that start to grow on the scions.

9. Inarching Trees

Inarching is a method whereby two plants are made to unite while growing on their own roots. With fruit trees, a young seedling is generally planted beside an older tree and grafted into the trunk. The usual procedure is to remove, from the trunk of the larger tree, a strip of bark as wide as the seedling trunk and 4 to 6 inches long, and then to lay the seedling trunk in this slit. The vertical cuts are best made with the round knife.

Prepare the trunk

About half of the part of the seedling trunk that lies next to the wood of the tree should be cut away to insure contact of the cambiums. Usually, in order to make the union more certain the end of the seedling is cut wedge-shaped, as in bark grafting, and shoved under the bark at the top of the slit.

Secure the inarch

The seedling should then be nailed into place, and the cut surface waxed. Some of the shoots that appear on the inarches should probably be saved for the first growing season, but they must be suppressed by pinching back their tips. After the union is well established, all shoots should be removed. The work described is best done in the early spring as soon as the bark of the injured trees will slip.

Uses of inarching

Inarching may be successfully used to save trees in which roots have been damaged by blight, gophers or other injury. If the tree has simply been girdled and the roots are alive below, bridge grafting is the best method.

10. Budding

Budding is the placing of a single, detached bud upon a plant called the stock. This method is used by the nurseryman to propagate his plants, and sometimes by the grower to change to another variety. Budding is a form of grafting, except a single bud is used instead of a section of a branch, shoot or twig. Budding is the more common method used in stone fruit, citrus and vines.

Select a method of budding

Some of the names given to methods of budding are based on the time of year in which the work is done. Spring budding is usually done in March or April; June budding in May or the first half of June; and late summer or fall budding in July and August or a little later. Other names used are based on the method of cutting and inserting the bud, such as sheild budding, patch budding, T budding, chip budding and other less important methods. In all these processes, success depends upon joining the cambiums of the stock and the bud.

Choosing season for budding

Budding, although usually done in July and August, may be continued into September and October, until the bark cannot be lifted.

Select Material at Proper Time

The budwood is collected from the current season's growth at the time the work is done, but may be stored a short while if kept cool and moist. The buds are placed either in trees that have grown from seeds planted in the spring of the same year, or, with apples, pears, and sometimes cherries and Myrobalan plums, in trees lined out in the nursery row in the spring. Grapes are usually budded on rootstock planted in the field.

Time to Bud

About the time growth starts in the spring after budding, cut back the top of the seedling rootstock to about ⅝ inch above the bud (that is, just above the crosscut of the T or top of the patch). Usually this cut slopes downward from the side where the bud is located. Remove all water sprouts appearing below the bud. The trees are dug in the winter after the buds have grown one season. Grapes remain in the field in growing position.

Fall budding popular: Late-summer or fall budding is the most important method used for deciduous fruit trees, although in recent years June budding has been used considerably to propagate some kinds of fruit trees.

June budding can be done in May: June budding may be done in May or in the first half of June. Some have made it a regular practice to propagate a considerable number of trees by this method.

June Budding Procedure

The usual procedure is to cut off the seedling top 2 to 5 inches above the bud three or four days after budding. Leave at least one leaf above the bud, and several below. It may be necessary to bud as much as 8 inches above the ground in order to have a sufficient number of leaves below the bud. These rootstock leaves help to manufacture food for the tree until the leaves produced by the bud are large enough to take over this function. Make a cut back to the bud 10 to 16 days after budding. Thereafter, any shoots other than those from the bud should be shortened, and when the bud has grown into a shoot 6 to 8 inches high and has enough leaves of its own, remove all other leaves and shoots.

Collect budwood from current growth: The budwood is collected from the current season's growth at the time of budding. As a rule, all the wood is removed from the bud shield except a small core in the bud. The easiest way to do this is to make the long cut, and then, at the upper end, to make a cut through the bark only, rather than through both bark and wood. The shield may then be removed with a sliding motion, and the wood remains attached to the bud stick.

Keep small core of wood attached: If the shield is pulled rather than slid from the bud stick, the small core of wood may become separated from the bud itself, and the result often is failure.

Peach seedlings most often used: Seedlings must grow rapidly in order to be large enough for budding in May or in the first half of June. Because the peach best meets this requirement, most June-budded trees offered for sale are on this rootstock. Nurserymen list various varieties of June-budded peaches, nectarines, almonds, apricots and plums.

June-budding generally is feasible only in regions which have a long growing season.

Spring Budding in the Nursery

The work is begun early in spring, as soon as the

METHOD OF CUTTING THE JUNE BUD

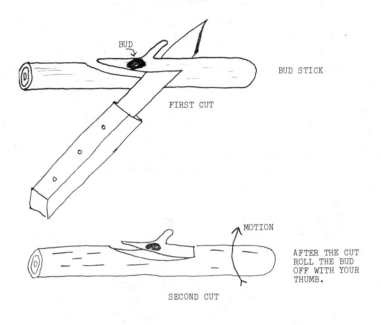

BUD

BUD STICK

FIRST CUT

MOTION

AFTER THE CUT
ROLL THE BUD
OFF WITH YOUR
THUMB.

SECOND CUT

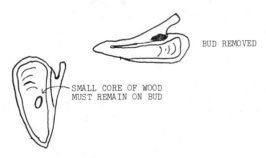

BUD REMOVED

SMALL CORE OF WOOD
MUST REMAIN ON BUD

Fig. 6.15—Method of cutting June bud.

bark of the stock slips easily from the wood and allows
the buds to be inserted, and should be completed before the trees have made much new growth. This will
usually be in March or April, depending on the kinds
of trees and the season. As a rule, the bud sticks are
collected in late winter, while dormant, and are stored
in moist sphagnum moss, peat moss or sand, in a cool
place. They can be used for T, or shield, budding without further treatment.

Treat Patch Budding Differently

For patch budding, however, the bud sticks must
be transferred to a warm location and kept there until
the bark will slip from the wood. By that time a few
buds will have started to grow. These cannot be used,
but others will be in good condition. Bud sticks for
patch budding may also be cut directly from the tree at
the time of budding, a practice thought by many to be
the best. When this method is used, bud sticks on which
part of the buds have started to grow are cut from
the trees. Some buds will be in the right condition, that
is, they will still be almost completely dormant, and yet
the bark of the patches can be separated from the wood
of the bud sticks—a requirement of patch budding.

Treatment After Budding

About two weeks after budding, the tops of the
stocks are cut off to force the buds into growth. The
next winter, after the buds have grown one season,
the trees are dug and sold. They are then essentially
the same as the one-year-old trees produced by late-
summer or fall budding.

This method is usually less satisfactory than late-
summer or fall budding, and should be used only for

trees that were not successfully budded during the fall, or in some other special cases.

SELECT BUDWOOD CAREFULLY

Buds for late-summer or fall budding and June budding should be taken from the current season's growth of the specified tree at the time of budding, but for work in the spring, dormant branches are usually selected and stored until needed. Although it is probably best to choose bud sticks that have leaf buds (wood buds) only, many propagators use clusters containing both leaf and flower (fruit) buds.

Choose leaf buds: Do not use flower buds exclusively, because these blossom and die. In plums, apricots, peaches and walnuts, a leaf bud usually occurs at each node or joint, either alone or associated with one or more flower buds. A single flower bud is occasionally found on the bud sticks of these species, but not often enough to cause the propagator much concern.

Difference between leaf and flower buds: Leaf buds are usually smaller and sharper-pointed than flower buds. Pear, apple and almond bud sticks often have a number of single flower buds near the apical end. (In the pear and apple, these are really mixed buds, but usually respond the same as ordinary flower buds.)

In all the fruit tree species discussed above, more leaf buds will generally be found on the most vigorous shoots. The danger of using flower buds can be greatly reduced by avoiding the shorter, less vigorous type of growth.

POSITION BUD

Budding is usually done as near the ground as convenient, but northern California black walnut stock, which is resistant to oak-root fungus, is often allowed to extend a foot or more above the surface of the ground. Other kinds of resistant rootstocks are commonly budded several inches above the soil surface.

Buds are usually inserted on the north side of the seedlings for protection against the sun during healing.

South Side of Trees Budded

In the hot interior valleys of California, however, where summer north winds are common, some propagators prefer to bud on the south side of the tree to prevent drying out of the bud, even though this practice may increase the possibility that the growing bud may be broken off by wind. There is another point in favor of the south side: After the bud has started growth, the short section of seedling trunk on the side below the bud is less subject to sunburn than is the side opposite the bud. Therefore, less injury will occur if the more resistant side is placed on the south. Not only is sunburn in itself serious, but the damage caused by it is often followed by the entrance of flat-headed borers.

Selecting method of budding

T, or Shield, Budding

This is the method most commonly used for deciduous fruits, except the walnut, pecan and grape. With some plants, better results have been reported when the wood has been removed from the buds, but with deciduous fruits this is done only when June budding is practiced and when (in a few instances) T budding is used for walnuts and persimmons.

STEPS IN MAKING THE T-BUD
(SHIELD BUD)

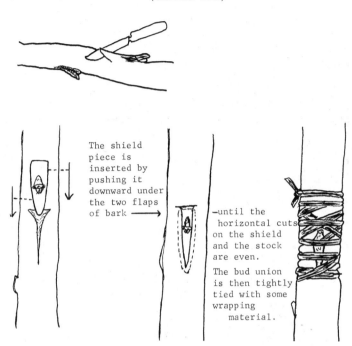

The shield
piece is
inserted by
pushing it
downward under
the two flaps
of bark ⟶

—until the
horizontal cuts
on the shield
and the stock
are even.

The bud union
is then tightly
tied with some
wrapping
material.

Fig. 6.16—T, or shield, budding.

PATCH, OR FLUTE, BUDDING

This type of budding is commonly used in propagating thick-barked trees, such as the walnut and pecan. A square or rectangular patch of bark is removed from the seedling and replaced with a similar one that includes the bud desired. This latter patch is slid rather than pulled from the bud stick so that the small core of wood in the bud itself will be retained. If the bark of the stock is thicker than that of the budwood, the stock bark must be pared down so that the patch can be tied firmly in place.

Fig. 6.17—Patch budding.

SELECTING PROPER WRAPPING MATERIAL

The usual wrapping material is waxed cloth or budding tape. String and rubber bands are not recommended because they are less effective in preventing drying out. Waxed cloth, budding tape or string should usually be cut in two or three weeks. If the stock is making very vigorous growth, however, it may be necessary to cut the wrapping material in about 10 days to prevent constriction. In cutting these materials it is best to make the cut on the side opposite the bud.

Do Not Use Ring Budding

Ring, or annular, budding is the same as patch budding except that a complete ring of bark is removed around the stem. This method is slower and has no particular advantage.

Chip Budding

In budding small grapevines, more consistent results have been obtained with chip budding than with other common methods. Rootstock rootings that are resistant to phylloxera or root-knot nematode or used for vigor in weak soils are planted in the vineyard in the spring and are budded the following August in non-irrigated vineyards, and September in irrigated ones. For good results, the buds must be taken from mature canes in which bark color has changed to brown. In addition, the stock must be growing actively at the time of budding.

Top Budding

Budding is done mostly by nurserymen to propagate their plants, but is also used by the fruit grower who wishes to change his trees over to another variety. The only differences between orchard procedure and that followed in nursery work are that the buds are inserted higher in the tree, usually in the branches, and late summer or fall budding is often done earlier. This earlier budding in the orchard is generally necessary

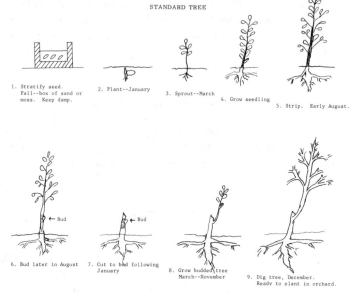

Fig. 6.18—Standard budded tree.

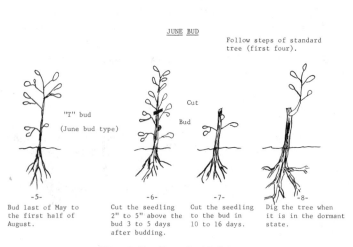

Fig. 6.19—June budded tree.

because the trees cannot be kept growing so vigorously in the field as in the nursery, and it is impossible to lift the bark later in the season.

Avoid large limbs

Fairly large limbs may be budded, but with difficulty. If old trees are to be budded, they are usually cut back the winter before in order to force out new branches in which to place the buds. It is usually best to top-bud only young trees and to use some method of grafting for the larger branches in older trees.

Chapter

VII

CULTURE

Most successful commercial growers practice some type of cultivation with two main objectives:

1. Plant responses to cultural practices.
2. Conservation of the soil.

Neither objective should be planned separately from the other because trees and vines respond directly to both. The more favorable the condition of the soil, the less problems of culture. It must be remembered that there is no one best system for all orchards and vineyards. However, listed below are some essentials that may fit most:

Activities Which Involve Approved Practices

1. Selecting cultural practices.
2. Practicing non-cultivation.
3. Using cover crops.
4. Choosing type of cover crop.

1. Selecting Cultural Practices

Use sod in some areas

Sod management cover crop is defined as a system

of soil management where plants are grown in soils without tillage of any kind. However, chopping grass may be necessary. If you select sod as your practice, you should apply adequate nitrogen.

Growing trees and vines in sod (grass) has certain advantages:

Fig. 7.1—Well managed sod culture in a young apple orchard. The grass is kept fairly short—4 to 6 inches.

1. It retards or prevents erosion from wind and water.

2. Land between rows is in better condition for many spring, summer and winter operations.

3. Color of fruit in eastern areas is more desirable.

4. Cultivation is easier in rocky or steep areas.

5. Chopping grass is less expensive than disking.

6. Often a balance can be developed between predators and pests to advantage. However, a disadvantage is also possible.

Choose Sod on Sloping Areas

There has been an increase in orchards and vineyards on slopes going into a sod type of culture. This has come about through the use of sprinkler or drip irrigation. Formerly these soils were irrigated by allowing very small streams of water to run down the slopes at rather widely spaced intervals. Under such a regime the soil was never evenly irrigated, and the small stature and yield of the trees and vines were evidence of this.

However, sprinkler and drip irrigation can be used on the slopes very successfully, especially when cover crops are grown to control soil erosion. These types of irrigation also result in a much more even and adequate irrigation. In turn, this gives larger plant growth, greater productivity and better size and quality of the resulting fruit.

Watch Sod Culture Closely

Some studies show orchards may begin to decline after sod becomes too thick. Many growers now plow, or turn it under in some manner, and re-seed as soon as sod becomes too heavy.

Use mulching in some areas

Mulching is a cultural practice that is successful in specific soil conditions. Mulching consists of organic material, such as hay, straw, corn, some animal and poultry wastes and tree products that is spread beneath a tree or vine. Mulching is good, but has limitations. The advantages often are overcome by disadvantages. A grower must decide by careful observation and make his decisions carefully.

ADVANTAGES

Growers find mulches tend to conserve moisture as well as increase the soil's ability to absorb moisture through the physical change caused by mulching. Others maintain a certain amount of nutrients are made available, and mulching also aids in erosion control. Soil temperatures are more constant, and a thick mulch will aid in "dropped fruit" being less damaged.

DISADVANTAGES

Nearly all areas using mulch materials report pests find this operation makes a fine home and hiding place for them and much to their liking. Rodents, for example, can cause serious damage to trees and vines, as well as irrigation ditches.

Nitrogen ratio in the soil must be watched because hay, straw and other organic matter demand nitrogen in their decaying process, thus causing a temporary deficiency in the soil.

Obtaining and putting the mulch around the trees and vines 2 feet from trunk and to skirts of tree) can be expensive, even when much of the material is readily available.

Fig 7.2—Natural cover crop. Orchard operations continue while the natural cover crop is growing. Later grass is plowed under.

Select clean culture

This practice favors temporary tree growth. Under a clean culture system many growers allow a natural or planted cover crop to grow during winter months and turn the crop under with various equipment in the spring.

Control of all weed and grass growth is continued during summer months.

2. Practicing Non-cultivation

Use with citrus

Non-cultivation has been widely adapted in the citrus orchards of central and southern California. Attempts to establish this regime in deciduous orchards have been generally successful, and there are instances where it appears to be an acceptable procedure. Experimentation is continuing in regard to the application of non-cultivation in many areas. During the first few years of establishing a non-cultivation practice, the costs of weed control usually exceed the alternative cultivation costs. However, after a period of a few years it should show an overall reduction in the cost of orchard operations. Grape growers have shown new interest in non-cultivation, and this will increase. However, this also means more use of chemicals around trees and vines for weed control.

3. Using Cover Crops

Cover crops are good for some soils and bad for others. Individual soils must be given an analysis.

Any crop grown between the plants and turned under may be considered a cover crop, even if it is a weed that volunteers. Such crops affect the problem of fertilization and the plants' response to fertilizers.

Types of cover crops

Annual cover crops may be divided into four groups: winter legumes, summer legumes, winter non-legumes and summer non-legumes.

WINTER LEGUMES

Among winter legumes, the most widely grown are bitter clover or annual yellow sweet clover, the vetches, and bur clover. Horse beans, fenugreek, lupine, and field peas have been successful in more limited areas.

Fig. 7.3—Two and one-half tons of oat hay was harvested from this cover crop. Note the trees are healthy. Adequate nitrogen should be added to help decay remaining stubble.

SUMMER LEGUMES

The following crops have had some use as summer legumes: cowpeas; velvet, mung, tepary and mat beans; soybeans; sesbania; and Hubam clover.

WINTER NON-LEGUMES

The most widely used winter non-legumes are: mustards (common, black and Trieste) and cereals (rye, oats and barley), together with some varieties of volunteer weeds.

SUMMER NON-LEGUMES

Where summer non-legumes are desired, orchard grass, Sudan grass and certain summer-growing weeds have proved satisfactory.

4. Choosing Types of Cover Crop

Choose cover crop for organic matter

The first objective in planning a cover crop is the addition of organic matter, not only as a source of nitrogen that will be released over a long period in the soil but also as a major factor in maintaining good tilth, or soil structure. With continuous cultivation, organic matter tends to disappear. It can be restored either by bringing it in from other sources, such as human and animal wastes, cereals or grasses or by growing it in place and working it into the soil. Manure or other suitable material is not often cheap enough to warrant the use of adequate amounts. In many orchards the growing of cover crops has tended to replace manuring. However, in recent years, farmers have been competing for treated human wastes that are high in nitrogen and other essential elements.

Measure effect on soil structure

It seems certain that in many soils water penetration is better after a few years of cover crops. The action of cover crops in improving water penetration may lie in either of two zones. One is the prevention of "surface sealing" which occurs in some soils when they are wet. The other is the improvement of the compacted layer below the depth of cultivation known as the plow pan or plow sole. At the University of California at Davis, for example, the latter effect was so great that the water from a 6-inch irrigation disappeared from the surface of a cover cropped basin in less than 24 hours, whereas, across a levee in an adjacent, clean, cultivated check, the time required was more than a week.

Fig. 7.4—Working a cover crop into the soil.

Manage properly to eliminate problems

More economical use of water and a better supply to the roots will result in the absence of plow pan. The use of cover crops is not, however, a substitute for careful soil handling. Cultivation when the soil is too wet will puddle many soils so badly that years of good care may be required to repair the damage. Good soil structure can be developed, moreover, and maintained without cover crops if sufficient care is taken to avoid compaction. Whenever such care is impossible because the soil is too wet, cover crops may be of great benefit.

Water penetration can be helped

A distinction should be made between the improved soil-water relations resulting from better penetration, and those from increased water-holding capacity of the soil. Under cool, humid conditions the soil's organic matter can be increased by annual cover crops, and with it the total nitrogen and, perhaps, the water-holding capacity. Under hot, semiarid conditions, this is not the case. The rate of destruction of organic matter is so great that there is little, if any, net accumulation.

Nitrogen increases with legumes

Much the same situation exists with regard to total nitrogen as with moisture-holding capacity. Leguminous cover crops with proper inoculation of nitrogen-fixing bacteria have given increases of total nitrogen in cool, humid sections. There probably was some fixation of nitrogen, but either it has been used, and therefore does not appear in analyses, or the amount is too small to be detected.

Cover crops should be considered in sandy soils

In sandy soils, where heavy rains might leach nitrate below the root zone, the absorption of this solution by the cover crop, with later release as the crop rots after being turned under, may save measurable amounts for use by the plants.

Cover crop steals nutrients

When organic material is incorporated into the soil most of it is decomposed by soil bacteria and fungi. These organisms, like other plants, need mineral nutrients for their growth and functioning. During the first part of the period of decomposition, the soil microorganisms increase in number, and may use nitrate from the soil solution as well as nitrogen from the decaying cover crop. The nitrate concentration is there-

Fig. 7.5—A well planned cover crop in sandy soil can save nutrients from disappearing during the winter season.

by reduced in the soil solution, leaving less for the plants. Strawy material, high in carbohydrates and low in nitrogen, may cause a depressed nitrate level for months after being turned under. However, mowing or chopping cover crop and leaving it on top to decay slowly does not use nitrogen noticeably.

Apply fertilizer to bulky cover crop

Any tendency toward nitrate deficiency in a soil will be much increased by the incorporation of large amounts of low-nitogen organic matter. Additional amounts of fertilizer will then be needed to supply both the soil organisms and the plant. Cover crops, furthermore, absorb nitrate while growing, and during that period may compete seriously with the tree or vine. An attempt should be made to correlate the timing of the growth of the cover crop with the fertilizer program and with the needs of the tree or vine.

Use cover crops on slopes

Cover crops may play an important role on slopes that are subject to erosion or in sandy areas where wind causes blowing sand. On slopes they increase the rate of water penetration, thus reducing runoff, and their roots tend to hold the soil in place, reducing the amount washed down by the water that does flow away.

Select crop with fast-growing roots

A crop to be used for erosion control must be one that establishes a root system quickly throughout the surface soil, unless a permanent sod is already established. Various crops of this type have been tried in most districts, and information about their use can be obtained from the local farm advisor.

Do not use cover crops in low moisture areas

Despite the advantages to be obtained from cover crops, they can be harmful in certain soils. Non-irrigated trees and vines in regions of low rainfall need all the moisture available to take them through the season. The use of any considerable portion of the supply by cover crops may result in failure to mature the fruit and during very dry years may cause severe damage to the trees or vines.

Fig. 7.6—This vineyard is under clean culture. The brush (prunings and grass) has been chopped with a brush chopper. French plowing or chemicals (between vines) and disking down the rows will be forthcoming.

On the other hand, cover crops growing in soils of high water holding capacity can be an advantage in drying out soils more quickly if such is desired.

Turn under cover crop early

Any cover crops used in light rainfall areas must be turned under early enough so that the late winter rains will restore the water used by these plants in the early winter. Under these conditions, large tonnages of cover crops cannot be expected, and conditions may keep the grower from turning the crop under in time to prevent some moisture depletion. The increase in rate of moisture penetration and the decreased loss by run-off may compensate for the water used when the practice has been carried on long enough to be effective. Since cover cropping must be practiced for several years before water penetration can be noticeably improved, this is still a hazardous program in non-irrigated areas.

Cover crops often inducive to disease spread

The growers of stone fruits have found a higher incidence of brown rot in orchards having cover crops at blossoming time. Generally speaking, if you have time and you believe your operations could be helped, try a cover crop. If it improves your overall situation—profit-wise included—a cover crop is recommended.

Chapter

VIII

PRUNING AND TRAINING

Pruning is an essential practice wherever profitable fruit is grown. It requires a thorough understanding of fundamentals such as the parts involved, growth cycle, bud growth, bud differentiation, effects of pruning, training, heading back and thinning out as well as winter, spring and summer pruning.

In addition to these general factors it is necessary that we have specific knowledge of the species or variety at hand. Pruning practices vary according to individual fruiting habits. However, a number of species are basically quite similar.

Pruning is like learning to swim—"once you learn the fundamentals you increase your skill with practice."

Activities Which Involve Approved Practices

1. Understanding the importance of pruning.
2. Deciding when to prune.
3. Deciding which species to prune.
4. Using pruning equipment.
5. Pruning young trees and vines.
6. Pruning bearing trees and vines.
7. Pruning grapes.
8. Treating pruning wounds.

Fig. 8.1—Nicely spaced primary scaffold. Framework such as this is not an accident. Understand the tree and its responses; then apply the proper skill at the right time as a learned and necessary practice.

Fig. 8.2—Breakage caused by poorly spaced primary scaffolds. Branches placed in this manner generally result in tremendous breakage and loss.

1. Understanding the Importance of Pruning

Pruning is the scientific removal of surplus or undesirable growth at the proper time of year to encourage new growth. Training includes some pruning to obtain the desired shape of the tree. Reasons for pruning:

1. To guide and control the growth of the fruit plant (height, shape, etc.).
2. To improve quality, color and size of fruit.
3. To insure a quantity of fruit.
4. To insure fruit bud differentiation for future years.
5. To facilitate cultivation, insect control, harvesting, etc.
6. To restore a balance between root and top growth.
7. To set a balance between growth and fruit production.
8. To remove injured, unncessary and diseased sections of the plant.

A good pruning practice can eliminate many undesirable natural growth patterns, and when done properly, takes advantage of the desirable qualities.

2. Deciding When to Prune

Prune during dormant period in moderate climates

This is often referred to as the time between leaf fall and bud swelling in the spring. However, prune when you have to, winter or summer.

Prune in spring in freezing climates

Some orchards are pruned in spring or at the

beginning of bud swell because of the freezing injury to fall or early winter pruned plants.

Avoid pruning early in freezing climates

In severe freezing climates, pruning in November and December is considered more hazardous than pruning later in the dormant season. However, it is often necessary when other orchard operations interfere, and pruning must be done even if timing is not to your liking.

3. Deciding Which Species to Prune

Pruning is an essential operation done during the winter, summer or spring period. All fruit species benefit from pruning, and for most it is essential for production of adequate crops. Peaches, apricots, grapes,

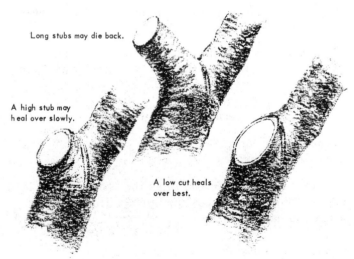

Long stubs may die back.

A high stub may heal over slowly.

A low cut heals over best.

Courtesy, University of California Extension Service

Fig. 8.3—Cut limbs close.

Fig. 8.4—Pruning during dormant period. Pruning does not have to be a "foul weather job." It is evident that the above trees are in a dormant state and the weather is pleasant.

plums, pears, apples, all require annual pruning for satisfactory commercial production. Many growers do prune lightly or remove dead wood only on apples and pears. The pruning of prunes or almonds may be done every other year, but annual pruning to some degree is recommended for these crops also. However, the pruning of mature orchards of almonds and prunes is usually accomplished more cheaply than for the fruits mentioned earlier by reason of limiting pruning cuts to larger sizes as these two species require less wood removal each year. Sweet cherries and some walnut orchards are pruned but infrequently, and then the pruning consists only of cutting out larger, older branches which have become diseased, or have died, or which are interfering with the growth of other portions of the tree. Older walnut trees require relatively little pruning at best. However for some varieties, such as the Franquette, a rather detailed pruning of older trees may be quite beneficial in invigorating the tree, resulting in stronger growth and greatly improving production.

Annual pruning necessary for production

For those fruits such as the peach, apricot, grape and shipping plums annual pruning is required and is quite severe. A large portion of last year's shoot growth is removed each season. This results in greatly increased growth of the remaining buds, giving more vigorous shoots and establishing a rather high leaf-fruit ratio for the properly thinned crop left. It also insures sufficient growth for the initiation and differentiation of fruit buds for the following year's crop. If a peach tree is left unpruned it will probably bear a very large, excessive crop the following year, during which it would make very little terminal growth, and in succeeding years the crop would be very light and the fruit probably small.

4. Using Pruning Equipment

Pruning of most deciduous fruits is still performed by hand, by use of the orchard ladder and hand pruning shears. Consistent attempts have been made by growers to mechanize this time-consuming and expensive operation. In the past 10 years, various types of pruning platforms have been tested with the goal of placing the pruner in the tree without the necessity of his climbing a ladder and moving it each time he needs to change position. A few of these platforms are still in use, but they have not been adopted widely. Earlier efforts to mechanize the pruning tool relied largely on pneumatic shears which have an action quite similar to the ordinary hand shears. In more recent years, air or electrically driven saws and shears have been used to some extent. Many orchardists are impressed with the mechanical tree pruners. Although the inaccuracy of the saw cuts down production to an extent, the savings in labor and the quickness with which a job

Fig. 8.5—Using a platform and air-powered shears to aid in pruning.

can be done, thus allowing other orchard operations justify its use. Platforms could be used conceivably in the thinning operation and perhaps even in the harvest operation also. The near future will bring about a more satifactory pruning machine that will be used extensively by many progressive orchardists.

Pruning can be described as an art perhaps more than a science, although the reaction of plants to various types of pruning cuts can well be predicted because of known responses. However, a normal growing tree presents so many opportunites to vary the pattern and severity of cutting that almost every grower has his own ideas as to what constitutes a well-pruned tree. In the early life of the tree, from planting until it reaches its final height or a mature condition, the phase of pruning known as training is very important. It is a well-established fact that the more severe the

TRAINING FOR THE OPEN CENTER SYSTEM

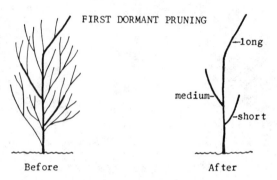

FIRST DORMANT PRUNING

—long

medium—

—short

Before   After

Select three branches (heavy lines) which are vertically and evenly spaced on the trunk. Remove all other branches. For best tree development the lowest branch should be the shortest, the highest the longest.

Do not have three branches arising at a single point.

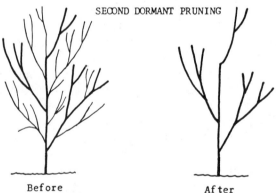

SECOND DORMANT PRUNING

Before   After

Select secondary branches (7 to 9) that are to complete the permanent framework of the tree.

Courtesy, University of California Extension Service

Fig. 8.6—First and second dormant prunings.

pruning the slower the development of the tree. Therefore, to encourage early production, training should
involve relatively light wood removal. On the other
hand, cutting is necessary to form a strong framework
for the load the tree will eventually bear. Training then,
whatever the system used, must balance these two requirements. The pomologists recommend a system
which, while developing a strong framework for the
ultimate tree, still requires a relatively small amount
of wood to be removed each season, which therefore
encourages early production. Extremely heavy "cutting
back" of the branches in the first two or three years of
the life of the tree is certainly to be discouraged for
all species, unless cuts are needed for a specific purpose.

5. Pruning Young Trees and Vines

At planting	Head 24″ to 30″ or even 40″.
	Apples 34″ to 40″.
	Primaries can be selected on some trees at this time. Stub to 6″.
	Some growers now leave all limbs on young trees.
	Summer prune later or not at all first year.
Summer pinching	Select primaries and pinch tips off of other shoots. This puts all growth into the un-tipped primaries.
First dormant pruning	Select primaries.
	Evenly distribute around trunk, 8″ to 12″ apart.
	Bottom primary 8″ to 12″ from ground.
	Should be about 120° angle.
Head scaffolds	Head primary scaffolds 1. Breast high.

TREE SCAFFOLDS

Explanation

    Numbers indicate secondaries at five-foot height from the ground. Notice that they branch lower than the five-foot level. Ordinarily if you can count five to seven scaffold branches five feet from the ground, the tree will have the right thickness of scaffold branches.

    A, B, and C identify the primary scaffold limbs. Three to four are the usual number.

Courtesy, California Polytechnic State University

Fig. 8.7—Tree scaffolds.

2. 15″ to 30″ or longer.
3. Greater growth leave longer.
4. Horizontal cut shorter.
5. Even cutting bad; leave top scaffold longest.
6. Height top longer.
7. Whorls off (cots).

(Avoid three limbs from one spot. Select proper crotch development.)

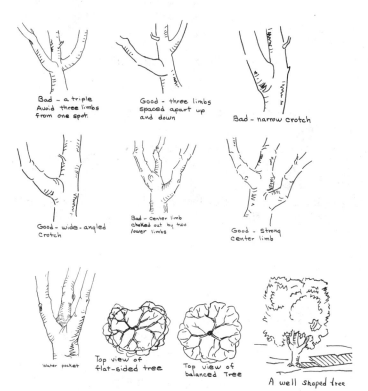

Courtesy, California Agricultural Teachers Association

Fig. 8.8—Tree crotches.

Second year

Remove laterals up to secondaries.

Select secondaries five to seven
at shoulder height.

Third and subsequent
dormant pruning

Thin out and eliminate crossing or interfering branches.

Remove watersprouts.

Encourage fruit spurs on
larger branches.

Open center to admit light.

Head at desired height.

Prune for heavy production of
good-quality large sized
fruit.

6. Pruning Bearing Trees and Vines

Collect supplies

The following supplies and equipment should be on
hand before starting:

1. Shears, hand clippers.
2. Oil, file, hone.
3. Saw, ladder.
4. Tree seal, Bordeaux paste, raw linseed oil,
white lead or other approved material for specific variety.

Decide which method—trees

LEADER TYPE

1. Occasionally found in some nut bearing trees.
2. Topmost branch encouraged to predominate.
3. Tree becomes pyramid-shaped.

MODIFIED LEADER TYPE

1. Mechanically strong framework.

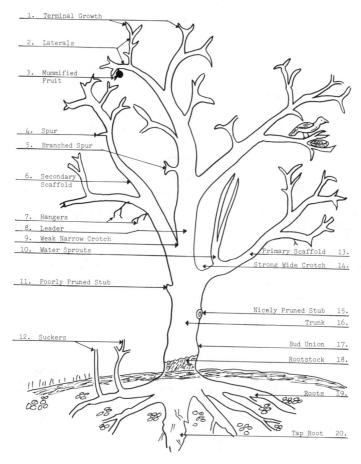

1. Terminal Growth
2. Laterals
3. Mummified Fruit
4. Spur
5. Branched Spur
6. Secondary Scaffold
7. Hangers
8. Leader
9. Weak Narrow Crotch
10. Water Sprouts
11. Poorly Pruned Stub
12. Suckers

Primary Scaffold 13.
Strong Wide Crotch 14.
Nicely Pruned Stub 15.
Trunk 16.
Bud Union 17.
Rootstock 18.
Roots 19.
Tap Root 20.

Fig. 8.9—Tree terms.

2. Topmost limb encouraged (several years).
3. Then cut to a lateral.
4. Results in four to six well-spaced scaffolds.
5. Used in walnuts, pecans and some apples.
6. For mechanical harvest of walnuts, more of this type coming into commercial practice.

"OPEN CENTER" TYPE

1. Most common in California—75%.
2. Uppermost branch left longest to avoid chocking out.
3. Centers kept open.
4. Wide angles, strong crotches.
5. Weakness to the system if not pruned properly.
   a. Scaffolds arise from one point.
   b. Water pockets form.
   c. Heart rot occurs in crotch.
   d. Results in heavy breakage.

7. Pruning Grapes

Ordinarily, grapevines (vinefera in California) are trained to develop three definite shapes according to their system of pruning. American and vinefera grape training will be discussed more extensively in the chapter on grapes.

Head pruning

The mature vine has a vertical trunk, up to 4 or 5 feet high, bearing at its summit a ring of arms or short branches. The bearing units (spurs) are left at the end of these arms. There are modifications such as a few spurs down the trunk also.

Cordon pruning

The mature vine has a vertical trunk 3 feet to 45 inches in height, and then branches in one or in both directions horizontally along a wire trellis. Along the horizontal portion of the trunk, arms are developed at intervals of 8 to 12 inches. Bearing units (spurs) are the same as in head pruning. Some growers train two sets of cordon arms under certain conditions.

Cane pruning

The mature vine has a trunk similar to that of the head type. The head of the cane-pruned vine is fan shaped, directed in the plane of the trellis. There are generally two arms on each side of the head. Fruit canes are 8 to 15 buds, 2 to 5 feet in length and are retained at the ends of the arms. These canes are then wrapped around the trellis wire support. Thompson seedless growers sometimes develop a modified head about 2 feet below the top of the vine and train canes along another wire. There it can increase production, but often at the expense of quality.

8. Treating Pruning Wounds

If a plant is properly pruned from the start, the removal of large limbs or spurs can usually be avoided.

Make cuts close

In removing large branches, make all cuts close to the limb from which the branch arises. This will promote rapid healing.

All wounds not treated the same

Treatment of pruning wounds depends largely upon local conditions. In a section where the foggy climate favors germination and growth of the fungi that cause wood decay, pruning cuts should be disinfected as soon as the wood has dried a little, but before any cracks have formed. Where the air is relatively dry, and no infectious diseases are apparent, pruning wounds seldom need disinfection.

Cover Large Wounds Properly

It is desirable to cover large wounds over 3 inches

Fig. 8.10—Cover large prune cuts. When one must cut large
branches, a great deal of damage is done. Pruner must not
allow additional injury to tree by infections through wounds.

with some protective substance—not to aid the healing
but to prevent the entrance of rot-causing fungi.

Bordeaux paste is a good disinfectant and wound
covering, but it must be replaced every year or two
until the wound has adequately healed. A more nearly
permanent covering is possible by combining Bordeaux
powder with a viscous mixture of white lead and raw
linseed oil. Enough Bordeaux powder is added to make
the mixture a light blue color.

Use Asphalt Compounds

Other materials that are not disinfectants are often
used for wound coverings. White lead paint mixed with
raw linseed oil has been widely used. Many proprietary

materials are on the market, most of which are asphaltum compounds or emlusions to be applied cold, such as "Tree Heal" or "Tree Seal," etc.

General Considerations

A tree or vine so responds to any kind of pruning that if its form is modified, its functions are influenced. To produce the desired responses, it is necessary to understand not only the various pruning operations, but also the nature of the plant's responses to cutting. Certain facts concerning a plant's annual cycle of growth and development in each locality are basic

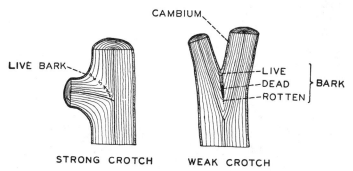

Courtesy, The Ohio State University

Fig. 8.11—Wide crotch angles insure strength. The angle of the crotch on the left is wide. Note relative thickness of the seven successive layers of wood (numbered) laid down by the cambium in this crotch angle. The angle of the crotch on the right is narrow. Observe that the bark of each branch in the crotch angle comes together before the crotch is filled with woody tissue. Annual layers of wood in the crotch are relatively narrow. A cleavage line results from the bark inclusions in the narrow crotch. Note that live bark, dead bark and rotten bark are found in succession down the cleavage line of the crotch, which prevent union and encourage decay. A narrow crotch is weak, splits down with overloads and is often associated with winter injury on adjacent bark. Use scaffold branches that leave the trunk with a wide angle.

to the adoption of sound pruning practices, and should be understood before extensive pruning is practiced. Consult your experiment station for these conditions.

A fruit tree or plant with its crop represents an accumulation of materials drawn from the soil by the roots and from the air by the leaves. When materials from either source can no longer be obtained, the plant ceases to live. Consequently, any plan for developing and managing an orchard or vineyard from its planting to the time it is no longer profitable must include the *treatment* of both *soil* and *plants*.

Learn how pruning affects growth and fruitfulness

Heavy cutting, whether on the young plants or old, generally results in rank vegetative growth and, with

PRUNING CLOSE TO LATERAL BRANCHES...

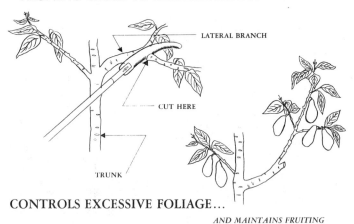

CONTROLS EXCESSIVE FOLIAGE...

AND MAINTAINS FRUITING

Courtesy, University of California

Fig. 8.12—Control excess growth.

Fig. 8.13—Severe pruning results in excess growth. Picture shows severe pruning in an attempt to cut back height of tree. Next pruning should be to leave one of the shoots about a foot long and force growth to lower part of tree.

trees or vines of bearing age, in reduction of fruitfulness. If, in addition to the pruning, the plants are irrigated and heavily fertilized, the new growth will be still ranker and more succulent, and little or no fruit will be produced.

Bearing trees must be pruned

In bearing trees and vines, on the other hand, a lack of pruning, soil moisture and nitrogen will result in scanty new wood growth and in a tendency toward overproduction. If this treatment is continued, plants soon reach a condition where little or no wood or fruit it produced. Between these two extremes may be found all gradations of vegetativeness and fruitfulness.

Pruning alone not enough

Unfortunately, many attempts have been made in the past to influence the wood growth and the productiveness of the tree by pruning alone. This is a mistake, since pruning is only one of the factors modifying plant growth and productiveness. Irrigation, application of fertilizers and insecticides (if needed) and cultivation (which kills the weeds that compete with trees for water and nitrogen) must also be considered.

Do not prune young trees too heavily

If young trees are severely pruned early in the summer, so that growth made from food stored the previous season is removed and, in addition, the leaf area is seriously reduced, the tree will fail to grow as much as one less severely pruned or not pruned at all, other conditions being the same.

Keep A Balance Between Growth and Fruitfulness

If the young vigorous trees are less severely cut back, the consequently larger leaf area will permit a greater manufacture of foods. Then, provided the nitrogen supply is not markedly increased, there will be a tendency toward a decrease of vegetative activities, with increase in carbohydrate accumulation, and the trees will gradually become fruitful.

Select the systems that fit you best

Every commercial grower should select his methods of cultivation, irrigation, pruning and the like with the idea of securing a proper balance between vegetative growth and fruitfulness. The production of a larger number of fruits is not profitable unless it can be continued, and for this purpose a constant supply of new growth must be maintained as well. By knowing some of the materials needed to maintain this condition and some of the means for their regulation, the fruit grower has a direct and fairly accurate method of securing the type of tree he desires.

Know relation of pruning to other cultural practices

Although pruning alone will not regulate the growth and productivity of the plant, it is one of the most important factors in determining the balance between carbohydrate and nitrogen supply. It is, therefore, important to understand the principles involved before adopting a pruning system for any particular set of conditions.

One condition present may not be enough

There may be an adequate supply of available nitrogen, but if soil moisture is so greatly reduced that the tree cannot utilize this food material, the pruning will maintain a proper balance. Pruning under such

Fig. 8.14—This four-year-old unpruned apricot tree shows good growth. Previous proper training and pruning are evident.

circumstances should probably be somewhat heavier in order to reduce the amount of water lost through leaf transpiration. It should also keep the proportion of nitrogen to carbohydrates the same as if sufficient soil moisture and nitrogen were available. Pruning can be affected by other conditions in the same way. Fertilizers, irrigation and cultivation affect the pruning practice by limiting or increasing the amount of soil moisture and available minerals, especially nitrogenous compounds.

Severe pruning may be necessary

Occasionally situations are encountered where poor drainage or a rising water table results in a restricted

SEVERE PRUNING CAUSES...

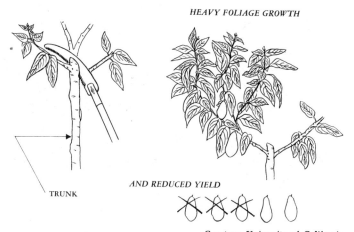

HEAVY FOLIAGE GROWTH

TRUNK

AND REDUCED YIELD

Courtesy, University of California

Fig. 8.15—Severe pruning results.

root development. Under such conditions pruning must be somewhat more severe so that the plant will not lose by transpiration more water than it can replace from the undesirable soil conditions.

Chapter

IX

FERTILIZING

Basically, four factors determine successful fertilizer usage: (1) the right kind at (2) the right time in (3) the right place in (4) the right amounts.

Available diagnostic methods may tell us the kind. Research and experience will tell us the time, place and amount.

One of the greatest changes in fertilization is the increased use of nitrogen. Perhaps the explanation for this is four-fold.

1. Our soils are getting older in many of the early orchards resulting in gradual depletion of the natural nitrogen supply.

2. As a result of urbanization, farmers are developing more marginal lands.

3. Fruit crops, specifically grapes, demand exacting climates for a certain quality fruit. Land in these climatic areas passed by because of soil problems are now being developed.

4. Growers are producing more fruit with intensive culture which demands more nitrogen. In general, trees use about 100 pounds actual nitrogen per acre per year; with some plantings like peaches this means 1 pound nitrogen per tree and almost 20 pounds per

tree where trees are spaced farther apart, as with walnuts. Mature grapes use between 40-80 units of nitrogen per acre, depending upon conditions. Some conditions do not require any addition of fertilizer.

Fertilizers Are Needed

Nitrogen still remains the most commonly deficient element in our agricultural soils, so far as trees and vines are concerned. The use of the other fertilizer

Fig. 9.1—Applying liquid fertilizer. There are numerous ways of applying various fertilizers to plants. Depositing the material where the roots are, such as in this young vineyard, is a good practice.

mineral elements, potassium and phosphorus, is generally indicated only when deficiency symptoms can be demonstrated. For many years only a few rather restricted locations showed potassium deficiency. Now it is being found in more and more of our soils. Again this is probably related to the more intensive culture and higher production per acre we now enjoy, as much as to any depletion of the soil potassium. Actually potassium is rather common in most soils so far as total potassium content is concerned, but the release of available potassium that can be used is extremely slow and at relatively low concentration levels. Until just within the past two or three years phosphorus was never found to be limiting in fruit or nut production. However, now there are proven cases of response to phosphorus fertilizers in walnuts and peaches in one or two very localized areas. The phosphorus requirement of fruit trees is extremely low as compared to many other crops.

Factors to consider for fertilization

A successful fertilizer program must take into account the condition of the soil, the age and species of fruit, and the nutrient deficiencies shown by the plants or by tests.

Success Factors Depend on Roots, Soil, Water

A fertilizer program depends upon a rather complex root-soil-water relationship. A mature tree or vine has a system of permanent roots extending throughout the available soil, plus many small, temporary feeder roots. The latter grow, die and are replaced by new roots one or more times each year. During growth, the surfaces of these feeder roots absorb water and mineral elements necessary for the normal nutrition of the plant.

Nutrients must be available

Many factors influencing the absorption of nutrients are concerned with the soil—its fertility, depth, texture, moisture, temperature, drainage and aeration.

Deep light soils are important

Trees and vines may secure as much from a good soil only 4 feet deep as from a poor one twice that depth, but they will rarely perform satisfactorily on a shallow soil even if it is a good one, properly irrigated and fertilized. In very coarse or very heavy soils, root branching may be unsatisfactory, and roots may fail to extract nutrients efficiently from a given volume of soil.

Soil moisture must be right

Roots will not grow in dry soil nor will most species grow in saturated soil. Such conditions reduce the active root surface and probably the efficiency per unit of root surface, thus limiting nutrient absorption.

Soil temperature is a factor

This absorption is also dependent on the correct soil temperature as determined for various species. For trees and vines, the lower limit is probably near 45°F., the maximum rate of activity, near 70°F. Above 90°F. there is little activity, and at slightly higher temperatures the roots will die.

Roots need oxygen

In order to grow and function, plant roots need oxygen. Saturated or tight soil through which the air can move only slowly will not provide a good environment, thereby actually suffocating the roots.

Fertilizers must be where roots are

In order that any added fertilizers may be absorbed, they must be brought into areas where the roots can come in contact with them. The depth to which they must penetrate will depend on conditions in the soil. If there is sod, for example, the roots may grow to within an inch of the surface, whereas in some clean-cultivated orchards there may be but few roots in the top foot of soil. In the latter case, the fertilizer must be a kind that will penetrate with rain or irrigation water, or else must be placed in the root zone mechanically in order to be absorbed by the roots.

Do you need fertilizer?

Some orchards and vineyards are on soils capable of supplying all the required nutrients. In such cases, addition of fertilizer is not profitable. However, some soils may have had low initial reserves of one or more nutrients, or may now be depleted of their original supply. These soils will require fertilization. No single, quick and easy method is available for determining whether a soil requires fertilizer. Some progress has been made with several methods, which are discussed as follows:

SOIL ANALYSIS SHOULD BE MADE

To be of any value, a soil sample must be taken near the roots, and must be representative of the area. If the change in soil character over the area is great, samples from each type of soil must be taken. Several types of kits for determining available soil nutrients are on the market.

PLANT ANALYSIS CAN HELP

Both laboratory and field methods have been developed for analysis of certain plant parts. As with soil analyses, results vary depending on modifying factors affecting the tissue tested. For example, leaf composition changes throughout the season. The character and rate of change differ for the different elements and will be modified by size of crop, seasonal conditions, and cultural practices, such as pruning, as well as by the available nutrients. The success of this method depends on experience and a knowledge of the fruit concerned.

DEFICIENCY SYMPTOMS USED BY MANY

The mineral elements known to be necessary for plant growth fall into three groups:

1. Commercial fertilizers—nitrogen, potassium and phosphorus. These elements are used in large amounts by plants and are often deficient in many soils throughout the world.

2. Elements usually present in sufficient amounts for plant growth—calcium, magnesium, sulfur—but possibly required in additional amounts to provide good soil structure.

3. Minor or microelements. There are several elements which can be grouped together under the generic name of minor elements or micronutrients. These elements are used in extremely small quantities by plants. Among these are some of the common mineral elements such as zinc, iron, magnesium, manganese and copper.

Zinc is an important minor element: Actually, zinc, next to nitrogen, is most commonly found to be deficient in most orchards and vineyards. Zinc deficiency can be corrected in a variety of ways, and the method used is determined somewhat by the species showing the deficiency. For example, dormant and foliage sprays may be used on most of the stone fruits. However, the sweet cherry does not respond to these types of sprays, and zinc glazier's points are still the standard method

Fig. 9.2—Little leaf on plum. Note the small leaves at the base of some normal leaves and at the top of the growing point.

of correcting zinc deficiency in it. On the other hand, some of the newer, so-called chelating compounds are being tested and show promise of correcting zinc deficiency in those species which were formerly considered to be difficult, namely, the sweet cherry and the walnut.

Iron must be considered: Iron deficiency is seen in many orchards, usually localized even within orchards. A common type of iron deficiency seen in California soils is the so-called lime-induced chlorosis. Under these conditions high pH or alkaline soil reaction results in the iron becoming unavailable to the plant so that a deficiency is seen. The slow but apparently sound method of overcoming this deficiency is through the use of acidifying soil amendments such as agricultural sulfur. Again some of the chelating materials may speed the recovery of some tree species from iron deficiency, though much of this work is still in the experimental stage.

Watch Your Trees and Vines at All Times

In addition to chemical tests for availability of these elements, the plants should be observed. Often they will show characteristic "deficiency" symptoms that indicate the need for a particular element. These symptoms are not completely reliable by themselves, but are valuable when considered in conjunction with soil or plant analyses. However, where deficiency of an element is suspected, application should be on a trial basis at first to determine whether large-scale application would be profitable.

Essential Elements

Nitrogen, as mentioned, is the most important element as a fertilizer. To produce maximum crops, trees and vines need additions of this material more than any other. A few soils, however, are plentifully supplied from reserves untouched.

Observe tree for nitrogen deficiency signs

In bearing plants, an acute nitrogen shortage is

Courtesy, Dow Chemical Co.

Fig. 9.3—Tree showing deficiency signs. When trees are "short of supplies," they have a number of ways to display their needs. It is up to the orchard manager to interpret the signs. Severe iron deficiencies, such as shown, also indicate poor management.

indicated by pale, yellowish-green leaves, smaller than normal; short vegetative shoots, usually small in diameter; profuse bloom, but very heavy drop, resulting in light set and poor crop; and small fruit maturing early, followed by early leaf fall.

Selecting the nitrogen carriers

There is a wide choice of nitrogen carriers that may be applied to soils. The most common chemical fertilizers are sodium nitrate, calcium nitrate and ammonium sulphate. In recent years the use of foliar feeding, ammonia, gas or liquid, has come to the fore.

Select the economical nitrogen source

Normally the most economical nitrogen source is the one to use, for there seems to be no difference in the reaction of the plants to the various sources of nitrogen so long as they are applied annually in a regular program. However, the best way to buy fertilizer is by the cost per pound of nitrogen.

Check soil conditions carefully

The use of sodium nitrate on a soil which is on the saline side might prove harmful. Sodium tends to deflocculate the soil particles, increase the difficulties of water penetration, and, of course, adds directly to the saline content of the soil. Under such conditions, calcium nitrate would be a much better source even though more expensive.

Do not use too much nitrogen

Excessive nitrogen may cause poorly-colored fruits, retarded ripening and unsatisfactory fruit quality. Light textured sandy soils, especially when fre-

THE PRINCIPAL COMMERCIAL SOURCES OF NITROGEN FOR ORCHARDS AND VINEYARDS

Name*	Compound Formula	Per Cent Nitrogen	Advantages	Disadvantages
Anhydrous ammonia	NH_3	82	High nitrogen percentage. Ease of application. No residue. Little danger of leaching.	(a) In irrigation water. Uneven distribution if irrigation system not adapted to its use. Cannot be used with sprinklers. (b) Dry injection. Some loss if ground is trashy or cloddy.
Ammonia solution	NH_4OH	Usually 20	Easier to handle than anhydrous. No residue.	Same as for anhydrous.
Ammonium sulfate	$(NH_4)_2SO_4$	21	Acid residue (for alkaline soils). Little danger of loss by leaching. Ease of handling.	Acid residue (for very acid soils). Delayed availability during nitrification.
Ammonium nitrate	NH_4NO_3	33	High N percentage. No residue. Half immediately available, half delayed.	
Ammonium phosphate-sulfate (16–20) mixture		16	Same as ammonium sulfate. Carries phosphate if needed for cover crop.	Same as for ammonium sulfate.
Ammonium phosphate	$NH_4H_2PO_4$	11	High phosphate content where needed for cover crops.	Low N percentage.
Calcium nitrate	$Ca(NO_3)_2$	15.5	Calcium residue (for acid or high sodium soils). Immediate availability.	May be leached.
Urea	NH_2CONH_2	42	High N percentage. Is not fixed if irrigated at once, before conversion to ammonium carbonate. No residue.	May be toxic in high concentrations.
Sodium nitrate	$NaNO_3$	16	Alkaline residue (for acid soils). Immediate availability.	Sodium residue undesirable on high sodium soils. May be leached.
Calcium cyanamide	$CaCN_2$	24	Alkaline residue (for acid soils). Calcium residue.	Danger of burning, especially at high rates or in growing season.

*Fruit growers will generally govern their choice on the basis of price per unit of N applied in the orchard. There is no serious trouble with the physical properties of any of these materials unless stored too long or under poor conditions.
Except for **calcium nitrate**, which has come largely from Norway, **urea**, from eastern U. S., and **sodium nitrate**, from Chile, these materials are produced on the Pacific Coast. California and British Columbia lead in tonnage.

quently irrigated, may need more nitrogen and/or split applications than heavier soil types.

Phosphorus may be needed

Phosphorus deficiency symptoms, less clearly defined in fruit trees, have been seen almost exclusively in potted culture experiments. Under these artificial restrictions, the condition developed is one of stunted growth and dark green or somewhat bronzed leaves, which may be thickened. Trees grow and produce well on a phosphate-deficient soil in which most annuals fail to make normal development.

Adding phosphate showed no gain

In a soil having the lowest phosphate-supplying power of any so far investigated, the common species of fruit trees failed to respond to added phosphate, although annuals increased growth five to 20 times that of their unfertilized checks.

Potassium is needed in some areas

Potassium deficiency has usually appeared as local spots varying in size from a few trees or vines to several acres, to orchards or vineyards of large acreage and including most of our fruit species. Treatment has not always been successful, particularly where symptoms are severe.

The plant will tell you its need

Deficiency may result in leaf scorch and die-back, sometimes with burning and shriveling of the fruit. Leaf scorch, observed in several fruit species, usually appears on the leaf margin, but may also involve most of the leaf blade. The reduced leaf area limits the food supply available to the roots, in turn, reducing the absorbing surface and the efficiency of the roots that result in further deficiency. The most severe and widespread potassium deficiency has been found with prunes.

Apply potash heavily

On nearly all soils (except sandy) 25 pounds of sulfate of potash per tree are necessary and will last about five years. Reappearance of symptoms will indicate treatment. Small amounts are not effective.

Calcium

Calcium has not been a problem in many soils. Calcium in the form of gypsum or lime has been of some value as a soil amendment in some areas. It is needed in small amounts by roots and shoots. Excess calcium gives bad effects by reducing availability of iron and potassium.

Magnesium

A few instances of magnesium deficiency have been reported, some in coastal areas of California. When it does occur, it is mostly in coastal areas. The basal leaves of affected plants develop brownish blotches and drop off. The tips may continue growth while more leaves drop and a few remain at the ends of bare shoots. Fruit bud production may be greatly reduced.

Sulfur

No evidence of soils being deficient in orchards or vineyards has been reported, although sulfur is an essential element. However sulfur is used as a corrective for alkali soils.

Manganese

Deficiency symptoms of a severe nature have been found in several species (notably walnuts), in some areas. In mild cases, yellowing occurs in the areas between the veins of leaves. In severe cases, these areas die, and many leaves fall prematurely. Some trees may be practically defoliated by late summer. Milder cases on peaches and apricots, and less often on other species, occur in both the coastal and the interior valleys.

Iron

Iron deficiency, generally referred to as iron chlorosis, is present in many western fruit districts. It is so frequently related to calcareous soils that it is also referred to as lime-induced chlorosis.

Scientists have long known that iron is essential for plants. Correcting iron chlorosis in fruit trees and vines is difficult. Recently, large applications of soil sulfur, 2500-5000 pounds per acre, have corrected iron chlorosis in several peach orchards for three to five years. Iron chelates have also shown some correction and may become commercially important when costs permit usage. As much as 300 to 500 pounds per acre is needed to correct the problem in some areas.

Boron

Boron injury was described before it was known that boron was essential. Now it is recognized that it is needed by many plants in very small amounts. A "little too much" results in severe burn and even death.

Fig. 9.4—Apricot leaves showing various stages of iron deficiency.

WORLD-WIDE PROBLEM

Orchardists and vineyardists all over the world have treated their plants for a boron problem which can be too much or too little. The amount needed is so small that one pound will supply 10 acres of healthy mature plants for one year.

Boron deficiency in the olive showed death of terminal buds; scorch of leaf tips; greatly reduced set of fruit; and deformed fruit known as "monkey face." The apple and pear in the same area may show "blast" of blossoms, dying back of shoots and the development of hard, brown, corky areas in the flesh of the fruit. The latter symptom seems much less common in coastal countries. In the European plum, brown, dry, pithy areas may develop in the fruit flesh. There may also be dying back of terminals. The prune has shown a witch's broom effect called "brushy branch." The walnut shows poorly-developed leaves, often misshapen, usually accompanied by dieback and chlorosis. So far, no evidence of boron deficiency has been found on the Japanese plum, even when growing among European plums with marked deficiency symptoms or where deficiency and excess situations occur within a few miles of each other.

Zinc

Zinc deficiency is also known throughout the world and has been called a number of things such as "little-leaf," "rosette," or "corral sickness." (Corral sickness has also been used to designate copper deficiency.) The most common symptom is a tuft of small, often deformed, yellowish leaves at the ends of shoots. Symptoms vary somewhat with the species. Fruit abnormalities are common, and crops are usually very small.

The most satisfactory and often-used method of zinc application to most deciduous trees except pear, grape and cherry is to spray in dormant season with a strong solution of zinc sulfate. 10 pounds each year per 100 gallons or 25 pounds every two years is often used.

Driving pieces of zinc or galvanized iron into the trunk and direct application to the soil are other methods of applying zinc. Zinc sulfate is usually sprayed or dabbed on grape cuts immediately after pruning.

Copper

Copper is an essential element, with only 1 pound needed for about 15 acres of trees for a year. Deficiencies of copper usually show up later in the year than some of the other deficiencies. Copper deficiency is rare but has been found associated with zinc deficiency in some corral spots and old Indian camps known as midden soils. Symptoms resemble those of zinc deficiency, but leaf scorch and roughened bark may also occur.

Molybdenum

Although essential for plant growth, it is needed only in minute amounts. On the basis of present information, deficiencies seem highly improbable, and have not been observed in deciduous orchards. However citrus orchards show widespread deficiencies in Florida.

Convenient fertilizers in the future

Scientists are working continuously on methods of applying fertilizers that will be available longer to the tree and be more convenient to the consumer. Pills to help get small plants off to a good start are becoming available. Our tests have not proven any benefits of this when used with the proper fertilizer program.

As applied today, fertilizers have a tendency to bring about an overabundance of nutrients immediately, then, a shortage later in the season. Fertilizers in plastic capsules may be released more slowly. The "delayed action" spreads the effectiveness of the fertilizer over longer periods of time, and we can look for other advances to help the producer use his fertilizer more efficiently.

Chapter

X

IRRIGATION

The water supply is one of the major factors affecting successful growth and production of trees and vines. Prolonged droughts in many areas have caused growers to focus their attention on irrigation in order to keep up with the increased competition in the fruit industry.

Eastern Irrigation

Many eastern orchards have shown definite results with the installation of various types of water systems. Other eastern growers work at conserving moisture such as mulching and weed control. Deep rooting is encouraged to lessen drought hazard.

Western Irrigation

The common irrigation practice in the West is in many forms. As rainfall does not exist between May and September in the great valleys of California and other southwestern states, conservation of moisture is practiced even in the areas of available water, but not much use is made of mulching. Deep rooting is, how-

Courtesy, California Polytechnic State University

Fig. 10.1—Soil in need of water. It is obvious that the soil in this picture will need water to grow successful crops.

ever, also encouraged. The cost of water ranges from being free in some areas to from $4 to $10 and up to $25 and $30 per acre-foot in other areas. Two to 3 acre-feet is the usual amount of water used.

Southern Areas

Many growers question elaborate water systems in light of areas that have summer rain. Some say a drought in one of five years does not warrant expensive irrigation systems. However, prolonged drought could harm or kill trees. Growers must take into consideration if the increase in crop and growth will offset cost of irrigation.

Purpose of Irrigation

The purpose of irrigation is to keep the soil supplied with readily available moisture for the plant as long as necessary for satisfactory growth.

Nothing is gained by keeping enough water in the soil to maintain a high moisture content at all times, but it can result in root problems as well as adding to cultural complications.

Rules of Thumb for Water and Plants

1. Results of approved irrigation practices, such as growth and yields, are cumulative and take a few years to determine.

2. Results of unapproved practices show in fast reaction, such as small fruit and less foliage growth.

3. No additional benefits are gained by adding more water than needed, but this can result in damage.

4. Withholding water does not force tree roots deeper into the soil.

Learn Proper Irrigation Terms

The following terms will help you understand your study of irrigation:

Saturation of the soil is the condition in which the pore spaces are filled almost completely with water. A soil is saturated or nearly so for a short time after water is applied, until drainage takes place.

Field capacity is all the water a soil will hold after drainage has taken place. During drainage, water moves downward by gravity, and, to a lesser extent, sideways.

At field capacity, each soil particle is completely surrounded by water but most of it exists in the form of wedges between the soil particles at their points of contact. It is from these wedges that plants get most of their water.

Permanent wilting percentage (PWP) is the moisture content of the soil below which the plants cannot readily obtain water; plants will wilt, and will not recover unless water is applied to the soil.

Wilting or drooping of leaves is the most common symptom that the PWP has been reached. Some plants will not wilt but show other signs such as decreased plant or fruit growth, or change of color of leaves.

Drooping of leaves, usually in the late afternoon, is a sign that soil moisture has been reduced close to the PWP. If this wilted condition is still noticeable when transpiration begins the following morning, for most soils this means that the PWP has been reached in that part of the soil which is filled by the major portion of the root system; the normal activities of the plant are then limited.

Readily available moisture is the moisture above the PWP. Soil moisture is also present below the PWP

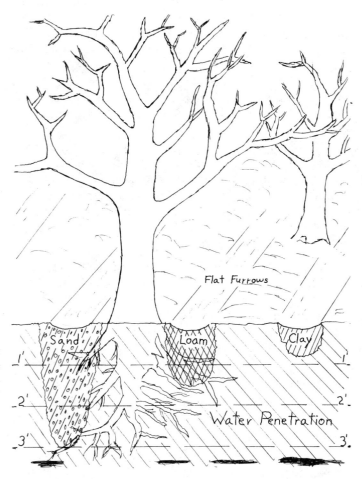

Fig. 10.2—Water penetration in soils. The penetration of water
varies, depending on soil type. Equal amounts of water
applied on above soils the same length of time result in the
pattern as shown: clay, about 1 foot; loam, 1½ feet; and
sand, 3½ feet.

but is held so tightly by soil particles that plant roots cannot absorb it rapidly enough to prevent wilting. The water in the soil above the PWP, throughout the entire range of moisture contents up to field capacity, can be used by plants with equal ease—it is readily available moisture.

The simplest way to determine the amount of readily available moisture in a soil at known field capacity is by growing a plant on it and finding the PWP.

The field capacity of clay soils is greater than that of sandy soils, but some sandy soils contain more readily available moisture than some clays. The readily available water varies from about one-quarter to three-quarters of the moisture equivalent. These differences do not depend on the textural grade (that is, whether it is clay, loam, or sand).

Soil texture is the size of the soil particles, indicating coarseness or fineness of the soil. In general, the fine-textured soils such as clays and loams hold more water at field capacity than the sands. This is so because most of the particles in fine-textured soils are very small, therefore have more particles in a unit volume of soil, and consequently have more water-holding wedges.

Soil structure is the pattern in which soil particles are arranged. It may influence the water penetration of the soil.

Uniformity concerns soil texture and structure. For instance, if a fine-textured soil (clay) overlies a coarser soil (sand or gravel), the zone immediately above the clay will have a higher field capacity than the clay would have if it were uniform throughout.

Soil depth is important as a shallow soil holds more water in a unit depth at field capacity than a deep soil of the same kind; but this difference is not marked in soils deeper than about two feet.

Presence of water table affects the soil condition above the impervious layer. The moisture content just above the water table is greater than that which the soil would have if it were drained. The distance above the water table affected this way is greater in clays than in sands. However, the amount of water held in the soil occupied by the roots is increased measurably only by shallow water tables, and not by deep ones.

Moisture equivalent is a common laboratory method of measuring soil-moisture conditions. It helps estimate the amount of water the soil will hold shortly after a rain or irrigation. It would be preferable to measure field capacity directly, but this is not always practical. The moisture equivalent measure agrees closely with the field capacity in most fine-textured soils, but usually is lower than that of the sands.

Water in Soils

How water is stored in soil

Soil is a porous material composed of particles of many different sizes touching each other, but leaving space in between. This space is called pore space and is the place where water in soil is stored.

Soil is a reservoir for water

The soil in which roots are growing is like a reservoir containing various amounts of water at different times of the year.

In some areas, the soil containing these roots is ordinarily filled to its field capacity at the beginning of the growing season. In unirrigated mature orchards or vineyards where drainage is unrestricted, the readily available moisture in the soil occupied by the roots is usually exhausted before the end of the growing season. The plants then remain wilted until fall rains renew the water supply. In other words, the roots use all the readily available water and then exist as best they can, which results in less yield and quality of fruit and injury to the plant. This situation can only be remedied by proper irrigation.

How soils are wetted

After an irrigation, the soil throughout the portion wetted is hopefully at uniform moisture content. The water moves downward mostly, by gravity; capillarity cannot be depended upon to distribute moisture uniformly.

Light irrigation

Soils must be wetted completely. A light irrigation simply wets a shallower depth to its field capacity than a heavy one does; it does not bring about a moisture condition less than the field capacity.

The field capacity may be exceeded, of course, in undrained soils. On the other hand, portions of the soil will remain dry where furrows are too far apart, as lateral movement caused by capillarity is very limited. A plow sole or decided changes in soil texture or structure will increase the lateral movement.

Measuring Soil Moisture

When is irrigation necessary? This question may be answered by measuring the amount of moisture in the soil. However, not all the water remaining in the soil at a given time can be used by the plant roots.

Soil sampling

The most accurate method of measuring soil moisture is by taking soil samples from various depths and locations, with a soil tube or auger, drying the samples in an oven, and calculating the water content. This method has the disadvantage of needing considerable equipment and requiring two days or so for the drying, weighing and calculating.

In parts of the West and South, the growing season is rainless or nearly so, and the climatic conditions affecting plants are similar year after year. After sampling your soil for several years you will find that, if the winter rainfall has been adequate and irrigations during the growing season have penetrated to a uniform depth each time, the dates when you need further irrigations will fall at about the same time each year.

Instruments with immediate readings

Various devices exist to measure soil moisture without the drudgery of soil sampling. In general, these instruments, such as the tensiometer and gypsum block have the advantage of immediate readings.

The tensiometer

When growing crops under irrigation, it is helpful to have a continuous record of the soil-moisture conditions in the root zone of the plants. Instruments have now been developed which measure the availability of water held by the soil, irrespective of the soil type. The soil-moisture tensiometer is one of several such instruments which can be used for estimating when to irrigate and for detecting drainage problems.

Fig. 10.3—Tensiometers are set in root zone.

The atmometer

This is an inexpensive device used to estimate the extraction of water from the soil (and thus determine the necessity for the next irrigation) by measuring the water evaporated from the atmometers.

Many fruit-growing counties of California are equipped with atmometers, and records of evaporation from them can be obtained from the farm advisors.

Methods of Irrigation

Your method of irrigating soils will depend on the

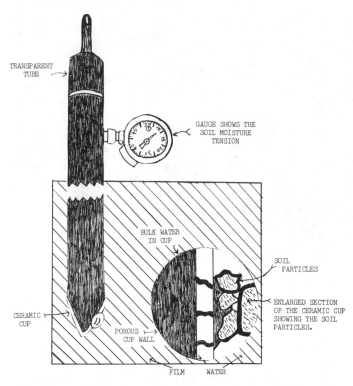

TRANSPARENT
TUBE

GAUGE SHOWS THE
SOIL MOISTURE
TENSION

BULK WATER
IN CUP

SOIL
PARTICLES

ENLARGED SECTION
OF THE CERAMIC CUP
SHOWING THE SOIL
PARTICLES.

CERAMIC
CUP

POROUS
CUP WALL

FILM   WATER

Fig. 10.4—Sketch of tensiometer in contact with the soil.

amount of water you have available, on topography, soil, climate and the general tendency to follow the practice prevalent in your locality.

Furrows are used

Furrows can be used if the slope of your land and the amount of your water are such that they will not result in erosion or loss of your water control. Space the furrows closely enough together so that the wetted areas through horizontal subbing meet and the water is kept in the furrows until it has accomplished both after

Fig. 10.5—Furrow irrigation is used in many areas.

a time relative to proper vertical subbing. Regulate the length of the furrow so that the difference in penetration between the upper and lower ends is not great. Also regulate the size of the irrigation stream in accordance with rate of water intake by the soil.

Flood irrigation

In some areas flood irrigation fits the need. It is fast and, if soil is uniform, does a good job. However, it must be used carefully as soils can remain saturated too long. That can affect fruit greatly.

Use sprinklers in some areas

Sprinklers can be used under a variety of conditions, and are adapted to rolling or steep lands. Their advantages for irrigating are that they need no leveling, they can make use of small streams of water, even distribution, help in temperature control, applying certain pest control material, fertilizers and soil conditioners.

Fig. 10.6—Flood-irrigated orchard. This is a common method of applying water; but land must be flat, or nearly so, for best results. Contour lines are often used in order to control water flow.

The disadvantages of sprinkling

Sprinkling requires high capital investment and maintenance costs.

Fig. 10.7—Sprinkler irrigation is used on various fruit.

The amount of water that usually can be applied at one setting of the pipelines is limited in case of portable equipment. The depth of application for a given time, which in orchards is generally limited by two moves of the pipelines in 24 hours, is controlled by the rate at which the soil will take water and the discharge rate of the nozzles. However, solid-sit sprinklers can apply water in small or large amounts. Their action is repetitive, and they do not require the time and labor to move them.

The operation of sprinklers is inflexible after the original design of the system is adopted. Low hanging branches in the case of orchards may interfere with the spray from the sprinklers and cause uneven distribution of water. This should be corrected quickly.

Drip irrigation

One of the most recent ideas in irrigation is keeping the soil constantly moist through mechanical devices known as emitters. The application rate is slow, from $1/2$ to 2 gallons per hour. Most of the water movement is downward. Wide interest has been created, and growers should check to see if it could benefit their situation.

Use of Water by Trees and Vines

Water taken from the soil by plants is almost entirely given off as water vapor through the leaves. This "transpiration" is like evaporation from a piece of wet paper; it may be controlled to some extent by internal conditions within the plant.

External factors influencing transpiration, other than soil moisture, are sunlight, temperature, humidity and wind. Of those, the amount and quality of sunlight are probably the most important. High temperatures are usually accompanied by low humidities. This tends to increase transpiration. Transpiration may be less on a calm than on a windy day, but does not increase in direct proportion to wind velocity. The effect sometimes noticed on leaves after a period of strong winds is probably due to the combination of low relative humidity, high temperatures, intense sunlight and mechanical injury.

Size of tree or vine does not influence the amount of water used by the plant. If the ground area shaded by the leaves is the same, the use of water is equal regardless of whether the plants are large or small. The shading or ground coverage more noticeable in orchards is determined by the spacing of the trees and their growth habit. What counts is not the number of leaves on the plant but rather the number of leaves directly exposed to sunlight.

Presence or absence of fruit does not materially influence the amount of water used by the plant. However, untimely application of large amounts of water can affect the quality and maturity of fruit.

Time of year

Transpiration by deciduous plants is confined almost entirely to that part of the year when leaves are present, although some water is used during the leafless period. Experiments with prunes, peaches, grapes and apricots indicate that the use of water depends upon the ground coverage of the plant, and not upon the particular kind. However, this may not apply to trees differing from deciduous trees as widely as the olive and orange, when the total seasonal use is considered.

Evergreen trees use water throughout the year, but the amounts used in the winter usually are much less than in the summer.

Tree and Vine Responses to Soil-Moisture Conditions

Plant growth is retarded, and other symptoms

appear, when the soil containing most of the roots has been reduced to the PWP. The degree of injury depends on the length of time the soil remains in this condition.

Irrigation experiments in California deciduous orchards yielded many results and observations on the response of fruit trees to various soil-moisture conditions, particularly those in which trees were allowed to remain permanently wilted for relatively long periods.

Short-term results

The response is immediate and takes effect the same season. In general, immediate results are usually harmful and follow changes in practice involving neglect or ceasing to irrigate, especially during certain critical periods. Decreased size in many fruits, including grapes, delay in maturity of pears and a lowered percentage of well-filled shells in walnuts are some of the results that immediately follow a failure to keep the plants supplied with readily available moisture.

Long-term results

The response to a given irrigation program appears slowly and is sometimes apparent only after several years. In general, the beneficial results are those requiring several years of good irrigation practice. Increases in yield, for instance, are as a rule the reward for the long-continued practice of keeping the plants supplied with readily available water throughout the year. In arid areas it is not uncommon for growers to apply water during dormancy during a late dry winter.

Fig. 10.8—This fruit reflects a good irrigation practice.

Relation of plant size to yield

Experiments dealing with the irrigation of trees and vines confirmed observations in many places about a general relationship between tree or vine size and yield. These results also indicate the relatively slow yield response of deciduous plants to irrigation.

Effect of irrigation on fruit size

Maintenance of readily available soil moisture allows the fruit to grow normally according to the characteristics of the particular kind of fruit. Lack of readily available soil moisture while the fruit is growing causes an immediate check in growth. Slow growth of fruit on peach, pear and prune trees as well as grapes has been repeatedly found when the soil moisture in the 5 or 6 feet of soil is reduced to the PWP.

Early fruits can be grown
without irrigation

In some areas, where winter or early rainfall is ample and the soil holds a comparatively large supply of moisture, certain early fruits may be grown to maturity without irrigation and reduction in fruit size, because the amount of moisture is sufficient to supply the needs at least until the crop is mature.

Reduction in size of almonds and walnuts is generally only noticeable in unirrigated areas following winters of exceptionally light rainfall.

Size of some kinds of fruits is also related to the number of fruits on the plant. If the fruits are not thinned, the final sizes may be unsatisfactory in spite of good irrigation. Of course, if the plants do not get sufficient water while the crop is growing, the fruits will be very small.

In general, fruits may be expected to attain normal size, if the usual thinning practice is followed, and if the soil moisture does not remain at the PWP while they are growing.

Fruits stunted in growth because of the lack of moisture begin to grow more rapidly than previously if the supply is replenished, but they always remain smaller than similar fruits not allowed to suffer from lack of water.

Effect of irrigation in soil with readily available moisture

If plants have readily available moisture, no measurable beneficial results are obtained by adding more water. In this case it does not follow that, if a little is good, more is better.

No benefits, neither immediate nor delayed, are achieved by this treatment.

Plants can take water readily from soil, no matter what its moisture content, as long as it is not reduced to the PWP. Transpiration will not decrease with decreasing soil moisture, growth will not be retarded, yields will not be lessened until PWP is reached. Neither will quality of the irrigated produce deteriorate under these conditions.

Local conditions and irrigation

Ordinarily, soil moisture is readily available between the limits of field capacity and PWP. Yet, local conditions often will determine when to irrigate.

"Soil moisture," means moisture in that part of the soil that is in contact with the absorbing portions of the roots. If the roots do not thoroughly penetrate the soil, there will be some parts of the soil that will not supply water to the plant. Under such conditions, soil sampling will not give a true picture of the moisture conditions. Observations of deciduous fruit trees and grapevines show that these plants have good root systems. There are, however, instances where the soil is too dense to permit root penetration.

Compacted shallow soils, high water tables, alkali and high salinity also may be controlling factors in timing irrigations.

Irrigation an important factor in fruit quality

It was believed that any irrigation at late periods of the growing season had an immediate and injurious effect on fruit quality. Experiments have shown that this definitely is not the case. The highest quality is obtained when trees and vines are supplied with available moisture throughout the year. However, a heavy irrigation at maturity can, in some fruit crops, increase yield without the expense of quality.

Canning peaches showed that maintaining readily available moisture in the soil up to and including harvest time did not injure either the shipping or canning quality.

On the other hand, lack of moisture for several weeks before harvest produced peaches of tough, leathery texture.

Under similar conditions of dry soil, pears frequently have a high pressure test, indicating later maturity than those kept watered; but this difference in hardness tends to disappear in storage. Delay in maturity may be serious in districts where early shipping is desired.

Benefits from good irrigation practice

The benefits derived from a good irrigation practice are cumulative. Increased crops result chiefly from increased size of trees and vines which in turn depends on the plants being kept healthy and vigorous. One of the chief factors in keeping them vigorous is an irrigation plan providing readily available soil moisture at all times.

There appears to be no irrigation formula that will quickly improve crops of deciduous fruits. Sometimes the benefits from irrigation may be slow in appearing, and are only apparent after several months or even years.

Irrigation During the Growing Season

Assuming a mature orchard with the trees 24 feet apart on the square system, and with the majority of roots in the upper 5 feet of soil, there are 2,880 cubic feet of soil from which each tree may obtain water. This volume of soil is essentially a reservoir that contains, when it is filled to its field capacity, a definite amount of readily available moisture.

Seasonal Irrigation

Spring

In some cases, irrigation during the spring is desirable.

If the winter rainfall has been insufficient to moisten the soil to a depth of six feet or more, this may be made up by spring irrigation. Again, if a cover crop has been allowed to grow so late that the readily available soil moisture in the feeder root zone is almost depleted, spring irrigation may be necessary. If a cover crop has not depleted the soil moisture, the first irrigation may be delayed until the readily available soil moisture is nearly exhausted, particularly if only one irrigation can be given before the crop is harvested.

Fall

Many deciduous orchards in California are allowed to remain in a dry condition for a long period each fall.

As long as leaves remain on the trees and can function, some transpiration takes place if evaporation conditions are favorable.

Very often after the crop is picked, either no further water, or only one irrigation, is given. As a result, the trees may reduce the soil-moisture content to the PWP, and then remain in a wilting condition for a long time. This affects some kinds of trees more than others. If it is necessary, however, to omit one irrigation from the regular schedule, the one in the fall may be eliminated with less danger of serious injury than one in mid-summer.

Influence of Irrigation on Root Distribution

Experiments do not support the belief that, by withholding irrigation, trees or vines may be made to send their roots deeply into the soil; that light irrigation tends to encourage shallow rooting; and that irrigating on one side of the plant only will result in confining the roots to that side. These ideas are not correct.

Plants which are normally deep-rooted cannot be made to keep their roots in the upper layers of soil if those at lower depths have a readily available supply of moisture and if no other adverse condition for root development lies below.

If the soil is wet to the full depth to which the roots would normally go at the beginning of the growing season, then later applications of water during the summer will have no influence on the extent of the distribution of the roots, unless they be frequent enough to produce conditions that are unfavorable for root growth.

The presence of water in amounts above the field capacity, a condition often called waterlogging, may injure the roots of some trees.

Fruit trees and vines cannot produce economically without water in some degree. Proper amounts for each type and condition are known. A successful grower has found out.

Chapter

XI

THINNING

"My trees were so heavily loaded that the branches broke," is a mistakenly boastful expression. If you have heard a grower say that, mark him as a questionable farm manager as he probably didn't thin or prune properly. The following activities involving approved practices will assist the grower to thin fruit properly when necessary.

Activities Which Involve Approved Practices

1. Understanding thinning.
2. Deciding which species need thinning.
3. Deciding when to thin.
4. Deciding how heavily to thin.
5. Spraying to thin fruit.
6. Spraying at the proper time.
7. Controlling blossom spray thinning.
8. Determining how much thinning—trees.
9. Thinning fruit by hand methods.

1. Understanding Thinning

Thinning fruit on trees or vines can be as neces-

Fig. 11.1—A peach tree properly thinned. This regular Elberta peach orchard produced 25 tons per acre. Trees were 11 to 12 feet tall. Each tree must produce about 500 pounds. Without thinning, this fruit would not be marketable. Note the heavy set of fruit and leaves. No two peaches are touching.

sary for success as your fertilizer and pruning program. Growers center their total operations on fruit "set," then many of them ignore the important job of thinning. Thinning of nut crops is seldom practiced in commercial orchards.

Many plants "set" more fruit than they can mature to good quality, size, color and taste. The need, time and method are important with each variety.

Reduce the number of fruit on a tree and vine

Experience in growing fruit for fresh market shows that in most seasons a reduction in the number of fruit per tree and vine is necessary for fruit which satisfies consumer requirements.

Thinning accomplishments

Everything thinning accomplishes is not known. However, it is known that thinning:

1. Increases the growth rate of fruit left on the plant. Larger fruit sizes at harvest result.

2. Reduces competition between the fruit and other growing parts of the plant, such as shoot growth (which forms leaves) and root growth. Thinning, with the increased leaf area, lets more energy materials go to the roots. This, in turn, results in the root's picking up additional nutrients and water to use in shoot and fruit growth.

3. Reduces breakage of limbs or shoots.

4. Permits culling of undesirable fruits.

5. Reduces total tonnage but normally increases salable tonnage.

6. Increases vigor of the plant and aids in producing uniform production each year.

Fig. 11.2—Young tree broken down because of too heavy a crop.

How does spray cause thinning?

Injury to flower parts, such as an ovary, causes the tree to "abort" the reproductive organ, or the flowers just do not set, and fall off.

2. Deciding Which Species Need Thinning

Such species as peaches, nectarines, shipping plums, apricots, apples and some table grapes should be thinned to meet market demands. Fruits of the pear, sweet cherry, prune and wine grapes also show benefit from thinning, although it is not a common practice and is perhaps used more with young plants to avoid overcropping.

3. Deciding When to Thin

It is logical to believe that the operation should take place at a time when the greatest effect can be expected from a minimum of effort and cost. Fruits are normally thinned as early as practical to fit into other work and to get the greatest advantage from the operation.

Thinning late in the season may relieve the tree and vine of some of its load but is not too effective in obtaining the desired results of earlier or proper thinning time. Too early thinning can result in split pit and gummy fruit in peaches as well as more labor to remove fruit and less ability to judge culls in others. Also, June drop may cause a shorter crop than planned.

Thin drupe fruits

For drupe fruits, thinning is practiced at the time they enter the so-called second stage of growth, that is, the period in which they are not increasing rapidly in size. For apricots, this may be early in April and usually occurs about mid-May for peaches. At this time the fruit is about half-grown and is readily removed from the trees by hand. Also the fruits are large enough that spacing may be accomplished with little difficulty. Thinning of table grapes varies with market and variety, while thinning of wine grapes can be combined with suckering and training in case of overcrop.

Space fruits properly

Spacing of fruit is essentially a hand thinning operation. Usually this is more or less in proportion to the final size of the fruit, i.e., apricots may be thinned from 2 to 4 inches apart on the branch or approximately one per fruiting spur. On the other hand, peaches may be thinned out up to 6 or 8 inches along the fruiting wood. In case of table grapes, part of the bunch is removed also. Hand thinning is done late enough in the season that the grower is practically assured that his crop will mature. For this reason it is used to regulate very closely the amount of crop.

4. Deciding How Heavily to Thin

Plan each year separately

Pomologists know that fruit will not always grow at the same rate each year, that is, in some years good-sized fruits are easily obtained, and in other years it is very difficult to cause the fruit to reach desirable commercial sizes. When the grower has advanced knowledge of the condition of his fruit in relation to these seasonal variations, he may adjust this thinning practice to accommodate them. This is used very extensively in the production of canning clingstone peaches where there is a definite size limitation for commercial pack.

Thin small fruits more heavily

Actually there is a relatively good correlation between the size of the fruit at thinning and final size. That is, if the fruit is relatively small as compared to other seasons at the time of thinning, a heavier job of thinning will be necessary to bring the fruit up to the size limit than if the fruit is relatively large. Thus, the canning cling peach industry makes surveys each year about the middle of May, surveys which are closely tied in to a readily determined biological index known as the reference date, from which they learn whether the fruits are abnormally large or small at the normal thinning time. Then, with additional estimate of total sets, growers can regulate thinning practice rather satisfactorily.

Records sometimes not the whole answer

Occasionally nature upsets the peach cart and even

with this knowledge the grower is unable to make a good estimate of his thinning response. 1959 was characterized by the shortest period on record between full bloom and the so-called reference date. In addition the fruit was extremely small at reference date. On the other hand, thinning was delayed somewhat because of the late time at which the cling peach marketing group determined the percentage of green drop (knocking a surplus to the ground), required to bring the crop down to market level. The result was that much late thinning and underestimation of the total crop on the trees resulted in very poor fruit size. In 1960, on the other hand, sizes were average or slightly above and the crop was not excessive so the peaches sized without difficulty.

Producer must know his outlet

Normally the grower will have some idea of the outlet his fruit is going to serve at the time of thinning. This is important for those fruits which have multiple outlets, such as the apricot and table grape. In this case the grower may ship, can or dry his fruit. Shipping fruit is picked relatively immature and the premiums for large sizes are substantial. Therefore, if the grower expects to market a proportion of his crop for fresh use, he must thin very heavily to secure the early size. On the other hand, if he is looking towards a canning or drying outlet where smaller fruits are readily accepted, and he will have a week to 10 days longer before harvest, he can leave many more fruits on the tree. Shipping apricots normally yield from 4 to 6 tons per acre, whereas apricots for cannery may run from 8 to 10 tons per acre, and this goes for grapes as well as some of the other products.

Thinning is necessary and expensive

It is readily seen that the thinning operation is

Courtesy, Food Machinery Corporation

Fig. 11.3—Applying chemical sprays. Sprays are applied heavily but with weak concentrations of the chemical. Flowers must be wet thoroughly.

important for the grower. It is also one of the most expensive operations he must perform, often accounting for nearly one-third of the total labor requirements when using hand methods. Any method to reduce this expense and still obtain the benefits of thinning would be most welcome. Certain practices are now becoming established in the industry which promise to accomplish this goal.

5. Spraying to Thin Fruit

One of the practices to consider is blossom spray thinning. Under this practice, the flowers are sprayed when trees are 85 to 95 per cent full bloom. Effectiveness of any one spray has not been uniform over all species. Fortunately, however, some of the crops with the greatest thinning costs per tree, or crops of insufficient value to support hand thinning, benefit from these sprays. For example, Japanese plums which commonly set extremely heavily and prunes respond quite well.

Use caution when blossom spray thinning

Blossom spray thinning has certain inherent dangers, and the grower should have good knowledge of his trees and vines, the climatic situation and other factors which may affect the results obtained. One of the greatest hazards in the use of sprays is that they are applied at bloom time, when frosts may still occur and materially reduce the set of fruit remaining after thinning. Thus a good thinning job could become a loss of the year's crop. Also, some chemicals cause early maturity which could be an advantage in some cases and quite a disadvantage in others.

6. Spraying at the Proper Time

Another disadvantage of this type of spray thinning program is the necessity for applying it at a definite stage of bloom. Under conditions of normal bloom or a sharp bloom this is not too difficult, unless the weather is bad at the time the spray should be applied. These factors tend to cancel each other out for under poor weather conditions set will probably be relatively lighter. On the other hand, in years following mild winters, the bloom may be distributed over a long period and it is impossible to time a single spray as required. Again, however, there are certain compensating factors in that under such conditions of prolonged bloom, sets are relatively light. The point is that the grower must recognize these variable factors and judge his spray program accordingly. In some years he will spray and in others he may want to omit the spray.

A good spray for thinning apples

For apples the most effective spray compound for some areas appears to be one of the growth regulators, naphthaleneacidamide. This substance has one advantage in that it can be applied somewhat later, usually from petal fall to a week or ten days thereafter. When applied at proper concentrations and under proper conditions it does a very good job in reducing the set so that good commercial sizes will result. The use of amid-thin in some apple districts is growing rapidly as a result of experimentation, as well as sevin.

New compounds look promising

A new compound, 3-chloro-proprionic acid, known

Fig. 11.4—Apple showing 75 per cent bloom.

Fig. 11.5—Apple showing 85 per cent bloom.

Fig. 11.6—Apple showing full bloom.

as 3CP, appears to be a very promising thinning agent for stone fruits. The advantage of this material is that it can be applied relatively late in the growing season. Such growth regulating materials are being used effectively on some fruit but must be used carefully.

Reduce costs

Of course the one tremendous advantage all of these chemical methods have over hand thinning is the much reduced cost. Even the most expensive chemical costs only a few dollars per acre for materials, and the cost of applications is rather moderate.

Advantages of blossom spray thinning important

The advantages accruing from blossom spray thinning have always proved of benefit when measured in terms of two to five or more years. This can even include the loss of an occasional crop. For example, the sizing benefits accruing from blossom spray thinning are substantially greater than from hand thinning. Also the trees maintain greater vigor under any given cultural regime. The latter is an effective aid in setting fruit buds for the following season. In prunes, where a very large crop one year results in light bloom and poor crop the next, blossom spray thinning evens out annual production.

7. Controlling Blossom Spray Thinning

The grower has less control with blossom spray thinning than with hand thinning. On the other hand, spacing does not need to be as regular as for hand thinning. That is, spacing becomes much less of an important factor and clusters of fruit do not need to be broken up to attain commercial sizes. This is apparently a reaction to the early thinning accomplished by this method.

Hand thin after spraying

In the case of some fruits a good spray thinning job may still leave need for a light hand thinning which can be accomplished at a much reduced cost.

Increase income indirectly

In the case of prunes, almost any gain is reflected in an increased income either in the year the spray is put on by reason of premium prices for larger sizes, or over a two- or three-year period by the more regular production of more desirable sizes. Therefore the benefits of this type of thinning, as mentioned before, must be measured in terms of two or more years rather than the net returns on the one year's crop.

8.   Determining How Much Thinning—Trees

When a tree has an overload of fruit it must be thinned to the amount that the tree can properly size and mature. Many orchardists find a tree will set 10,000 fruit. A normal size drupe will only develop 3,000 to market demand. This means that 7,000 green fruit or blossoms must be removed.

Important factors to consider in thinning amounts

1.   If fruit tends to be grouped in clusters.
2.   Heavy set on just a few limbs. Make room for fruit growth and prevent limb breakage.

3. Poor soil—trees showing low vigor, leaf area/ fruit.

4. Older trees—fruit on older trees in some sections tending to become smaller. Will need more thinning than young trees/leaf area.

5. Water availability for season.

6. A cull never a marketable fruit.

7. Use of some thinning chemicals harmful if deposits fall on cover crops (dinitros).

Good growers find that calipers are as important to thinning as shovels are to irrigating.

9. Thinning Fruit by Hand Methods

First size up the tree. How does the fruit on it compare with the block as a group? If the fruit on one tree is larger than that on surrounding trees, more leeway in thinning can be made. If the fruit is smaller, then more must be removed if the harvest size is to be comparable. In general, the more fruit on a tree, the smaller the average size. Trees that are weak will not do a good job in sizing their crop. They should not be expected to carry as many fruits as the more vigorous ones. Trees that are noticeably larger or extremely vigorous can size more fruit. They should have more than the average number left on them.

Remove culls and small fruit

Fruit to be removed can be classified in one of two ways—those that will be culls at harvest time and those that will be the smallest. The reason for removing obvious culls needs no explanation. Removing the smallest fruit leaves fruit on the tree with a larger average size which lets the tree have an easier job sizing the crop.

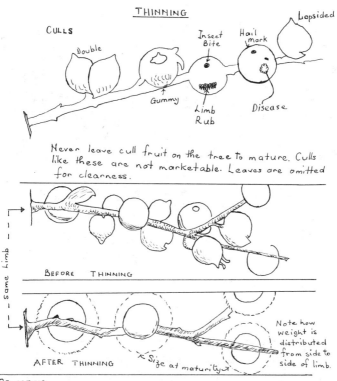

THINNING

CULLS

Double

Insect Bite

Hail mark

Lopsided

Gummy

Limb Rub

Disease

Never leave cull fruit on the tree to mature. Culls like these are not marketable. Leaves are omitted for clearness.

— Same limb —

BEFORE THINNING

AFTER THINNING   ← Size at maturity →

Note how weight is distributed from side to side of limb.

SELECTING

1. First size the branch up to decide which largest and best fruit to leave; then remove all other fruit. Do not loosen fruit to be left.

2. It is better to leave the correct number of fruit on the tree with even spacing along branches, than to space evenly and leave poor or cull fruit.

3. Strong vigorous branches will size more fruit than weaker branches.

4. Leaves will help indicate the vigor of the tree.

Fig. 11.7—Thinning chart.

Consider thinning methods

Hand Method

Simply grasp the fruit with the hand. Remove the excess fruit by twisting, flipping, pulling or pinching

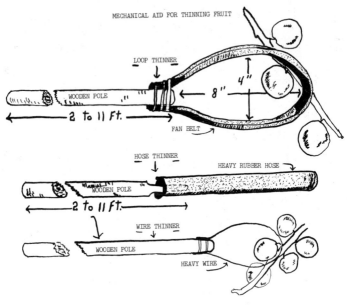

Fig. 11.8

them off. Throw fruit away from the tree. Hand shears and knives have been used on some fruits, such as the apple. However, it is slow and expensive.

POLE METHOD

The pole method will not produce a complete job but does speed up the operation. Some use a straight pole with a rubber hose or wire hook to remove unwanted fruit. Caution must be used in breaking up clusters.

MECHANICAL THINNERS

Because of the speed with which mechanization is gaining on the orchard operator, labor-saving devices for thinning are being tried. Some growers use almond

Fig. 11.9—Tricycle type tree shaker being used in the thinning
program. The clamps encircle a main scaffold branch and,
with hydraulic shaking action, shake the fruit from the tree.

mallets for pre-thinning, then follow up by hand in a week or so.

Shakers have also been used. However, again, as with the mallets, it is difficult to control the amount that either falls to the ground or is jarred loose but does not fall immediately. The problem, of course, is not being able to control accurately the amount you want to remove. At any rate, hand thinning should follow.

Thinning grapes

Thinning of grapes to improve salable quality pays. Some of the results of thinning are: less decay and cost in packing and picking; more uniform color, which encourages a better balance of leaf and berry ratio; and production of the maximum amount of fruit a vine can mature.

A word of caution! Thinning is a practice one must develop first hand. Call your farm advisor or other knowledgeable person before you start.

Thinning basically is done according to one of three methods:

1. *Flower clusters:* This method increases number of leaves in proportion to fruit resulting in proper amounts of nutrients going to its remaining fruit. The operation should be done as soon as possible, particularly when bunches to be removed can be pinched off by fingernail and thumb. The bunch growth should be far enough along to where they are easily seen above or out away from the leaves, and not too far into bloom.

2. *Cluster thinning:* This system involves removing the entire cluster after berry set, and it is a recommended way of not only reducing a heavy crop but also can be considered a type of grading or sorting of clust-

ers early in growth. Also, close observing workers will remove undersized or too large bunches as well as those that are shaped poorly.

3. *Berry thinning:* This involves removing part or parts of the cluster so that the vine has left only what the grower believes it can produce for the proper market. Timing is important, and a grower should start soon after berry set or shatter. Growers are well aware that when berry thinning is done properly, the weight of a seeded berry can increase from 25 to 30 per cent, and so will the price. Seedless grapes have less effect on thinning. However, when berry thinning is practiced, it is more for attempting to control compactness when using plant growth regulators, or in some cases, girdling.

Chapter

XII

PROTECTING TREES AND VINES
FROM COLD AND ANIMALS

The factors affecting the economics of protecting vines and trees from damage by frost, animals and pests are complicated.

Proper use of approved practices will tend to reduce damage from these hazards.

Activities Which Involve Approved Practices

1. Protecting from spring frosts.
2. Deciding which equipment to use.
3. Determining cost per acre-hour.
4. Providing money for frost protection.
5. Protecting individual areas.
6. Utilizing cultural operations.
7. Protecting trees and vines from animals.

Protecting trees from winter injury has been covered in another chapter.

If a grower selects a site in an area that has a large number of frosty nights or freezing temperatures, the crop must be of sufficient value to carry the investment in the necessary equipment to give protection.

1. Protecting from Spring Frosts

Because most fruit comes from flower buds that were initiated the previous season, early blooming varieties may get their blossoms killed, resulting in limited fruit set.

Temperature tolerance

The following table shows the temperatures (F.) various deciduous fruits will endure for 30 minutes or less.

TEMPERATURES DECIDUOUS FRUITS WILL ENDURE FOR 30 MINUTES OR LESS

Fruit	Buds Closed but Showing Color	Full Bloom	Small Green Fruit
	----------(degrees F.)----------		
Apples	25	28	29
Peaches	25	27	30
Cherries	28	28	30
Pears	25	28	30
Plums	25	28	30
Apricots	25	28	31
Prunes	23	27	30
Almonds	26	27	30
Grapes	30	31	31
Walnuts (English)	30	30	30

Protect longer than bloom period

Just as the buds begin to swell they become considerably more susceptible, and for most species, temperatures in the low 20's may cause killing of these buds. As they develop and the flowers come into full bloom they become still more susceptible to low temperature damage. Open flowers of our common deciduous fruits are normally able to withstand temperatures of 26° to 27°F. If the colder temperatures follow several cool days they may withstand a degree or two colder. After the fruit is set the young fruits become increasingly susceptible to low temperature damage and temperatures of 30° to 31°F. may result in the death of the young developing fruit. Therefore frost protection is given, not only during the bloom period, but for some time thereafter.

Citrus, for example, needs protection not only for buds and tree but also for the maturing fruit. Mature deciduous fruit also gets frozen in some areas, but seldom has there been special efforts made to prevent it.

2. Deciding Which Equipment to Use

Expensive equipment needed and the management problem involved might cause growers to question the use of artificial heat.

Growers use smudge pots, wind machines, irrigation water and in some cases, spray or sprinkle water. Sprayers and helicopters are used to mix air.

Perhaps most commonly used are oil burning smudge pots, in-return stack heaters, wind machines and water, used in various ways. The capital investment in wind machines is quite high, most running from $4,000 to $6,000 per installation and each being capable of protecting a maximum of 8 to 10 acres. In addition to this, many areas are so located that wind machines are relatively ineffective as compared to heating. The reason for this appears to rest mainly with the location of the acreage to be protected. They are characterized generally by high inversion layers and low temperature differentials. This means that the wind machine is able to draw in air only slightly warmer than that occurring at the ground level. Average results might be characterized by saying that the wind machines may afford two or three degrees protection against frost, whereas orchard heating under the same conditions would usually give five to six or

RETURN
STACK
HEATER

manually op-
erated heater

AUTO
CLEAN STACK
HEATER

automated
system

Fig. 12.1—Orchard heater showing use of return stack to conform to pollution control policies.

seven degrees protection. A method of using ground
level wind machines in conjunction with a much reduced number of oil burning heaters appears to be
relatively successful in experimental trials to date.

Use area heaters

Area heaters are being used by a relatively few
growers. These heaters are characterized by a very
high heat output driven through the orchard or vineyard by an air blast. The heater itself is mounted on

wheels or skids and is pulled through the area to be protected. On firm, dry ground this appears to be feasible, but one can readily visualize ground conditions in the spring of the year when it would be impossible to move such heaters.

Use water

The use of water is an excellent means of frost protection if all conditions are right. The requirement is that the total area can be covered quickly and that usually a free water surface can be maintained for the period of danger. As frosts sometimes occur two or three nights running, or more in specific years, or several frosts may occur in a relatively short period, the maintenance of the free water surface may be difficult. Nevertheless because of its high heat of vaporization, water or water treated ground affords an excellent means of warming up the air immediately above the ground level quite rapidly. There are increasing experiments with mist and fog making devices that look encouraging, and the use of overhead sprinklers in grapes has also proven to be successful. Frost control is serious business and growers must carefully check new ideas.

3.   Determining Cost per Acre-Hour

The cost per acre-hour for different methods of frost protection varies considerably. Not only are different methods responsible for variations in per acre-hour costs, but the number of hours of operation influence to a large extent the costs involved.

Wind machines versus heaters

According to tests, wind machines and heaters

show no marked difference in cost per acre-hour for 10 hours of annual operation. The combination of machines and heaters at 10 hours have a wider range of costs than wind machines alone or heaters by themselves. However, both of the gasoline machines (a single 100 h.p. on 10 acres and a dual 100 h.p. on 15 acres) in combination with heaters, show less cost per acre-hour than heaters alone.

Per hour costs

In comparing per acre-hour costs of gasoline and electric wind machines, the following tendencies seem apparent from a study of the data: Up to 40 hours, both the dual and the single 100 h.p. machines are less expensive to use than the electric. At about 80 hours of annual use the two gasoline machines are still cheaper to own and operate than the 50 h.p. electric but cost about the same as the $12\frac{1}{2}$ h.p. electric (on five acres) ; at about 160 hours, the $12\frac{1}{2}$ h.p. electric is the most economical machine of all, with the single 100 h.p. gasoline next, and the dual 100 h.p. gasoline and 50 h.p. electric about the same in regard to per acre-hour costs. The electric machines become progressively cheaper to use in comparison to gasoline machines per acre-hour, as the number of hours of operation annually is increased.

It should not be overlooked that wind machines are usually operated more hours than heaters in a corresponding season. This is because most growers start wind machines earlier at about 30°F., and light heaters at about 29°F. for lemons and 27°F. for oranges.

4. Providing Money for Frost Protection

If frost control measures are going to be financed

from receipts from a crop, then each presents a problem of determining what sum is available from the sale of fruit, after deductions have been made for expenses other than frost protection, including sums for family living, payment of debts and maintenance of the equipment, trees and other capital items.

Thus, if data are compiled showing the economic situation for a given orchard or vineyard, an idea can be obtained as to ability to pay for heating either from (a) current earnings; or (b) an increase in the quantity or quality of fruit sufficient to meet the expenses of frost protection after these increased expenses of caring for a large crop—picking, hauling, etc.—are first covered.

5.   Protecting Individual Areas

From the material discussed, the fact is clear that each situation presents individual problems both as to the best type of frost protection and the justifiable investment in frost control measures. Several factors justify this view.

1.   There is no uniformity in the frost occurrence pattern. Prevalence of frost sufficient to require heaters or wind machines, or both, varies markedly from year to year in both a given locality and a given field. Operation of heaters or wind machines thus follows no definite pattern. Much use may be needed some years and little or none in others.

2.   Selection of proper equipment for the project depends on the size, shape, topography and direction of prevailing winds, as well as other local conditions.

3.   The use of frost control measures varies with the kind of fruit. Lighting of heaters customarily takes place when the thermometers drop to 28° to 30°F. in the case of lemons, and to 26° to 28°F. for oranges. However, in the case of deciduous trees and

vines, frost control measures may begin at 32° or even 33°F. depending upon the overall picture. In the case of frost control with wetted, firm base ground, control measures may start three to four weeks before an expected frost.

Wind machines are usually turned on when temperatures drop to 20° to 32°F. in lemon groves and 29° to 30°F. in orange groves. However, the time of lighting heaters or starting wind machines is by no means standardized. Growers are inclined to exercise some individuality in selecting the temperature for frost control measures. These practices at one or two degrees above or below the figures cited are not uncommon.

4. The danger of frost damage also varies with the condition of the orchard. Young trees and vines that are one, two or even three years old are more susceptible to frost damage than older plants, and the degree of dormancy of older plants will influence the amount of damage. Semidormant trees and vines will withstand more frost than those that are still in the succulent growing stage.

6.   Utilizing Cultural Operations

Time cultural practices

Proper timing of the customary cultural practices also can diminish frost hazard. A firm soil with a bare, or almost bare, surface provides a good storage of heat. On clear nights the air will be kept warmer above such ground.

Compact soil

You must provide, therefore, a compact, bare soil. This you can do by turning under cover crops or heavy weed growth. This alone, however, will not be enough, because loosened soil is as hazardous in frosts as soil with vegetation. A good rain after turning under the ground cover can reestablish the desired compactness of the soil; irrigation or rolling the surface certainly will.

7. Protecting Trees and Vines from Animals

Choose deer control program

Many orchards and vineyards are damaged seriously in a short time by deer browsing on the new growth. The male deer also finds the trunk a fine place to rub his antlers while the family makes its lunch off the fruit limbs or shoots.

Young Plants Injured Most

Young fruit plants need all their leaves to supply growth substances to the shoots. Deer destroy both, as well as break the young scaffold branches. The lower shoots being eaten causes the growth to be pushed to the upper portions and the grower finds difficulty in training to the desired type.

Fence May Be Your Choice

An 8-foot fence around the area is effective but expensive. Some use a lower fence slanted out, and it seems to confuse the deer for a while, besides being cheaper than the 8-foot fence.

Use Individual Tree Wire Protector

For young trees two posts, or perhaps three, are used around the tree, and wire stretched around them. This prevents both rubbing of horns and low browsing.

Fig. 12.2—Young peach tree after deer attack. It is obvious there is not the proper ratio of 40 leaves per fruit for good fruit quality.

REPELLENTS MAY BE USED

There are various repellents on the market that seem to do a good job of keeping deer away. Extreme caution must be taken in making up home remedies because of possible injury to the plant. Small bags containing about 2 ounces of naphthalene flakes, tied to the outer branches of the trees, give some help. Some sprays are also used. Seek local advice as repellents react differently in particular locations.

ENCOURAGE HUNTERS

Hunters will do a good job of eliminating a lot of deer if you let them know they can hunt there—in season.

Control gophers

A number of systems to eliminate gophers are at the disposal of the grower. Traps are used nearly all year, and irrigation cuts down the population, especially with a good dog present. Poisoned bait in the burrows is effective, and gas is also used. Exercise caution when using carbon disulfide, as it can injure plants. The barn owl and the gopher snake will also aid in gopher control. The "gopher machine" that digs its own gopher burrows, laying bait such as poison grain in the burrows is an effective control in use. It works off a three part hook-up and operates much like a single-row corn planter.

Squirrels and mice need controlling

Poison is very effective when used properly. Traps,

Fig. 12.3—Young apricot grove attacked by deer.

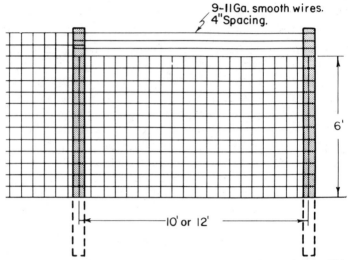

9-11Ga. smooth wires.
4"Spacing.

6'

10' or 12'

Courtesy, University of California Extension Service Circular 514

Fig. 12.4—Deer fence may be effective.

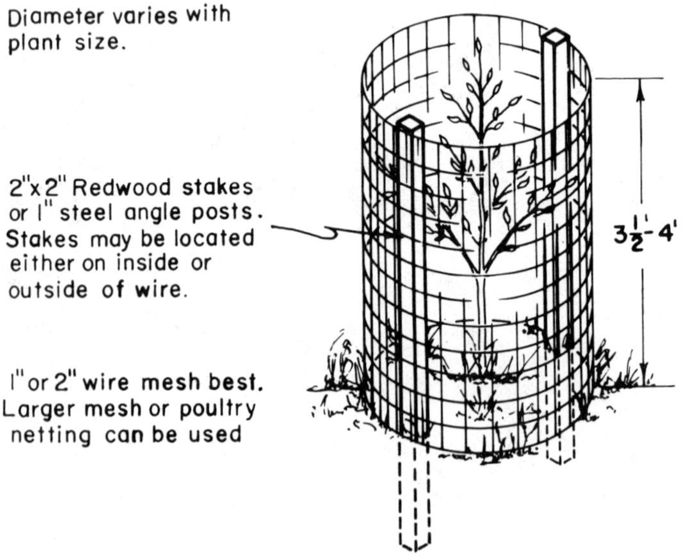

Diameter varies with plant size.

2"x 2" Redwood stakes or 1" steel angle posts. Stakes may be located either on inside or outside of wire.

1" or 2" wire mesh best. Larger mesh or poultry netting can be used

$3\frac{1}{2}$'- 4'

Fig. 12.5—Individual tree protector.

gas and shooting all combine to be effective controls also.

Rabbit damage can be serious

Most damage by rabbits is to young plants. The bark is gnawed, which girdles the trees and vines and many young shoots are destroyed. Shooting, using various types of protectors, spraying repellents and installing fences are effective deterrents.

Consider bird control

Birds can cause tremendous damage to ripening fruit. Various types of noise-making devices are in use and do a good job if used sparingly. Before using any type of poison, consult the local agricultural commissioner for approval.

Chapter

XIII

CONTROLLING PESTS
AND DISEASES

Farmers are engaged in a constant battle against agricultural pests. "Pests are our rivals on earth," said a famous scientist, "and perhaps our successors." During the years of severe insect visitations from Biblical times down to this very day, the destruction wrought gives point to such a dismal expression.

Research Gives Man Upper Hand in Control

The results from research, on the other hand, lend hope that man will overcome his insect foes and reduce the extent to which he provides food and livelihood for the hordes of pests that compete against us.

Careful Planning Essential

A successful campaign against the multitude of pests in our fields requires every type of weapon and carefully planned strategy—and a good farmer-operator will win. He must.

Courtesy, Niagara Chemical Division, F.M.C.

Fig. 13.1—Developing effective new pesticide formulations is a continuous task.

Activities Which Involve Approved Practices

1. Learning fundamentals of pest control.
2. Controlling pests that suck sap.
3. Controlling pests that produce worms in fruit.
4. Controlling pests that chew foliage and fruit.
5. Controlling pests that bore in bark and wood.
6. Controlling pests that feed on roots.
7. Controlling bacterial diseases.
8. Controlling virus diseases.
9. Controlling fungus diseases.
10. Controlling physiological diseases.

1. Learning Fundamentals of Pest Control

Use right materials

The right material mixed with another that is also recommended to do the same job may lose the effectiveness of both—this is known as being incompatible. Also several sprays when mixed together may cause injury to the plant, while if used separately, they would be effective. Select a material that will do the best job economically. However, there are a number of materials that can be mixed together that control different pests at the same time. Agricultural jargon often refers to this as "shotgun application." Most chemical companies will provide you with a "compatibility chart."

Select the proper time

Most successful pest controls are based on prevention rather than cure. Therefore, if you have the right material to start with, then you must pick the best time.

Fig. 13.2—Applying spray material on time. This orchard operator is spraying to kill the adult stage before eggs are laid that result in worm damage later.

Know habits of pest

Habits and life cycle of the pest must be known for an effective program. In most cases the material need not be on the plant at all times. It only needs to be present a little before, during, or slightly after the outbreak. It is important that the material be in contact with the pest, generally immediately. However, in some cases one type of material irritates a pest causing it to move around so it does come into contact with another pesticide that results in control.

Do a thorough job

In general most sprays or dusts must completely cover the parts of the plant likely to be affected. You will get little control even if you have the right material and have selected the proper time if you do not have the material on the parts of the plant subject to control. Complete coverage inside, outside, top and bottom is essential if such a pest requires it.

SPRAY STAGES FOR DECIDUOUS FRUITS AND NUTS

Timing	Crops	Explanation
Postharvest	Pear	Within two or three weeks after harvest; to control bud and blister mite.
Fall	Peach, apricot	Nov. 15 to Dec. 1; to control peach blight (Coryneum).
Dormant	All fruits	Jan. and Feb. or up to bud swell period; safest for the tree.
Delayed dormant	All fruits	Bud swell to cracked buds; timing for certain insects and still safe for dormant spray materials.
Green tip (crack bud)	Pear, apple, prune, plum, cherry	Leaf tip beginning to emerge from bud; timing for insects and diseases.
Red bud	Apricot	Fruit buds emerged before petals show; brown rot spray.
Pink bud	Peach, nectarine	Petals showing, flowers not open; peach blight spray.
Popcorn	Almond, prune plum, cherry	White petals showing, flowers not open; brown rot spray.
Cluster bud	Apple, pear	Flower buds separated but clustered together; scab and blister mite spray.
Finger (pink)	Apple, pear	Flower buds spread apart, petals showing, flowers not open; scab and blister mite spray.
Full bloom	All fruits	90% of flowers open, no petals off; apricot brown rot, etc.
Petal fall	All fruits	90% of petals off; apricot brown rot, etc.
Prebloom	Walnut	Before pistils of female flower are expanded; walnut blight spray.
Postbloom	Walnut	After 90% of female flowers are pollinated; walnut blight spray.
Jacket	Stone fruits	Calyx clinging to small fruits; twig borer and mildew.
Calyx	Apple, pear	All petals off and before calyx lobes close.
Foliage	All fruits	Whenever leaves are present, as distinguished from dormant period.
Cover	Pears, apple	Codling moth spray on fruit.
Preharvest stopdrop	Pear, apple	7 days before harvest or just as first fruit is about to drop. Prevents fruit drop.

Check weather conditions carefully

Weather conditions and proper dilutions of materials singly or in combinations are also important pest fundamentals.

Don't underestimate problem of control

Control of injurious insects has always been a major problem of fruit growers. In recent years the

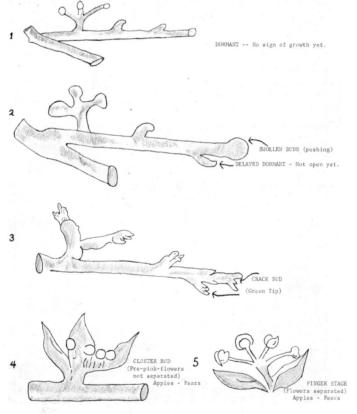

Fig. 13.3—Fruit crops—spray stages.

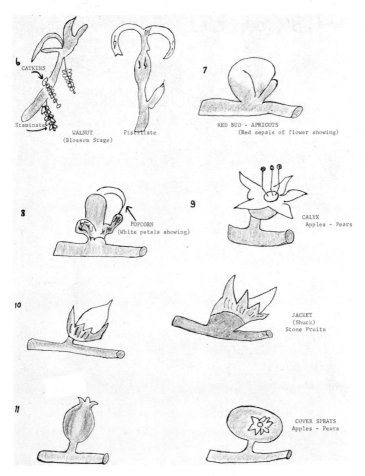

Fig. 13.3 (continued)

pesticide industry has provided new and superior weapons for grower usage. However, insect control promises to continue as a major problem in all phases of American agriculture.

Modern fruit farmers must compete on the basis of quality. In most instances quantity is also important.

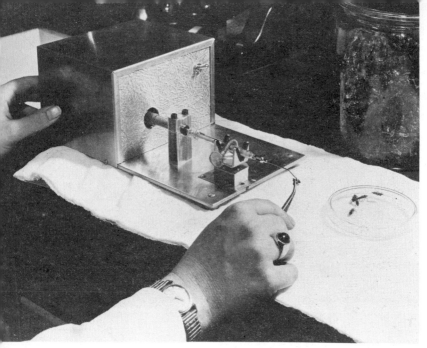

Fig. 13.4—Putting equipment to work. A specially designed laboratory device for applying pesticides to test insects. Used in research efforts to determine effective controls.

Insects represent a major limiting factor of both quality and quantity in fruit production.

Understand life history

Growers are finding that variations in effectiveness and prices of insecticides have a great deal to do with efficiency in fruit production. It is thus important that they understand the life history and control fundamentals of their major insect pests in order to get the best returns from insect control chemicals.

Positive determination of insect problems is important for efficient control. Because recommendations for chemical control vary from year to year, no suggestions of this type are given. Commercial growers should consult the current revision of Extension Bulletins from local farm advisors, the Agricultural Commissioner or field men for chemical recommendations.

2. Controlling Pests That Suck Sap

Pests that suck sap are among the most injurious pests of fruit trees. Injury is sometimes overlooked because the pests are often small and feed on parts of the plant other than the fruit. A weakened plant and improper bud development usually result from such feeding. In years of drought, heat or inadequate moisture supplies, injury is more severe.

Learn life cycle of sucking insects

The sap-sucking pests have a life cycle known as incomplete metamorphosis, that is, they have only three life stages—egg, nymph and adult. In certain instances, as with many aphids and scale insects, the egg stage is missing and only young (nymphs) and

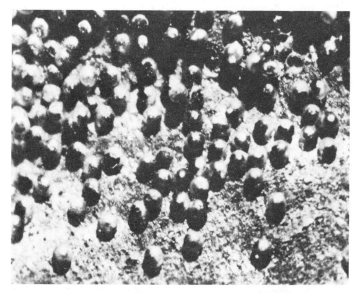

Fig. 13.5—Red mite eggs. Once these eggs hatch, a serious infestation will be underway.

adults are present. In these cases adults give birth to living young.

Insects with only three life stages often have a very rapid life cycle. Some have several generations each year. Both nymphs and adults represent active feeding stages. Most of the other fruit pests have four life stages and usually do not reproduce so rapidly as sucking pests (notably aphids and mites). This is an important consideration when planning control measures.

Select contact sprays for sap pests

Because they have piercing-sucking mouth parts, pests that feed on the sap must be controlled with pesticides having contact fumigating action. Materials that kill largely by stomach poison action are worthless or of little value against sucking pests.

Systemics

Sucking insects as well as others can also be controlled by applying material to the plant that is absorbed by the plant. The insect then consumes it when it sucks on the juices.

Aphids

Aphids are among the most serious of the sucking pests in many areas. They are found to some extent on practically all of our fruit plants.

Aphids are small, soft-bodied insects, usually identified by two small cornicles (horns) on the end of the abdomen. They usually feed in groups. Winged and wingless individuals are often present in the same colony.

Fig. 13.6—Aphids, among the most universally troublesome and costly fruit crop foes, can be seen busy at work on a leaf in this microphoto.

PREDATORS HELP CONTROL APHIDS

Natural enemies of aphids are common in most sections of the country. Ladybird beetles feed on aphid colonies both as adult beetles and as immature larvae. Syrphid flies, often seen hovering in mid-air, produce legless larvae that forage readily on aphids. Lace-wings lay eggs on silken stalks, which hatch into active "aphis lions." Tiny wasps destroy aphids by feeding as internal parasites. Unfortunately, most present-day insecticides destroy many of these beneficial insects.

PLANT DISEASES CAN BE CARRIED BY APHIDS

Some aphid species are carriers of certain plant

IDENTIFICATION OF SOME COMMON FRUIT PESTS AND AREA OF DAMAGE*

Injury	Apples	Almonds	Apricots	Pears	Peaches	Cherries	Plums	Grapes	Usual Identifying Characteristics	Pests
Pests suck sap	S	L	L	M	L	S	M	L	Small, slow-moving pests live in colonies	Aphids
	S	S	L	L	L	L	S	L	Minute 8-legged pests	Mites
	L	D		L	L		L	S	Greenish insects, often run sideways	Leafhoppers
				S					Small insects, secrete honeydew on pears	Pear psyllas
	D	S	S	D	D	D	D	D	Hard scales, numerous on bark, some soft with tufts	Scale insects
				D	D				Quick insects, larger than other sucking pests	Plant bugs
									Spittle masses secreted by young nymphs	Spittlebugs
										Mealy bugs
Worms in fruit	S	D	D	M	S	S	S		Worms with brown head but no legs	Plum curculios
	S			M					Worms with head and legs, work in core	Codling moths
			D		S		D		Worms with head and legs, in peaches	Oriental fruit moths
	S		D						Worms (larvae) without head or legs, in apples	Apple maggots
						S			Worms without head or legs, in cherries	Cherry fruit flies
Pests chew foliage and fruit	S			M	S	S	S	S	Gray-brown snout beetles about ¼ inch long	Plum curculios
									Worms, roll leaves and feed on fruit	Leaf rollers
	D			D	D	D	D	D	Long-legged tan beetles, congregate in groups	Rose chafers
	D			D	D	D	D	D	Cutworms, climb plants at night early in season	Climbing cutworms
Pest bore in bark and wood		S	S		S	D	D		Large worms, work near soil level under bark	Peach tree borers
		S	L		S	D	D		Medium-sized worms, work on trunk and large limbs	Lesser peach tree borers
	D		S	D	D	D			Small borers, produce shot-hole pattern in bark	Shot-hole borers
Pests feed on roots									Large grub worms, chew off roots	White grubs
									Small grubs, feed on strawberry roots	Strawberry root weevils
		S	S		D	D	D	S	Microscope reveals eel-like worms	Nematodes

*The degree of injury to plant if pests are not controlled is indicated by: S—serious; M—medium; L—light; D—depends on location and season; blank—no particular problem.

Courtesy, Extension Service, Michigan State University.

diseases. Viruses of strawberries may be transported from one plant to another by winged adults.

Start Control Early

Some species of aphids require control early in the season, and protective sprays are needed in plantings with a history of infestation. Under these conditions, control is advisable whether pests are seen or not. Aphids requiring this type of control are the rosy apple aphid, black cherry aphid and currant aphid. Most satisfactory control is obtained with pre-bloom applications.

Select Control When Damage Appears

Green apple aphids and various other aphids which build up on other fruits during the summer can be controlled when damaging infestations are observed.

Mites

Mites are similar to aphids in that they have a high reproductive rate and feed on a wide variety of fruit crops. Although mites are not true insects (having four rather than three pairs of legs) their injury is similar to that caused by other pests with piercing-sucking mouth parts. A magnifying lens is usually required for observation of their four pairs of legs, and for positive identification of species.

Mites Found in Large Numbers

Mites are very small and are often found in great numbers. Weather factors such as warm, dry periods favor mite build-up. Also certain spray materials used against other pests sometimes destroy mite enemies and allow an increase. Under such conditions, mites can become extremely injurious.

RED MITE MAY HAVE EIGHT FAMILIES PER YEAR

The European red mite, which is a pest of a number of fruits, remains on the trees throughout the summer. Eight or more overlapping generations occur each season. In areas where European red mites are a persistent and perennial problem, a prebloom application of an effective material is often advisable.

The two-spotted mite, as the name suggests, can usually be recognized by prominent dark spots showing on its back. Although they are sometimes pink or salmon-colored, two-spotted mites tend to be lighter and of a more greenish appearance than either European red mites or clover mites.

SELECT PESTICIDE FOR BEST CONTROL

Some pesticides, while not specific against mites, tend to hold down infestations when they are applied during the regular spray program. The use of such materials is advisable. However, a close watch should be maintained throughout the summer as mite populations can build up very rapidly, especially during warm, dry periods. It is best to control them before noticeable injury occurs.

SELECT COMBINATION OF MATERIALS

When mites do build up to damaging numbers during the summer, an effective miticide should be used immediately. It is most economical to choose a material with ovicidal (egg killing) properties or one with long residual effectiveness so that one application will provide effective control. Some growers favor a combination of two materials—one for adults and nymphs, the other for eggs. Unless eggs are destroyed, a second application may be necessary to kill young mites which hatch 5 to 10 days after the original application.

Leafhoppers

Several species of leafhoppers are injurious to varying degrees on fruits. Early in the season the most serious is the grape leafhopper, which requires control every year in most vineyards. Several others feed on such crops as apples, pears, strawberries and brambles.

Leafhoppers Do Double Damage

In addition to sucking sap, some leafhoppers are capable of spreading certain virus diseases, and when allowed uncontrolled interfere with fruit picking, notably in vineyards.

Select Contact Spray for Control

Being active individuals, leafhoppers come into contact with a leaf surface more than do several of the other sap-sucking pests. Most are controlled readily with pesticides having contact action.

Other leafhoppers can be controlled with materials used against other pests in the spray program.

Pear psylla

The pear psylla is a small, aphid-like insect that feeds on pears. Like aphids and scale nymphs, the pear psylla secretes a sweet substance known as honeydew. If infestations are not controlled, the discharge of this waxy fluid leads to a sticky, blackened condition on the foliage caused by a black fungus growth which develops readily on honeydew.

When viewed through a magnifying lens, the adult psylla is similar in appearance to an adult cicada. Overall length is approximately $\frac{1}{8}$ inch for adults and fully grown nymphs.

Scale insects

Several species of scales are injurious to fruits. The San Jose, European fruit lecanium, and Forbes scales are the most serious offenders throughout the United States.

The scale insect itself is a small, soft-bodied individual. However, these insects secrete a hard, protective, terrapin-like covering which is very resistant to insecticidal materials.

The San Jose is a small, circular scale about the size of a pin head that attacks nearly all fruits. It is usually dark brown to black and has a raised, dull yellow, nipple-like center. The overall appearance during winter is an ashy-black condition on the bark.

The Forbes scale attacks many fruit trees, but is more serious on red tart (sour) cherries than others. It is similar to the San Jose scale but is slightly larger, and the overall appearance tends to be brown, rather than dull black or ashy. Adults have a raised, orange-colored, central nipple.

The European fruit lecanium is a pest of blueberries, peaches and plums. It is much larger than the others mentioned, is brown and has a terrapin-like appearance. Mature lecanium scales are $\frac{1}{8}$ to $\frac{1}{6}$ inch in diameter.

USE DORMANT SPRAY ON SOME SCALES

Heavy infestations of San Jose and Forbes scales

are best controlled with a dormant application of an effective material. Dormant or delayed dormant oil sprays, sometimes applied in combination with other active ingredients, are ordinarily used.

Unless populations of San Jose or Forbes scales have built up in an orchard, a contact type insecticide in the regular spray schedule during the month of June tends to hold them in check in some areas. At this time, the young scale nymphs (crawlers) are migrating over the plant. Migration continues about one week before the small crawlers insert their mouthparts into the plant tissue and take up permanent residence on the spot. The hard scale covering is secreted soon thereafter and the insect is no longer susceptible to the usual summer insecticides.

Lecanium Scale Easily Controlled

The lecanium scale can ordinarily be controlled by applying effective materials soon after the crawlers have emerged. Apply one treatment when approximately 70 per cent of the eggs (present under the adult female scale) have hatched. The eggs turn from white to salmon color immediately before hatching.

Plant bugs

Plant bugs are larger than most of the other sap-sucking pests. Adults range in size from about 1/4 inch long (tarnished plant bugs) to the stink bugs which sometimes attain a length of 1/2 inch.

Tarnished plant bugs are perhaps the most serious of this group on some fruits. They infest strawberries, pears, peaches and brambles. Feeding injury on the fruit portion leads to a deformed condition often referred to as "catfacing" on peaches or "button-berries" on strawberries.

Time Right for Plant Bug Control

Plant bugs can ordinarily be controlled with early-season applications of effective materials. These sprays are directed against adult insects which emerge from hibernation and feed on young plant growth. Although plant bugs may have two or more generations each year the late broods are ordinarily controlled with sprays used primarily against other pests.

Spittlebugs

In the adult stage spittlebugs closely resemble leaf-hoppers. Adults are brownish individuals often seen in great numbers in hay and grain crops during the late summer. Many of the females lay eggs at the base of strawberry plants.

"Champagne" Type of Pest

Spittlebugs generally hatch by early May. In addition to sucking sap, the young nymphs blow bubbles which produce a spittle mass.

Preventing Spittlebug Best Procedure

A spittlebug infestation can be prevented with an effective, long residual-type material applied in the prebloom period. This is ordinarily before many spittle masses have appeared. If control is delayed until the postbloom period, when spittle masses are plainly evident, an effective material labeled for use in the postbloom period should be selected.

Other sap-sucking pests

Additional insects that are occasionally troublesome on fruits as sap-sucking pests include treehoppers

Fig. 13.7—Tarnished plant bug.

and cicadas. Pests of this type vary tremendously according to the year, location and weather factors and often cause more injury to twigs by their egg-laying activities than they do by actual feeding. They can ordinarily be controlled with insecticides effective against other sucking insects.

3. Controlling Pests That Produce Worms in Fruit

Insects that produce worms in fruit have a life cycle known as complete metamorphosis. In addition to the egg, larva (worm) and adult stages, there is an additional stage called the pupa (resting stage) in which the insect transforms from the larva to the adult. The pupa is similar to the egg stage in that it is inactive and quite resistant to many insecticides. Often the pupa is enclosed in a cocoon, or is otherwise protected so that pesticides cannot reach it.

Select proper insecticide

For the most part, pests that produce worms in fruit have chewing mouthparts at some stage of their life cycle. Often they can be controlled with insecticides showing only stomach poison action. However, insecticides that exhibit stomach poison, contact action and sometimes fumigating action, usually work best. Such ingredients provide a "shot-gun" effect and often destroy two or more life stages of a given pest.

Kill adults early

To prevent worms in fruit, it is usually important to apply protective sprays prior to or during periods when adults are active. Control largely depends upon destruction of the pest at adult or immature stages, before the fruit is infested.

Plum curculio

The plum curculio is a brownish-gray beetle about $\frac{1}{4}$ inch long and differs from other curculios by having small humps on its back. It has a long snout with chewing mouthparts at the tip. Adults emerge from hibernation in and around orchards about the time peach trees are in the shuck-split stage. They injure the fruit by external feeding and egg-laying activities.

SELECT A PROTECTIVE SPRAY FOR CONTROL

In some areas, apples, pears, plums, peaches and cherries usually require protective sprays against the plum curculio. To prevent egg-laying, effective materials should be applied whether adults are seen or not. Stone fruits that are infested ordinarily drop, while apples and pears usually hang to the tree but bear egg-laying marks.

ONE GENERATION TO CONTROL EACH YEAR

Larvae (worms or grubs) grow quite rapidly when the infested fruit drops. Full grown larvae leave the fruit, enter the soil and change to the pupa stage. Later in the summer, adult curculios emerge from the soil, feed for a while on unsprayed fruit and then enter hibernation quarters in the soil or under debris. Hence, only one generation occurs each year.

Codling moth

The codling moth is a serious pest of apples and other fruit wherever they are grown in the United

States. Protective sprays are always needed. Although pears are usually damaged to a lesser extent, they also require protective sprays.

The codling moth spends the winter as a full-grown larva about ¾ inch long in a partial cocoon under flakes of bark. The larva changes to the brown pupa stage in the spring and emerges as a moth during the latter part of May and throughout June. The adult moth is slightly over ½ inch long and has a dark, chocolate-colored band along the base of the wing. The moths fly late in the evening and deposit eggs singly on the foliage and fruit.

Young Worm Enters Stem End of Fruit

Larvae that hatch from eggs (about one week after they are laid) often migrate to the calyx end where they enter the fruit. Before the appearance of DDT and other organic insecticides, a calyx spray of lead arsenate was standard procedure. This left a poisonous residue in the calyx end of the apple before the sepals closed and provided protection for young larvae. Present-day insecticides destroy larvae largely by contact action before the larvae can enter the fruit and cause injury. Some materials (especially those with fumigating action) act against adult moths and eggs as well.

Second Brood Appears in Some Areas

In the Midwest a second brood appears late in July. Spray dates based on the emergence of adult moths are determined by the Department of Entomology at most state universities. Announcements of spray dates are made by county agricultural agents and district horticultural agents in the various fruit areas. Thorough sprays during June against the first brood

ordinarily tend to keep second brood numbers greatly
reduced.

SOME LARVAE AREN'T KILLED OUTRIGHT

Larvae that pick up a slight amount of insecticide,
but do not die until they enter the fruit, produce defects known as "stings." Worms killed by fumigating
action of some insecticides soon after they enter the
fruit also produce this condition.

Oriental fruit moth

The oriental fruit moth is a very serious pest on
peaches. Three full broods and a partial fourth occur
each year. In some areas, the adult moth is approximately ⅓ inch long, and is of a basic dark brown color.

MOTH LIKES EVENING FLYING

Like the codling moth, adults fly late in the evening. Females deposit their eggs on peach twigs, foliage
and fruit. Injury from the first brood is caused by
cream-colored larvae which enter the terminal growth
and tunnel inside succulent twigs. Larvae from later
broods enter the fruit and are the most common worm
in peaches at harvest. The larvae work near the pit and
attain a length of approximately ½ inch. When full-
grown many turn pinkish in color.

They are largely eliminated by present-day insecticides used against other pests in the peach schedule.

CONTROL A CONTINUOUS PROBLEM

In many fruit areas, it has become highly important to continue an active spray program against
the oriental fruit moth until peaches are harvested.

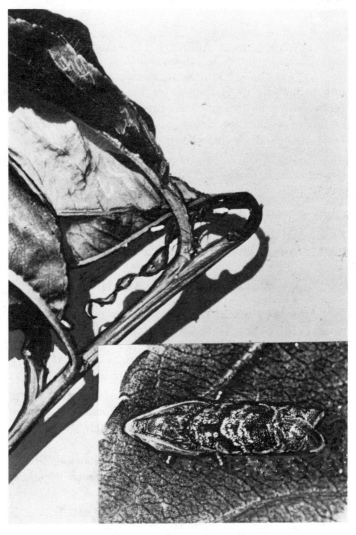

Courtesy, Union Carbide Co.

Fig. 13.8—Oriental fruit moth.

Otherwise, small larvae often enter the ripening fruit near the stem and tunnel in beside the pit. Such peaches may appear sound until they are opened. To prevent this, select an insecticide which has long enough residual action to provide protection until the crop is harvested. Also, choose an insecticide that will not exceed the tolerance established for that particular material on peaches.

Apple maggot

The apple maggot is a serious pest on apples and several other fruits. Protective insecticidal applications are required each year during July and August on crops.

Injury is caused by a maggot (typical fly larva, lacking a head and legs) which tunnels inside the fruit. Because of the winding nature of the tunnel, this pest is sometimes called the "railroad worm."

DESTROY ADULTS FOR BEST CONTROL

Control depends upon killing adults before eggs are laid. Thus it is important to apply the first protective spray after adults emerge, but before egg-laying begins. Because adults continue to emerge from the soil throughout July, protection is needed well into August.

Some county extension agents announce the timing for the first spray against apple maggot. Announcements are based on observations made in the field by entomologists checking for adult flies.

Cherry fruit flies

The cherry fruit fly and black cherry fruit fly are very closely related insects.

Injury Is Similar to Apple Maggot

These flies are related to the apple maggot and injure the fruit in a similar manner. There is but one generation each year. Control consists of poisoning adults within the 7- to 10-day interval between emer-

Fig. 13.9—Cherry fruit fly.

gence and the start of egg-laying. Like the apple maggot, cherry fruit flies sponge food from the foliage and fruit and have dark bands across their wings.

Additional worms in fruit

Several other worms are sometimes troublesome in fruit. These include cherry fruitworm, mineola moth, peach twig borer and drosophila (fruit fly). In orchards (especially cherry) with a history of such problems,

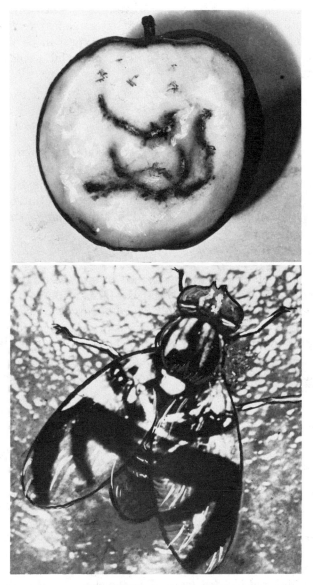

Fig. 13.10—Apple maggot.

the forms can normally be prevented by choosing an insecticide with a wide range of effectiveness for use during June. Most materials of this type can be used alone or combined with a specific material used for control of another pest.

4. Controlling Pests That Chew Foliage and Fruit

Like the pests that are troublesome as worms in fruit, the insects that chew foliage and fruit have biting (chewing) mouthparts. They also have the complete metamorphosis type of life cycle. Control is directed largely against the adult and/or larva stage.

Plum curculio

The plum curculio, described in more detail on an earlier page as related to larvae infestation in fruit, is also a pest in the adult stage. Injury from adult feeding often occurs in the spring prior to and during egg-laying time. Small circular holes are cut in the sides of young fruit. Chewing injury of this type is usually quite minor in comparison with the more serious egg-laying activity.

Leaf rollers

As the name implies, leaf roller larvae usually fold or roll fruit leaves. They often attach leaf edges to a fruit and feed on the leaf and fruit surfaces.

Two very serious types occur each year on fruits in some areas—the red-banded leaf roller and strawberry leaf roller. Others, such as the fruit tree leaf roller and oblique-banded leaf roller, sometimes occur on fruits. Their injury is more sporadic than perennial.

The *red-banded leaf roller* attacks a wide variety

Courtesy, Union Carbide Co.
Fig. 13.11—Red banded leaf roller.

of fruits. Winter is passed in the pupa stage on the ground. Adult moths, almost ½ inch long with a rusty band near the center of their wings, emerge early in the spring. Egg masses resembling miniature fish scales are deposited on the slick bark of apple and other fruit tree limbs. Egg-laying by the first brood is ordinarily at its peak just before and during bloom on apples. Applying effective materials soon after the bloom period greatly reduces first brood numbers. If the small worms are not controlled at this time, control becomes more difficult as the young larvae soon roll leaves and gain protection from spray materials.

CHECK EARLY TO SAVE INJURY AT HARVEST TIME

A second brood of red-banded leaf rollers occurs in July and August. It is highly important that growers

Fig. 13.12—Red-banded leaf roller in action.

be on the lookout for egg masses and young larvae on leaves during this period. Unless control measures follow when these signs are present, serious loss at harvest time may result.

ADDITIONAL CHEWING INSECTS

Various other chewing insects occasionally injure the foliage or fruit—in either the adult or immature stages. These include the grape flea beetles, certain scarab beetles, grasshoppers, various fruit worms, saw-flies, caterpillars and cut worms.

Insects of this type can normally be controlled by prompt treatment with some effective material when infestations are first noticed.

5. Controlling Pests That Bore in Bark and Wood

There are a number of troublesome borers in fruit orchards. Mechanical injury to the trees results from their feeding activity and makes the tree more susceptible to drought and to disease organisms. Most serious are the peach tree borer, lesser peach tree borer and shot-hole borer.

Peach tree borer

The peach tree borer works largely on peach trees, but is sometimes a problem on other stone fruits, especially those with peach root stock. Injury is caused near the ground level where borers enter the bark and feed on the cambium and associated plant tissue. Injury is ordinarily limited to a 12-inch area from 6 inches above the surface of the soil to 6 inches below the surface.

The adult is an active day-flying moth. It is steel blue in color. The males, which lack scales on their wings, resemble large wasps. Females have an orange strip across the abdomen. Eggs are deposited near the ground level on the trunk and sometimes on weeds nearby. The young larvae hatch within a few days and bore directly into the cambium.

Use a Drenching Spray for Borer

To control the peach tree borer, it is important to apply drenching sprays with a gun at about 150 pounds pressure. Sprays should be applied when adults are actively laying eggs. Effective materials destroy the adults, eggs and/or larvae before injury is caused. Some areas still use a fumigate crystal at the base of the tree (PDB).

There is but one brood each year, but unlike many other fruit pests, adult emergence is spread over a considerable period of time—usually from late June until late August, with the peak around mid-July. It is most important to have protective sprays on the trees from early July until mid-August.

Lesser peach tree borer

The lesser peach tree borer is closely related and similar in appearance to the peach tree borer. However, it is somewhat smaller and the larvae work higher in the peach tree. Injury most often occurs around cankered areas on scaffold limbs, at crotches and the upper trunk.

When both the peach tree borer and lesser peach tree borer are troublesome in plantings, select a material that is effective against both pests. The period when protective sprays are needed in this case extends from late June until mid-August.

Shot-hole borer

The shot-hole borer is one of several small bark beetles that attack fruit and forest trees. Injuries occur both from adult feeding at the base of twigs and from galleries made by the tunneling larvae. Common host plants include cherry, peach, plum, apple and pear.

Borer selects trees in trouble

The borers breed primarily in weakened trees or those that have been freshly killed. Female beetles enter the bark and construct an egg gallery parallel to the grain of the wood. Young larvae which hatch from eggs deposited in this gallery bore outward at a right angle to the egg gallery. As the larvae grow and consume more food, the injured area becomes fanlike in appearance, with the larval galleries radiating from the parent egg gallery like the ribs of a fan.

When the larvae complete their development, pupation occurs at the end of the individual galleries. Later, adult beetles emerge from these sites and produce the characteristic shot-hole effect commonly observed on the bark surface.

Insecticides normally used in fruit spraying schedules during June serve to control this pest in bearing orchards. However, non-bearing trees, especially in locations where populations are allowed to breed unmolested, may suffer severe injury. To control, apply effective materials early in June and/or August when adult beetles appear.

6. Controlling Pests That Feed on Roots

White grubs

White grubs (the larvae of the common May beetle) are often troublesome in strawberry and sometimes bramble fields where grass sod has been plowed. They feed normally on grass roots but shift readily to the berry plants. They have a brown head and attain a length of approximately 1 inch. The hind part of the abdomen is usually darkened in color due to the fact that soil particles in the abdomen show through.

Sod Harbors Many Grubs

The most effective means of controlling white grubs is to avoid planting in a newly-plowed sod field, or to treat the soil with an effective chemical labeled for soil usage.

Nematodes

Nematodes are minute microscopic animals found in great numbers in practically all soils. Many types feed on decaying organic matter and are beneficial to plant life; others, however, feed on plants. These are called plant parasitic nematodes. Some are serious pests on fruit crops.

Various Names for Nematodes

Plant parasitic nematodes are sometimes named according to the type of injury they produce. The root knot nematodes cause small gall-like growths on the roots of hosts. The pin nematodes have mouthparts equipped for piercing root tissue.

Nematodes capable of attacking roots of fruit trees and vines often build up in tremendous numbers in plantings of susceptible host plants. The establish-

Fig. 13.13—Peach tree killed as result of nematodes.

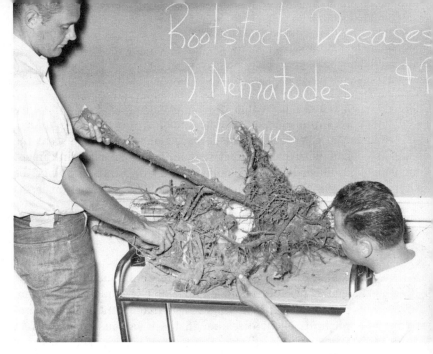

Fig. 13.14—Close-up of roots of tree in Fig. 13.13. Picture shows knots and twisted roots that caused death of the tree.

ment of a new fruit planting on sites heavily infested with such species can be very unprofitable.

CHECK SOIL CAREFULLY

It is often advisable to have the soil checked for nematodes prior to planting an anticipated fruit crop. Such tests can determine kinds of nematodes present and the advisability of fumigating or otherwise treating the soil. Nematode-resistant rootstocks have proven beneficial in many areas, as well as treating areas with chemicals after planting.

Use proper management practices

Another means of control, which works well against certain pests, is to raise a non-susceptible host plant one or more years on the site before establishing a fruitful planting. In this way, the life cycle can be interrupted so that chemical means of control is avoided.

In infested fields a means of control is to treat the soil with some effective fumigant. Special equipment is needed for this purpose, and application should be made only by experienced operators. Resistant rootstock is advisable.

Fruit Diseases

Fruit diseases are often more difficult to recognize and control than insect pests. Consequently, prevention, in the form of good management, is most important. Fruit diseases, in their various forms, affect roots, trunk, limbs, fruit and leaves. Diseases are classed according to the cause—bacteria, virus, fungus or a disorder referred to as physiological.

Fig. 13.15—Oak-root fungus damage. Author with agriculture instructors explaining management problems leading to death of tree.

7. Controlling Bacterial Diseases

Bacterial diseases damage fruit, foliage and other parts of the tree usually above ground. Bacteria are microscopic plants or organisms and are difficult to control by sprays or dusts.

Remove infected areas and destroy

Infected areas such as limbs damaged by blight or crown gall on stems are often removed from the tree and destroyed by burning. The pruning wound is then disinfected with various materials depending on type of tree and disease. Sterilization of the tools used, with alcohol, lysol or similar material is advisable to avoid further contamination.

Consider antibiotics for blight

Orchardists report some success in controlling blight with streptomycin. The author used a spray at 60 p.p.m. on pears during blossom stage, and control was improved. However, the cost of materials is considerably higher than the often used Bordeaux and phenyl mercuries.

Crown gall

Crown gall continues to be a serious problem on peaches, almonds and grapes. Annually many plants are weakened, stunted and even killed by crown gall. But the disease is both avoidable and curable.

The bacterial organism which causes crown gall lives in the soil and establishes itself in a tree or vine only when introduced through a wound. Once the bacteria get inside the plant tissue they multiply and cause rapid, disorganized growth of plant cells.

The subsequent galls are large, roundish swellings that have rough bark on their exterior surface. Galls appear on roots and on the trunks of trees and vines at the soil surface. Occasionally they are seen on limbs where the bacteria are introduced in pruning wounds.

The incidence of crown gall can be reduced by careful cultural operations. Avoid hitting the crown of a plant with a disk or shovel. Injuries caused by implements make a perfect entrance site for the bacteria.

The crown area (trunk of tree or vine at soil surface) is the most serious place for a gall. The progressive enlargement of a gall in this area can partially or entirely girdle the plant.

Corrective measures can be taken for these galls. The greatest value from treatment is derived by young trees or vines, two to six years old, because galls are usually fairly small.

Also young trees and vines are vigorous and have rapid healing capacities. Treatment of old plants and roots is usually not practical in a commercial venture.

The best time for treatment is the fall-winter period. Galls are easier to get at and labor is usually available. Some plant injury may occur during extremely hot weather.

Crown galls should be cleaned or removed before chemical treatment. The galls can be removed with a chisel or they can be left on the plant and cleaned thoroughly with a dry paint brush. If a gall is left, it must be free of dirt to permit proper coverage and penetration of the chemical.

After the galls are prepared, a mixture of elgetol and methanol (synthetic wood alcohol) is brushed on the area to be treated. Paint the exposed surface and ½ inch to 1 inch of good bark around the edge of the wound, if the gall is removed.

UNTREATED GALL
INFECTION

CHISEL OFF ALL GALL
INFECTION TO THE WOOD.

REMOVE INFECTED CHIPS
AND DESTROY THEM.

IF THE GALL SURROUNDS
THE TRUNK, DO NOT TREAT
OVER 1/4 OF THE TREE
IN ONE YEAR.

Fig. 13.16—Treating crown gall.

When the gall is left on the plant, paint the gall and ½ inch to 1 inch of good bark around the edge. Do not treat more than halfway around the trunk of a tree or vine.

The elgetol--methanol mixture is prepared by mixing one part of 20 per cent elgetol and four parts of methanol. If only 30 per cent elgetol is available, the mixture should consist of one part of 30 per cent elgetol and six and one-half parts methanol. The mixture should be taken before each treatment so that the ingredients remain well mixed.

Galls treated with the elgetol-methanol mixture die gradually over a period of a few weeks to several months. All wounds made during preparation for treatment should be disinfected with a light dressing of elgetol-methanol mixture and covered with a sealing agent.

Fig. 13.17—Bacterial canker. Vigorous suckers growing below severe canker.

Galls on most grape vineyards do not result in serious economic damage. Keeping soil away from its crown will often cause galls to dry up.

Bacterial canker

Interest in bacterial canker has been renewed because of severe outbreaks in some peach and plum orchards.

CAUSE OF THE DISEASE

A bacterium which gains entrance through pruning wounds or natural openings in the tissues is the causal agent. It produces cankers in the bark during the dormant season and in early spring. Heavy fall rains appear to be important in inducing the severe outbreaks of the disease. When heavy rains occur in the spring, a blasting or blighting of blossoms, leaves, and green shoots may also occur.

TREES AND PLANTS ATTACKED

This disease is known to attack the almond, apricot, avocado, cherry, peach, nectarine and plum. Bacterial blight of the lilac and blast of citrus, pear and rose are caused by the same organism. Peaches are usually less susceptible than apricots, cherries and plums; however the disease is bad on the peach in some years.

Fig. 13.18—Bacterial canker on apricot. The twig of this infected branch broke and fell over where the infection occurred. Note the gummy substance at the break. Normal leaf is displayed.

VARIETIES SHOW DIFFERENCE IN RESISTANCE

There seems to be some difference in susceptibility among varieties, especially in plum where Beauty and Kelsey are highly resistant, Santa Rosa is moderately susceptible and Duarte and President are highly susceptible. The disease is also quite serious in some French prune orchards. There is no general agreement as to the relative susceptibility of sweet cherry varieties.

KNOW SYMPTOMS

This disease causes the bark to die in elongated areas or cankers on the trunk or limbs, and in time the trunk or limbs may be girdled and killed. Young fruiting wood and spurs may be attacked and the buds killed. After the tissues are infected, an amber gum usually forms, and this has accounted for the common name of bacterial gummosis. But in some cases a thin ooze with little gum develops and the diseased tissues become brown, moist and sour-smelling. This form of the disease is often called "sour sap," but should not be confused with sour sap caused by poor soil drainage around the roots and crown.

ALL GUMMING NOT CANKER

It should also be remembered that gumming may be caused by other things than bacterial canker; for example, peach tree borer. The disease is extremely variable from year to year. In years of epidemics, very heavy losses have occurred in California.

OTHER SYMPTOMS

Although the most serious aspect of this disease is the cankers that girdle and kill large branches or sometimes the entire tree, other symptoms occur that should be briefly described. During rainy periods in the spring pear and stone-fruit blossoms are sometimes blighted, the destroyed blooms usually remaining attached to the twigs. This blighting of the blossoms

Fig. 13.19—Bacterial canker. Note glob of pitch material hanging from tree in the lower right corner. This 35-year-old produced a good crop of apricots in the spring. The tree had to be removed in the fall.

is often referred to as blast. Rains that occur after the blossoming period often give rise to a spotting and eventual shot-holing of the leaves and to a blighting of the young green shoots. This condition appears to be more prevalent in plums and apricots than in the other stone-fruit species. Infection of the young fruits of apricot, cherry and pear infrequently occurs and results in the formation of small, black, firm, depressed lesions.

APPROVED PRACTICES BEST CONTROL

There is no adequate control of bacterial canker, but certain practices may aid in reducing the severity of the disease.

CONSIDER CANKER REMOVAL

If the cankers are not too large or too numerous, surgery to remove the dead bark, followed by disinfection of the wound, may prove of value. Girdled or severely diseased branches should be entirely removed, using care to make the cuts somewhat below any evidence of infection. Such surgical treatment should preferably be done in the summer when the disease is inactive. If done at this time of the year, covering the wound with Bordeaux paste should provide adequate protection against reinfection and should discourage invasion by woodrotting fungi.

USE BORDEAUX

Another measure that has offered some promise is the application of one or two fall sprays of a 6-6-50 or an 8-8-50 Bordeaux mixture. For maximum protection it is thought that the first application of Bordeaux should be made as the leaves begin to fall, with a second spray being applied when most of the leaves are off. A Bordeaux spray at the popcorn stage of bloom has shown promise on cherries in England, but it has not been adequately tested in other areas. Since the disease is generally more serious in young than old trees, the first spray application should be made in the fall, at the end of the first season's growth.

ROOTSTOCK SELECTION MAY HELP

In establishing a new orchard or in replanting in an old orchard, it would be well to consider the effect of the rootstock on disease severity. Observations in commercial orchards and data from an experimental orchard indicate that plums and French prune on Lovell peach root suffered considerably less from the disease than where Myrobalan or Marianna 2624 rootstocks were used. In planting plums on peach root, care should be taken to keep the union well above the soil line. Peach rootstock should not be used in heavy, poorly drained soils. In apricots, the rootstock has had no consistent effects on the severity of bacterial canker.

Fire blight of fruits

Fire blight, known also as pear blight or simply blight, is a common and frequently destructive bacterial disease of plants belonging to the rose family (Rosaceae). Pears and quinces are extremely susceptible. Apples and crabapples are also frequently damaged. Temperatures are important in disease growth.

Development of this disease is favored by a combination of temperatures of 70° to 85° F. and high humidity created by rain, fog or even irrigation, especially overhead irrigation. Dry weather usually prevents new infections and retards existing infection.

Fig. 13.20—Fire blight on pear, early stage.

Fig. 13.21—Fire blight on pear, advanced stage.

Recognize Symptoms

Fire blight is characterized by a shriveling and blackening of the blossoms, tender shoots and young fruits. The affected parts look as though they were scorched by fire; hence the name, fire blight. An infection may progress down a shoot and into the bark of larger limbs where dark, sunken cankers are formed. These cankers slowly enlarge and may eventually girdle the limb.

Know Disease Cycle

The bacterium which causes the disease survives the summer and winter in blighted twigs and cankers, which serve as sources of new infections the following year. During moist weather in early spring, the bacteria ooze from the holdover cankers in small, milky, sticky drops.

Bacteria Need Transportation

The bacteria are carried to the blossoms and tender shoots by flies, ants, beetles and other insects and by splashing water. Bees and flies play a major role in spreading fire blight from blossom to blossom, but the beehive is not a holdover source of infection.

Control When Symptoms Show

During the summer, prune out and burn the diseased twigs and branches. Cut well below the edge of the infected area. On large trees, such as pears, cut back 18 inches or more where possible. After each cut, sterilize the cutting tools and the cut surface with a disinfectant to avoid further spread of the disease. A 5 per cent Lysol or a 4 per cent Amphyl solution may be used. Both materials are available from drug stores as liquid concentrates.

WATCH MANAGEMENT PRACTICES CAREFULLY

As a rule, fire blight is much worse on succulent growth. Excessive nitrogen fertilization, combined with heavy irrigations and other cultural practices that promote rapid growth, should be avoided where the disease has been a problem.

START CONTROL IN THE SPRING

Blossoms are the most susceptible part of the plant. They may be protected from infection by copper-containing sprays or dusts. A minute amount of copper in the blossom is effective. A very weak Bordeaux spray ½-½-100 or its equivalent has proven highly successful in controlling the disease on pears.

ANTIBIOTICS SHOW PROMISE

Streptomycin sprays or dusts may also be used. Streptomycin must not be applied after the first fruit is visible on pears, quinces, apples and crabapples or streptomycin residue may be present on fruit at harvest. The number of applications necessary depends upon the period of blooming. Make the first application at or before 10 per cent bloom and repeat at four- to five-day intervals until all late bloom is over. For pears this will mean 5 to 12 applications per season.

8.   Controlling Virus Diseases

The virus diseases are complex and mysterious. They can transmit their disease from one plant to another by mechanical means, such as pruning or grafting; by insects traveling from tree to tree and by other means. Viruses must be in the plant cells before they are able to regenerate themselves. Tree and vines may be infected with viruses that may or may not show symptoms.

Recognize the mosaic type viruses

This type of virus is familiar to the grower in the form of symptoms. The green leaf color is mottled dark and light. Brambles such as raspberries are susceptible.

Virus yellows

The entire leaf when affected with virus yellows is off color, resulting in eventual loss of fruit production. Most stone fruits are especially susceptible to yellows. They are often spread by sucking insects. Peach yellows and russet ring on apple are important virus yellow diseases.

Viruses cause other symptoms

Stunting of the plant growth and fruit, crumbly fruit and low production often are evident with virus infection. Death of the plant may also result. The grape industry has made giant steps in propagating vines that are free of any known harmful virus.

Remove plant and burn

No satisfactory control for virus is known once the plant has been infected. Growers should remove the plant and destroy it by burning to eliminate the disease organism.

Courtesy, U.S.D.A.

Fig. 13.22—Yellow virus of peach in an advanced stage.

Control vectors

An important factor in controlling viruses is to control the means of transmission from plant to plant. Spraying with an insecticide to eliminate aphids and leaf hoppers, known virus vectors, is practiced. Sanitation and good management will go far in eliminating

Courtesy, U.S.D.A.

Fig. 13.23—Ring spot affected leaves of peach showing rings, spots and chlorotic pattern.

serious virus infections. Research in the form of re-sistant varieties shows promise as a means of virus control.

Virus Diseases in Propagation

Ring spot is common

The most common virus encountered in grafting over trees of stone fruits is the ring spot virus. It may cause killing of scions or buds usually accompanied by gumming at the unions. Scions or buds that survive ring spot reaction are delayed but may make good growth later in the season and usually recover by the next season following grafting. If the same or a re-

Courtesy, U.S.D.A.

Fig. 13.24—Ring spot on peach, advanced stage.

lated strain of the ring spot virus is present in the scions and buds as in the stocks, no shock reaction, killing or gumming will occur.

Stubby twig, a serious disease

More important than ring spot virus are some

other viruses that may be present in the scions or stocks. While the main damage from ring spot occurs during the first or second season after grafting, certain other viruses are damaging year after year. Stubby twig is one of the viruses most likely to be present in trees of peach or nectarine varieties introduced the last 10 years. This disease does not kill trees or even cause complete infection in the trees. It occurs on portions of trees and reduces the amount and quality of the crop, causing damage year after year. Stubby twig can be detected in orchard trees by visual observation during the proper season. It is difficult and unreliable to attempt detection of stubby twig in the nursery or in one-year-old orchard trees.

Check for Symptoms in Spring

Inspection for stubby twig can be made in the spring when shoots on normal trees or branches are 6 to 8 inches long. In branches affected with stubby twig the terminal buds do not produce shoots but produce a cluster of leaves showing symptoms resembling nitrogen deficiency. Some leaves produced from lateral buds or spurs on affected branches show a dark green sectoring, and these leaves usually are somewhat misshapen and of a tough or leathery texture. Shoots originating from the basal portions of affected branches or from other branches tend to cover up these symptoms of stubby twig. Frequently leaves on current season shoots will roll and become yellow or pink. In severe cases considerable portions of the trees will be affected.

Necrotic leaf spot

Another disease found commonly in peach and nectarine varieties is necrotic leaf spot. This disease

Courtesy, U.S.D.A.

Fig. 13.25—Stubby twig symptoms on peach. A normal growing branch on the right.

is usually not serious in bearing trees but can cause
considerable leaf dropping from current season shoots
originating from new scions. This may delay growth
and predispose these shoots to sunburn and attack by
twig borers. Necrotic leaf spot virus may be related
to ring spot virus, but the disease differs from ring
spot in peach and nectarine in that necrotic leaf spot
may recur each year. As trees get older the effects of
the necrotic leaf spot disease become less obvious.

Select virus-free wood

Growers should insist that nursery trees or vines
be propagated from inspected orchards and vineyards
or that all possible precautions be taken by the nurserymen against propagating plants with virus diseases.

Fig. 13.26—Necrotic leaf spot. Large leaf shows early stage, with middle and end leaves displaying severe damage. Infected leaves often are more subject to attack by pests such as aphids, as shown on severely damaged leaf.

9. Controlling Fungus Diseases

Perhaps the most common diseases affecting trees belong to the fungal organisms. They affect roots, stems and fruit, as well as leaves. Fungi survive as parasites on or in cells and tissue of trees. Fungi do not have chlorophyll, therefore lack the green color we see in higher plants. They are usually microscopic but can be seen when grown in colonies. Fungal diseases include the mildews, rusts, leaf spots, leaf curls, apple scabs, wilts and others.

Fungi seek free ride

Fungi spores travel to their new home by a variety

of conveyances. Wind is their favorite, as well as slight air currents. Rain can spread them, as can insects. Man-made machines also do their share in distributing the organisms, especially those that affect roots.

Select fungicides for disease control

Sulfur and copper have long been used to control fungus diseases. Sulfur can be used as a dust or spray. Finely ground sulfur is best when dusting or when combined with a wetting agent to form wetting sulfur. Combinations of lime-sulfur must be used with care as they can be toxic to plants.

Copper compounds to control diseases have also been used extensively. Bordeaux, for example, is a combination of lime, copper, sulfate, and water. Bordeaux also can be toxic under high humidity conditions. A material known as low soluble sulfur is used more in orchards as it is not so toxic as Bordeaux.

Research develops new control for above-ground infections

An organic fungicide called Captan is effective against numerous diseases. It is known to have a low toxic level against plants and has become popular with growers. Ferbam, a fungicide even more widely known than Captan, is also effective against many diseases.

A number of mercurial compounds are also used as organic fungicides.

Peach leaf curl

Peach leaf curl is a widely distributed fungus disease of peaches, ornamental flowering peach and nectarines. The most serious damage occurs on the first spring leaves which, when infected, are yellow

Courtesy, U.S.D.A.

Fig. 13.27—Peach leaf curl with natural size leaf.

to reddish in color, thickened, crisp in texture and somewhat curled. As such leaves develop they produce a dusty white coating of spores. Many of the infected leaves drop, and a second crop of leaves soon replaces them. Such a loss of the initial leaves, together with production of a second leaf crop in one season, has a weakening effect upon both tree growth and crop production.

When peach leaf curl infection builds up and is left uncontrolled over a period of several years, trees may ultimately decline to the point that they must be removed. While most infected leaves drop, a few remain on the tree throughout the season. These tend to hang in clusters, standing out because of their dark brown color. When such leaves are shaken or tapped, clouds of spores are seen to rise in the air.

Infected twigs and shoots are usually distorted, often becoming thickened. The peach leaf curl fungus occasionally attacks blossoms, causing them to drop. Fruits are sometimes attacked, the symptoms being a reddish, irregular, roughened growth on a portion of the fruit surface. Typical infected areas are variable in size, later in the season becoming corky and having a tendency to crack.

CONTROL MEASURES

Commercial plantings: As the leaves are falling between November 15 and December 15, apply 10-10-100 Bordeaux spray or a fixed copper fungicide plus adhesive, prepared according to the manufacturer's directions.

These sprays must be applied as a fully dormant application before the buds begin to swell in the spring. Thorough tree coverage is essential for effective peach leaf curl control as leaves developing from buds not covered by the fungicide will probably become infected.

Controls for soil fungi

Control of soil fungi is much more difficult than above ground infections. However, satisfactory control has been achieved with carbon bisulfide and chloropicrin. These materials are used as fumigants in various management practices, and in some cases, have proved to be the only effective control used. One should keep in mind that if these organisms are known to exist beforehand, crop rotation and resistant root-stock should be considered.

10. Controlling Physiological Diseases

Physiological diseases are caused by one or more unfavorable conditions of the tree's environment. Some growers refer to these as "environmental disorders." Weather conditions are known to cause problems as well as nutrient unbalance. An incompatible stock-scion relationship also is classed as physiological.

Jonathan spot on apples is a result of uneven temperatures when they are in storage, or it can be observed when apples have been harvested when overmature.

Little leaf is a result of inadequate amounts of zinc available to the tree. Corkiness in apples can be controlled somewhat by proper addition of boron. Scald, black end of pears, bitter pit and internal breakdown of apples and pit burn of apricots are also considered physiological diseases. Most of these diseases are the results of local conditions, and adjustments to control them vary. It is advisable to consult local extension specialists for their recommendations.

Chapter

XIV

HARVESTING

The peak of the fruit season for a grower is the harvest, and the profitable sale of fruit is the ultimate objective of the commercial fruit grower. Profitable sales depend on the variety and quality. They also depend on proper maturity, preharvest treatment, post-harvest handling, precooling, storage, processor, picking and shipping containers, picking and delivery schedules and, finally, market outlets.

Mechanization of Orchard and Vineyard Operations Is Inevitable in Processed Fruits

One of the greatest changes in farm history is now taking place in the mechanization of fruit growing—namely harvesting. Some types of fruit are moving along faster than others because of labor problems and adaptability to mechanical means.

Most of the crops are still some way from total mechanization of their harvest. This is especially true for those fruits which enter the market as shipping fruits. For such things as clingstone peaches and perhaps freestone peaches, total mechanical harvesting

Fig. 14.1—Preharvest treatment of fruit. The Wealthy apples at the right were treated with Color Set 1004 at the rate of 20 p.p.m. three weeks prior to harvest. They are of much better color than the untreated apples on the tree at the left and will bring higher returns.

is but a few years in the future. Mechanization of certain grapes for fresh marketing looks dim, but for wineries it is here.

Growers and Processors Must Consider Certain "Harvesting" Problems

Undoubtedly there will have to be considerable reorganization of the grower's and processor's thinking regarding such crops before mechanical harvesting can become an accepted practice. Certainly for some fruits mechanical harvesting will result in some loss of total crop because of the difficulties of harvesting to a given maturity, damage from the mechanical means used and other factors being not so fully under the control of the grower as in the case of hand harvesting. However, recent tests on some grape varieties show more actual tonnage from mechanical harvesting than from hand; still there remains some question as to the quality delivered.

Yet the savings in labor and timing of operations could well offset the total loss, though many old-timers say, "It will never come about."

Some Orchards and Vineyards Can Be Completely Mechanized

Not too many years ago, the same old-timers said the same thing during the development of mechanization in walnuts, almonds, prunes, grapes and others. Today, if he chooses, the grower's product in the above-mentioned fruits and nuts need not be touched by human hands—complete mechanization!

Fig. 14.2—Walnut shaker saving many hours of hand labor.

The Fruit Orchard, and Often the Market, Determines the Practice

It should be pointed out that there exists, and always will exist, considerable variability in orchards and vineyards in relation to the operation of mechanical harvesting procedures. There are various kinds of shaking machines, catching frames, pickup machines and other implements connected with mechanical harvesting, which allow quite a variation in practices. The method to be adopted may be influenced by the nature of the fruit itself, topography of land and demands of the processor.

Watch for Problems in Mechanization

Some fruits ripen on the trees and vines all about the same time and can be harvested in one operation. Others are picked three, or even four times, according to their particular maturity. This involves a great deal of moving of large equipment, resulting in marked inefficiency. This is also true in some grape varieties.

Consider Cost of Mechanization

One of the main drawbacks of mechanization of our harvest is the cost of the machines. Only large growers can afford to invest the capital needed to mechanize the harvest. On the other hand, the smaller grower will benefit by the use of contracted custom harvesting.

When the mechanization of these crops was first attempted, the main goal was to reduce the harvest costs. In most cases substantial reductions in total harvest costs have been accomplished.

Fig. 14.3—Prunes stored after mechanical harvesting. Orchard owner comparing fruit in "hand picking box" with machine harvested prunes in the bulk bin. The fruit is good in either case.

Mechanize When Labor Is High or Unavailable

At the present time, the thinking is more that mechanization is justified on the basis of its labor-

Fig. 14.4—Mechanical harvesting on side hill. Because of extreme side-hill operations, this machine is mounted on special tracks. This particular operation is picking up the nuts and loading them in sacks.

saving features. For some of these harvests, labor is scarce and relatively expensive compared to the value of the crop, at the time of harvest. Thus, even though mechanization may be equally expensive, the grower has the harvest under his own control and does not need the large labor force necessary for hand harvest.

Be Alert to Bulk Handling of Fruit

The feature of mechanization which goes somewhat beyond the scope of many fruit areas is the trend toward bulk handling of many of our commercial crops, especially those that go to processors. The cling peach

Fig. 14.5—Standard size bulk bin in use. Bin is 28¼ inches high by 4 feet square. Empty weight is approximately 130 pounds, and the bin will hold around 1,000 pounds of fruit.

industry, for example, is undoubtedly on the way to a complete turnover from the lug box to the so-called bulk bin. These containers have a longer life, are much less expensive and, apparently, when used with proper precautions, can handle the fruit as safely as the boxes can. However, additional machinery is needed.

The apricot, some grapes, berries, citrus, nuts, cherries, etc., all adapt to mechanical harvesting to some degree. But, hang on—someone, maybe you, will come up with an idea for the "impossible harvester."

Discussion of harvesting for individual fruits will be continued as specific fruits are covered.

Chapter

XV

DECIDING HOW TO MARKET THE FRUIT

Produce a Quality Product

Quality fruits, fresh and processed, have good markets and should be in sufficient quantity throughout the season to enable them to become an established commodity. If the customer is used to good fruit, he will be back. A number of Federal and state laws affect the marketing of fresh and processed fruits.

Federal laws apply to interstate commerce, while state laws apply to marketing operations within a state.

Federal laws provide definite standards for containers, inspection services and labeling and branding.

Most state laws parallel the Federal requirements, and some states are even more strict.

Roadside Stands Can Be Profitable

Successful marketing of fruit from a stand depends on a number of factors:

1. Fruit clean and attractive as well as the premises and operator.

2. Fruit available over prolonged periods of time.
3. A variety of fruit available at the same time.
4. Location near population center or near traffic.
5. Fair price to all.

Sell Directly from Orchard and Vineyard

Sales from the orchard and vineyard to the consumer dispose of fruits in another way. The sales are usually quite small and undependable, and the consumer wants high-quality fruit, but this market can be good, particularly in areas where relatively few trees and vines are located.

Try Local Packers

Packing shed operators generally are located near the center of fruit-producing areas. They are usually reliable businessmen who purchase the load of picked fruit from the grower. The packing shed operator buys and receives the fruit, grades, packs and loads it for shipment, and usually has contacts where it can be sold. Packing sheds may be cooperatives, local growers, or independent enterprises.

Select a Capable Broker

Brokers and wholesalers are usually located in distant terminal markets and buy or accept consignments of packed fruit from packing shed operators who sell to the retail merchants.

Successful marketing by this method depends partly on the ability of the broker. An aggressive broker will buy volume fruit that is of good quality. He will attempt to promote a close relationship between the grower and the store.

Fig. 15.1—Fruit pack of pears. Quality fruits, such as displayed in this standard pear box, are one reason for good sales.

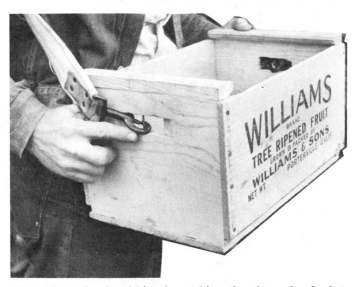

Fig. 15.2—A handy picking box taking the place of a bucket. This box, developed by the California growers, has been very successful. Filled boxes are palletized and hauled to sheds. This eliminates much bruising caused by dumping, as the box is filled from the tree.

Maintain Close Relationship
with Stores

Local stores, chain stores and supermarkets constitute outlets that may prove very profitable to the grower. Success will depend upon a clear understanding between the grower and outlet and a close working relationship.

Courtesy, Wooden Box Institute

Fig. 15.3—Fruit ready for shipment.

The grower will find he must supply clean, high-quality and attractive fruit.

Some Outlets Not Always Dependable

Direct orchard sales or those made to buyers coming to the orchards are practical in parts of the country. Truck drivers, for example, like to buy produce from a section and "back haul" to produce dealers upon their return. In this manner they do not have to return with an empty truck. Often the trucker will buy lower grades of fruit, or even combinations, to get the product cheaper. If the trucker has arranged for a market, he may only seek top-grade products. However, this type of outlet is not too dependable.

A Future in Freezing

Fruit products for the various forms of processing, like drying, canning and freezing, are developing rapidly. Some sections of the United States consider processing as a supplementary outlet to fresh fruit. Most West Coast fruit-producing areas consider fresh fruit markets as a somewhat inconvenient obligation.

Processing Is on the Increase

Trends point out that nearly all areas of the United States will soon take advantage of processing when more improved techniques are developed in both production and processing. A number of fruit co-ops and promoters provide customers with instructions for home processing.

Let Consumers "Rough It"

A number of producers, usually small in acreage, have reported an increasing number of customers wanting to *pick their own fruit*. These customers bring the family and the picnic basket and make a day out of it. Michigan, California, Florida and Texas have reported some advantages, such as overcoming labor shortage, savings on labor, obtaining retail price and obtaining new outlets.

Marketing and Harvesting
of Wine Grapes

Markets for wine grapes have changed consider-

Courtesy, Wooden Box Institute

Fig. 15.4—Fruit packed in shredded paper. Fruit packed carefully arrives at its destination in good condition.

ably the past few years, as well as the methods of harvesting. Wineries that require large tonnages, made up of most all varieties grown in the various areas, have long-term contracts with quality standards and delivery schedules for each variety. Also fieldmen representing the wineries keep close supervision on the cultural practices, size of crop and progress of maturity.

Methods of harvest range from picking boxes and 2-ton gondolas to mechanical harvesters that pick up to 100 tons per day and deliver to wineries in 20- to 25-ton trucks. There is also a trend in crushing the grapes in the vineyard and hauling the juice in closed tanks to the processing plant. Experiments in all phases of the harvesting and handling of wine grapes will be with the industry for a long time.

Select Shipping Containers Carefully

A successful shipping container should: (1) transport produce to market in the *best condition possible,* (2) be attractive in appearance, (3) identify the product and (4) create a memorable and pleasing impression of the product. The container also should be strong and easily stacked and protect the produce from bruising. It should be easy to pack and handle, should display the product neatly and attractively and should be inexpensive.

Courtesy, Wooden Box Institute

Fig. 15.5—A fine looking display of fruit. Attractive displays such as this lead to higher sales.

Regardless of construction, bulk containers have certain common weaknesses. Some of the fruit in the bottom of the container are bruised by the pressure from above. When fruit is stored for any length of time, various kinds of rots spread through the container.

Each major type of container has some particular advantage.

APPROXIMATE AVERAGE NET WEIGHTS OF FRESH FRUITS IN SPECIFIED CONTAINERS

Commodity	Container	Net Weight
		(lbs.)
Apples	Carton	40
	Box	44
	Bushel	45
Apricots	Lug	25
Avocados	Flat	13
	Lug	26
	Box	39
Bushberries	Flat	9
Cherries	Campbell lug	16
	L. A. lug	25
Dates	Flat	15
Figs	Flat, 1-layer	6
	Flat, 2-layer	15
Grapefruit	Carton	33
Grapes	Lug	28
	Lug (dessert)	24
	Tapered lug	20
Lemons	Carton	38
Loquats	Lug	25
Nectarines	4-basket crate	27
	Lug, 2-layer or carton	22
	Box	17
Olives	Lug	25
Oranges	Carton	37½
Peaches	Peach box	18
	Lug, 2-layer	24
Pears	Pear box	47
	L. A. lug	24
	1-way lug	46
Persimmons	Flat	12
	Box	17
Plums	L. A. lug	25
	4-basket crate	27
	Box	18
Pomegranates	Lug	26
Prunes	Lug	25
Quince	Lug	25
Strawberries	Crate, 12-pint	11½
	Crate, 24-pint	23
Tangerines	Carton	37½
	Lug	30

Baskets

The bushel basket has been the most popular container for shipping some fruit to market. However, it does not give adequate protection from bruising for

Courtesy, Wooden Box Institute

Fig. 15.6—Four-basket crate of plums. Individual baskets can be removed and sold separately.

the mature type demanded by consumers. Recently cardboard baskets that fit a particular crate have gained in popularity.

Wirebound boxes

To overcome some of the objections to the round wooden basket, various types of wirebound boxes appeared on the market. Evaluation studies revealed that these boxes somewhat reduced the bruising of fruit for distant shipment. They stacked better in storage than regular baskets and made a fairly attractive pack.

The wirebound box is used mainly in shipping some green mature fruit. It is a major competitor to the basket. Its principal advantages are that it can be stored in a flat condition, thus reducing space, and that it is easily stacked for shipment and storage.

Lugs

For many years, West Coast growers have used the conventional peach lug in combination with paper cups for individual fruit. This container has been accepted readily by all supermarket managers because of its many desirable features. It is a small, easily handled container that stacks well, offers maximum protection to the fruit and can be used for display. With the increasing demand for ripe fruit, some losses do occur in the bottom layer of the pack. The thin cardboard pad, which separates the two layers of fruit, does not always protect the bottom layer from bruising.

Recent experiments with a thin veneer shelf, supported on cleats between the two layers of fruit, showed that it was possible to give the bottom layer adequate

Fig. 15.7—Peaches packed in a "Party Pack" display. Top pad and three-slat lid.

protection. Several types of molded cup trays, designed for use with the standard peach lug, are now available. They would replace the fruit cups and eliminate the need for the supported shelf but would again pose the problem of careful sizing. These trays do not seem so practical as the crinkle cup which does not require careful sizing of the fruit.

Fiberboard containers

Many kinds of fiberboard boxes, designed for bulk packaging, have been developed in recent years. Some of them are in one piece and can be assembled rapidly by folding at certain points. The newer types are using a moisture-resistant fiberboard that prevents the box from collapsing in moist storage. They are attractive and can be used for displaying fruit in the store. Recently designed fiberboard containers have many desirable features of the wooden lug. A container with a sturdy shelf that would be fully equal to the lug in all respects could be constructed.

Cell containers

Several years ago it seemed that cell containers might be the answer to the growers' problem of giving the fruit more individual protection. Initial studies indicated several objectionable features of the early types. Since the cells were not interchangeable, the grower was required to stock many different sizes of boxes for various-sized fruit. The boxes frequently lacked sufficient strength and were not moisture proof. Unless the fruit was carefully sized, it rolled about in the individual cell, resulting in considerable bruising. Recent improvements in construction, along with interchangeable cells for one standard box, have made these containers more acceptable.

APPROXIMATE SHIPPING SEASON OF FRESH FRUITS BY STATE OF ORIGIN

State	Apples	Cherries	Grapes	Peaches	Pears	Plums and Prunes	Strawberries
Arizona	October		June-Aug.			June-July	April
Arkansas	June-April		July-Sept.	June-Aug.	Sept.-Oct.		April-June
California	June-May	April-July	June-Feb.	May-Oct.	June-May	May-Sept.	April-May
Colorado	Sept.-April	July		Aug.-Oct.	Aug.-Nov.		
Georgia	June-Jan.			May-Aug.	July-Sept.	June	April-May
Idaho	July-May	June-July	Sept.-Oct.	Aug.-Sept.	Sept.-Dec.	Sept.-Oct.	July
Illinois	June-May		Aug.-Sept.	June-Sept.	Aug.-Oct.		May-June
Indiana	June-May		September	July-Oct.	Sept.-Oct.		May-June
Kentucky	June-March		October	July-Aug.	Oct.-Nov.		May-June
Maryland	June-April			July-Sept.	Aug.-Oct.		May-June
Michigan	July-May	July-Aug.	Aug.-Nov.	Aug.-Oct.	Aug.-Nov.	Aug.-Oct.	June-July
Missouri	June-May		Aug.-Sept.	July-Aug.	Sept.-Oct.		May-June
New Jersey	June-May		October	July-Sept.	Aug.-Sept.	Sept.-Oct.	May-June
New York	July-June	June-Aug.	Aug.-Dec.	Aug.-Oct.	Aug.-March		June-July
Ohio	July-May		Sept.-Oct.	Aug.-Oct.	Aug.-Nov.		May-June
Oregon	July-May	June-Aug.	October	Aug.-Oct.	Aug.-April	Aug.-Oct.	May-June
Pennsylvania	July-May		Sept.-Nov.	Aug.-Sept.	Sept.-Oct.	September	
South Carolina				June-Aug.	August		April-May
Tennessee	June-Sept.			July-Aug.	Sept.-Oct.		April-June
Virginia	July-June		August	July-Sept.	Sept.-Oct.		April-June
Washington	July-June	June-July	Aug.-Oct.	July-Oct.	July-May	July-Oct.	May-July
West Virginia	July-June			July-Sept.	Sept.-Oct.		
Wisconsin	Aug.-Feb.	July-Sept.					June-July

Source: Agricultural Marketing Service, U.S.D.A.

Chapter

XVI

ALMONDS

History

The almond came to America from the Old World. Scientists believe it is a native of Western Asia and after many years, eventually was brought to America.

How to pronounce the word "almond" often leads to some embarrassment. The story goes as follows: As almond growers know, the nut must be "knocked" from the tree, sometimes with quite a blow from a rubber type mallet. When the almond is still attached to the tree it is pronounced with the "L" as almond. After the limb or tree is struck with the mallet and the nut has been dislodged from the tree and is lying on the ground, it is thereafter referred to as an "ammond." The reason for this is because, in the operation of dislodging the nut from the tree, one had to knock the "L" out of it!

The earliest almond trees in the United States were those grown from seed introduced from Mexico and Spain when the missions were established in California. Apparently, these trees died after the missions were abandoned. No further attempts at almond growing in the United States were made until 1840, when some trees imported from Europe were planted in the New England states. The climate was too severe there and the attempt was not successful. In time, plantings were made down the length of the Atlantic seaboard and into the Gulf States. But everywhere the almond's exacting climatic requirements ruled it out as a profitable crop.

In 1843, some almond trees brought from the East Coast were planted in California. California is now the only important almond-producing state in the country. But there are many areas in this state where almonds cannot be grown profitably.

Present Outlook and Trends

There appears to be little slowing down in planting almond trees, with an average of 15,000 acres per year for the past six years. Prices also continue to be favorable and markets are expanding readily— 268,000 acres presently, so 300,000 acres is not far away. Almonds produce between 1,500 to 2,200 pounds of meats per acre.

Hundreds of varieties have been grown throughout the world. European varieties were used exclusively in the early California areas and most were of inferior quality. One of the choice almonds in Europe, the Jordan, usually fails in this country.

The successful varieties, planted in this country were developed here—some by careful breeding and selection, and some by accident—but with wise observations. One grower, Mr. A. T. Hatch, of Suisun, was responsible for three important varieties. In 1894, he planted a quantity of seed. Of the resulting seedlings, he left about 200 unbudded. From this group of seedlings, three varieties were named. These included the IXL, Ne Plus Ultra and the Nonpareil.

Spain, Italy, Morocco and Iran also grow almonds.

Activities Which Involve Approved Practices

1. Selecting a suitable location.
2. Deciding on varieties.
3. Planning orchard planting system.
4. Determining nursery supply.
5. Pruning—training.
6. Selecting preharvest practices.
7. Determining harvest procedure.

1. Selecting a Suitable Location

As most almonds are grown in California, one would perhaps assume they can be grown throughout the state. This is not true with almonds any more than it is with other fruits.

Choose area of proper winter chill

The wood of the almond as well as the flower buds are damaged slightly more than peach with cold weather. Almond flowers grow at colder temperatures than peach. Almond chill requirement is similar to many peach varieties, but the early blooming habit subjects it to severe damage by frost and brown rot. Areas of warm winters such as low elevations of Southern California do not produce a satisfactory almond crop.

Select frost-free site

Almond buds, because of their early opening habit, open under the most undesirable weather conditions of any fruits. Frosts damage the young flower and fruit seriously in many areas. Several areas of Northern California need frost protection equipment up to six nights a year, often two years out of three. Good air drainage and warmer spring areas would help.

Fig. 16.1—This almond orchard displays proper response to the selection of location, soils, planting and other approved practices. There is only four months' growth between the time these two pictures were taken.

Spring rains also a problem

Spring rains in the almond growing districts are damaging to flowers and fruit by their aid in brown rot and green rot infections. Fog during the summer causes spotted fruit.

Select deep loam soil

Almonds will grow on a wide variety of soils, from the finest valley soils to the rocky soils of the foot hills. However, they grow and produce best in deep, well-drained loam, and the trees are most productive in such soils. In deep soils the roots of an almond will grow to a depth of 12 feet. However, they extract most of their nutrients and moisture from the top 6 feet of soil. They will not do well in heavy or poorly-drained soils and should not be planted in such locations.

Choose some irrigation practice

Irrigation has been correctly called the most important cultural operation that the grower has under his control. Its purpose is to keep the soil supplied with readily available moisture at all times.

At one time, most of the almonds in the state were nonirrigated, even in the interior valleys. However, growers found that almonds responded so markedly to irrigation in terms of tree vigor and tremendously increased production, that a nonirrigated orchard is relatively uncommon now.

2. Deciding on Varieties

Be sure to weigh the economic aspect of the varieties you are going to use as well as the pollination effectiveness of the secondary varieties. The Nonpareil variety is the key variety and economically demands the lion's share of the space in an orchard. Mission almond is also a heavy producer as well as a good pollinizer, and even though the per pound price is less on the Mission, generally, the extra poundage it gives helps to offset the price consideration.

Almost all almond varieties are self-sterile. So, in the selection of varieties, pollinators are necessary.

Almonds are divided into three types:

1. Hard shell—Jordan, Peerless, Drake, Mission.
2. Soft shell—IXL, Ne Plus Ultra, Jordanola.
3. Paper shell—Nonpareil, Kapareil, Merced.

Choose a good variety

Nonpareil is the leading almond today, being very well accepted in the commercial trade. It produces small, thin, sweet, kernels, is well adapted to all almond-producing areas and blooms in the mid-season. Mission, Ne Plus and Kapareil are considered good pollinators.

MISSION (TEXAS) IS ALL-AROUND GOOD VARIETY

A medium-sized, hard-shelled almond with well filled, plump, sweet, kernels, the Mission is the leading pollinizer for Nonpareil at this time. It blooms late, has a late harvest period, is vigorous-growing and is relatively pest-free. Nonpareil and Drake are pollinizers. There are a number of new varieties being tested and many look promising.

Provide bees for pollination

Most almond pollen is carried by the honeybee from flower to flower. For this reason it is important to see that the bee colonies you have are active and healthy. Minimum requirements are two hives per acre.

Place pollinators on windward side

It is important to note that pollination varieties should be placed on the windward side of any orchard

Fig. 16.2—This is an arrangement which theoretically meets the requirement of having a main variety next to a pollinizer. During good pollinating seasons, this arrangement may be satisfactory, but it may not provide enough pollinizers for adverse years.

as much as possible since the wind will assist by carrying the pollen across your trees. Also, the honeybee is smart enough to fly into the wind, empty of pollen. When he picks up pollen he returns with the wind and works back over the trees from the windward side. Hives should be placed on the downwind side.

SELECT NONPAREIL AS THE IMPORTANT VARIETY

Most growers believe that two Nonpareil rows to

one pollinizer is better and, in some plantings, single rows of Nonpareils have a pollinizer on each side. Because blooming dates of the different varieties vary from year to year, at least two varieties of pollinizers are now frequently used. There are numerous possible planting arrangements of varieties.

The following diagram shows a popular orchard layout in order to insure maximum pollinization. Used when minimum number of Key Variety is desired.

0—Key Variety (Nonpareil)

#—Pollinator No. 1

X—Pollinator No. 2

```
# 0 0 # 0 0 # 0 0 #

X 0 0 X 0 0 X 0 0 X

# 0 0 # 0 0 # 0 0 #

X 0 0 X 0 0 X 0 0 X

# 0 0 # 0 0 # 0 0 #
```

3. Planning Orchard Planting System

Orchardists should plant the maximum number of trees per acre that will grow well. In most new plantings on good valley soils the trees are planted 24′ x 24′ and some 25′ x 25′. Planting closer is not recommended on good soil. This results in 75 and 69 trees/acre respectfully on the square system, 150 and 138 on quincunx and 87 and 79 on hexagonal.

Select square planting system

The square system of planting almonds is popular. Trees are planted from 22 to 30 feet apart depending on varieties and soil conditions.

Planting filler trees

Sometimes a grower wonders about planting more trees per acre to get higher yields in the early years of the orchard, with the idea of removing some of them eventually. This is not recommended for almonds because the trees grow very rapidly and crowding results before much additional income has been realized. It is then not only costly but also difficult to remove the extra trees.

Choosing intercrop carefully

If a grower must raise intercrop, beans and grains offer good possibilities. Even these crops are only practical in areas where it is easy to have the harvesting done. The soil should not be allowed to dry out.

Tomatoes and cotton aid in Verticillium disease build-up, so they should not be planted.

Grass cover crop

As almonds require considerable pest control in winter months, a good grass cover crop used with non-tillage makes it possible to get into the orchard soon after rains.

4. Determining Nursery Supply

Select rootstock

Almond rootstock is preferred for almond trees. On deep, well-drained soils, it is the best available rootstock because it is the most vigorous, and over a long period of time makes the most productive tree.

Use Peach for Some Conditions

Peach rootstock is used in many parts of California. It has a shallower root system than almond. This helps it to tolerate high water table conditions. In some areas, it is considered to have a shorter life than almond rootstock.

There are peach roots that are resistant to root-knot nematode and these may be used in nematode-infested soil. However, a certain number of trees may fall over, due to the large growth of the almond tree on the nematode-resistant peach stock.

Choose Marianna for Fungus Infection

Marianna plum (2624) is resistant to oak-root fungus. It is often used as a rootstock where almonds on other stocks have been killed by this disease. However, this stock is considered compatible only with Peerless, Texas, Ne Plus Ultra and Jordanolo. Trees on Marianna stock are smaller than those on almond or peach rootstock and can be planted closer together.

Approved practices such as nursery, care of de-livered trees, land preparation, young tree planting and care and management of the developing almond orchard are the same as for peaches.

5. Pruning—Training

Actually, the first pruning is done at the time the trees are planted. At this time the trees are cut back, or headed, to the height at which it is desired to have the permanent branches arise. Modified leader type pruning system is popular.

Prune trees high

The tendency now is to head trees higher than in the past to avoid damage from orchard equipment.

Mechanical pickup machines require more space below the scaffold limbs, and all farm equipment is becoming larger and heavier. Many growers now head their trees at a height of from 24 to 30 inches.

Use side branches properly

On the trees that have grown vigorously in the nursery, there will be a number of small side branches, when they are received. In addition to heading the tree, these small side shoots should be cut back, but not entirely cut off. At least one base bud should be left on each shoot, and some shoots can be left 4 to 6 inches long. When these side shoots are cut off entirely, the grower may not find new shoots properly placed for permanent scaffold branches later on.

Pinching back should be considered

Some trees grow vigorously and later growth must be pruned away—perhaps wasted.

In practice, each tree should be examined when the new growth is 3 to 4 inches long. The shoots that are selected for main scaffold branches are left alone. All other shoots, which will not be wanted, are pinched back to only a few leaves to shade the trunk. Normally, after four to six weeks, it is advisable to check the trees again to make sure that no new undesirable shoots are growing.

Cut back scaffolds

If you notice your selected scaffolds are growing vigorously, pinch their ends back to within 30 inches of the trunk. This will cause them to branch. This causes larger trees, in shorter time.

Choose permanent scaffolds carefully

The selection of permanent scaffold limbs requires some thought, whether summer training is done or the whole job is left to the dormant pruning season. The tree structure should start with three or four scaffold limbs beginning at the trunk. Ideally, they should be spaced 6 to 8 inches apart up and down the trunk and should be evenly spaced around the trunk.

All trees will not supply properly located limbs

It is seldom possible to find a young tree on which the scaffolds can be spaced in an ideal manner. Still, this arrangement should be kept in mind, and as close an approximation to it as possible should be made. Care should be taken to leave the top scaffold branch longer than the others so that it will not be choked out.

Training during second year

Training should continue with the same type in mind that was used the first year. Eliminate unwanted limbs and keep tree growing to fit your training system.

Pruning mature tree

Pruning the mature almond tree does not involve the details of the peach or apricot. Some growers prune every second or third year. Taking out dead or crossing limbs as well as those interfering with cultural operations is most of the job.

Continue spur development

On the average, spurs are considered to be fruitful for only about five years. It is necessary, therefore, to prune in such a way that new wood with new spur growth is coming along constantly to replace the spurs that are no longer fruitful. To accomplish this, pruning is confined to the removal of the older branches ½ to 1½ inches in diameter. Very little thinning out of smaller wood is done except to remove unwanted water sprouts or suckers.

If the pruning is done every year and if enough wood is removed, it should result in the growth of sufficient new wood to maintain spur growth without heavy cuts.

6. Selecting Preharvest Practices

The cultural operations before harvest differ in a few respects from others. Pest controls are similar but ground preparation is a major operation.

Knock almonds on ground

The ground must be scraped, floated and in some areas packed, to aid the mechanical pickup machine.

In more and more orchards the nuts are knocked to the ground and picked up mechanically. This is more economical than the old method of knocking them onto canvas, but it does introduce other problems in connection with worm control, handling and hulling facilities.

7. Determining Harvest Procedure

Harvest early

Harvesting at the earliest possible date is necessary to avoid worm damage to nuts. The date will vary from year to year. Growers should remember that mallet wounds are a source of considerable damage to tree and, if knocking is attempted too early, it will

Fig. 16.3—Almond harvesting by machinery. This photograph shows the "clean sweep" effect of the rake action.

take harder blows to dislodge the nuts. On the other hand, if knocking is delayed, the infestation of such worms as the navel orange worm will be increased.

Orchard handling of nuts changing

When nuts are knocked onto a canvas, they are sacked and moved out of the orchard at frequent intervals. Now, growers like to knock several rows, or even the total orchard, of the same variety at one time. The nuts may then be windrowed, or at least raked away from the trees. Then the pickup machine is brought in.

Speed of operation is desired

Every day that the nuts are left on the ground

greatly increases the chances of rain or worm damage, often to a serious degree. Mechanical harvesting is here to stay, but every effort should be made to pick up the nuts and get them out of the orchard as soon as possible after they are knocked. Almonds should not be stored in a warm, damp place as rancidity results. Properly cured they will keep in a dry, well ventilated building six months or more.

Hull almonds soon after knocking

After the nuts are harvested, they should be hulled as soon as possible to cut down worm damage. Small operators normally have this operation done by a custom huller. Larger operators usually do their own hulling. After hulling, the nuts are sacked or loaded into bulk bins and taken to the receiving station.

Cooperative handles the almonds effectively

About 70 per cent of the almond crop is handled by the California Almond Growers Exchange. This cooperative is owned by about 4,500 growers. Its main office and plant are located in Sacramento. Twenty receiving stations, where members may deliver their crops, are maintained in the principal growing areas.

Chapter

XVII

APPLES—KING
OF FRUITS

History

The apple, a pome fruit and a close "kinfolk" of the pear, originated in Southwestern Europe and the Caspian Sea area. A number of varieties were named in 300 B.C. The apple is grown in more parts of the world than any other fruit.

Johnny Appleseed, a nickname given to a real person, John Chapman, 1814-1845, truly is a legend. He lived, traveled widely, planted apple trees and seeds wherever he roamed and asked nothing in return. Midwestern folks took care of him and his trees. They both responded and to this day we look to Johnny Appleseed and folks like him as an important part of America.

Present Trend and Outlook

Varieties having high quality dessert characteristics show an increase in demand. Such varieties as Delicious, Golden Delicious, Neuton, Gravenstein and Cortland have responded to demand.

There has been an increase in production per acre. Per capita consumption of 25 pounds will rise as quality, shipping, processing, new products such as apple wines, blends and juice, storage and advertising improve.

Statistics of Interest

There are between 5,000 and 6,000 named apple varieties tested and recorded.

Presently there are 400 varieties of some commercial importance in the United States. Thirty-five varieties make up 90 per cent of the annual crop.

France produces over 210 million bushels of apples; of these, 90 per cent are pressed into cider.

The United States produces a little more than 100 million bushels from over 550,000 acres, half as much as France, yet receives more income for the higher-quality products. Commercial orchards produce 15 tons per acre in California.

Major Apple-producing Areas of U. S.

Pacific Northwest continues to increase as a major producing area. The state of Washington produces about 25 per cent of all apples in the United States; adding California and Oregon brings the western states up to 38 per cent.

The northeastern United States, including the important areas of the Ohio Basin, areas of the central and north central Atlantic states and western mountain areas, continue to supply good products to many local markets. The southern areas are somewhat limited to smaller plantings except in the higher elevations of North Carolina, Tennessee, Missouri and New Mexico. Thirty-five states have commercial acreages of apples.

Activities Which Involve Approved Practices

1. Selecting a suitable location.
2. Deciding on varieties.
3. Planning orchard planting system.
4. Determining nursery supply.
5. Caring for delivered trees.
6. Preparing land before planting.
7. Selecting proper planting time.
8. Planting the young trees.
9. Caring for trees after planting.
10. Managing the developing orchard.
11. Pruning.
12. Selecting preharvest management practices.
13. Determining harvest procedure.

1. Selecting a Suitable Location

Growing apples for commercial production anywhere should only be attempted in locations recognized as growing areas. Apples are grown in nearly every state for limited use; however, approved areas are essential for profitable growing. Selecting a location unfavorable to apple production will nullify good approved practices.

**Choose area that supplies
proper chilling**

A number of apple varieties require more chilling for normal growth than many other deciduous fruits. Northern Spy and McIntosh are two. Others, such as Yellow Newton, Gravenstein and Delicious, are quite moderate. Improper chilling causes more damage to apple fruit buds than to stone fruits.

Select deep soil

Because apples have an extensive root system, it is recommended they be planted only where the roots can penetrate at least four feet.

Choose clay or sandy loam

Apple orchards are planted and grown on nearly all types of soils. However, one must consider cultural operations, drainage and fertility as part of his selection. Some apple varieties are more adapted to specific soils, but this has not been determined to be of great importance.

Choose proper water drainage

Apple trees will not produce efficiently with "wet feet." Prolonged water logging will kill the tree. Good drainage, man-made or natural, is a recommended and essential practice.

Good air drainage can cut frost hazard

Many apple orchards depend on an effective, natural air drainage system. This allows the colder air to move down the slopes of the orchard into the lower elevators.

AIR CIRCULATION HELPFUL IN OTHER OPERATIONS

Apple growing areas subject to rain and fog can use air drainage to advantage. If foliage is damp or wet over a period of time, fungus and mildew take over. Good air movement on a sloping orchard site will facilitate drying and virtually eliminate much of the problem.

Sites near bodies of water are often selected because of air currents created by land and water, resulting in good air circulation.

2. Deciding on Varieties

Your choice of a variety should depend not only upon where you will grow it, but the use you will make of it. The best varieties for commercial fruit growing are not always best for farm orchards or backyard gardens. The large-scale commercial grower needs relatively few varieties that produce heavily every year.

Select varieties to fit your market

The fruit must handle and ship well and have an attractive appearance for fresh markets. If you are planning on selling your fruit for commercial canning or other processing, such as making juice or a type of wine blend, or on freezing or shipping, it is suggested that, before you plant, you talk to the fieldman for the processor or shipper who will buy your fruit. He may only accept certain varieties and will pay more for certain ones than others.

Provide for pollination

Because most apples are self-unfruitful, it is necessary to have cross-pollination from another variety. There are some that are self-fruitful but even these produce better, under certain conditions, with pollinizers. Some varieties such as Gravenstein and Winesap don't even produce fertile pollen. So be sure to seek professional help. Your farm advisor or nurseryman will help you with these local conditions. Keep in mind that insect activity is important for pollination.

Fig. 17.1—Apples galore going to market. Selecting the right variety always results in a ready market.

Choose several varieties for home planting

For home use, more varieties may be chosen. Heavy yields are less important. The emphasis should be on high quality, value for canning and freezing and adaptability to local conditions. For limited commercial production for *local market* a larger number of varieties should be grown than for large-scale production for distant markets. There can be less attention to the ability of the variety to stand handling and shipping, but more attention should be given to high dessert quality and suitability for canning and freezing.

Seek professional advice

Your extension agricultural agent, nurseryman or vocational agricultural instructor can usually help you. The McIntosh is planted in most northern areas; York Imperial and Winesap are leaders in the South. Delicious, Newton, Gravenstein, Jonathan and Wealthy are other popular varieties. Delicious varieties are increasing in all sections of the West.

3. Planning Orchard Planting System

The apple orchard is a long-term investment. A little exercise with a sharp pencil before the vigorous use of a strong back will save unnecessary work. With the pencil, plan roadways, ditches, contour and turning areas.

Topography must be considered

On steep slopes, one must plan to place the tree rows along the contour to avoid excess erosion and improve safety in operation of equipment.

Use square system

The trees are set on designated corners of a square area. With the rows straight in all directions, approved orchard practices are easier. The system is rather simple to lay out, and it is readily adapted to fillers (trees removed later).

The rectangular, quincunx and triangular or hexagonal systems are discussed fully in Chapter 5.

Planning turning area for equipment is necessary in all systems.

Space according to area and variety

The proper spacing of apple trees is directly

associated with the region, type of soil, variety selected and cultural plans. For example, apple trees in the Northeast may grow larger than ones in a region of the South or West. Some varieties have smaller limb areas, 30 to 40 feet, such as Golden Delicious. A McIntosh may have a spread of 50 feet. For soils of average fertility, a distance of about 35 feet on the square system is recommended for good growing varieties, such as Golden Delicious, Winesap and Jonathan. Trees of larger growing habit, McIntosh, York Imperial and Baldwin, should be placed 40 feet apart on good soil.

Don't plant too close

Most of the mistakes in planting are made in planting too close. Crowding of trees creates many problems such as shading, root crowding, reducing available nutrients and moisture, and cultural, pest and harvesting operations.

Intercrop for cash

Your objective is the trees, not the money a cash crop brings in. If, in any way, vegetables, field or small fruit crops interfere with the progress of your trees, eliminate interplanting. The cash crop must be considered secondary. A well-planned and managed intercrop can be profitable and actually benefit trees.

Consider filler trees for large space planting

An increasing number of growers are planting semi-dwarf trees between permanent trees that are planted around the 40-foot plan. In this way, income is obtained earlier and the trees are rather easily removed when crowding seems apparent.

4. Determining Nursery Supply

Select good nursery stock

As quickly as possible after selecting your planting system, make plans to select and order your trees. The nurseryman usually makes financial adjustments on orders a year or so in advance. This will also assure you of a complete order of healthy, sturdy, uniform trees on desirable rootstock.

Select rootstock for the area

Many seedlings of the common apple varieties are considered good rootstock for apples. French seedlings were imported from France at one time but are considered the same as our own seedlings.

Virginia crab apple is used in some areas that have cold winters, but consideration must be given to varieties not compatible to it.

Quince can be used as rootstock quite satisfactorily with Winter Banana where wet soil is a problem.

Choose reliable nurseryman

It isn't so much that a nurseryman will knowingly sell trees of questionable name, but a reliable one knows his trees. It takes an apple tree from five to seven years to bear. If you have the wrong variety and it is not of the type accepted or is not doing well, it has cost you money.

A number of nurseries have inspections to verify trees. This method cuts down accidental or intentional errors. You can ask the nursery if it has this service.

Order trees by grade

Apple trees are graded according to the diameter

of their trunk measured at two inches above the bud union. The approximate height of the tree may also be given. For example, a ½-inch tree is usually from 4 to 6 feet high.

Order young trees

Young trees, one year old, do better when transplanted than older trees. Two-year-old trees are satisfactory, but trees three or more years old need special care and handling, and growing them should not be attempted, at least on a commercial orchard venture.

Consider dwarf trees

An increasing number of trees are sold on dwarf stock. Some growers report that cost of production is less on trees 8 to 10 feet tall than on full-grown trees. Research so far indicates the rootstocks are weak and may need constant support. The East Malling group is a common stock for dwarfing.

5. Caring for Delivered Trees

When you receive your young trees from the nursery they are in good condition. You must continue to keep them that way. Good, healthy, early growth depends on your care. If trees arrive in poor condition —return them!

Heel in trees

If you are not planning to plant your trees in the field in a few days, heel in your trees. Simply dig a trench deep enough to hold the roots, put the trees in carefully and cover roots again with soil. Water if soil is dry or becomes so later.

CHOOSE AREA "FREE OF ACTIVITY"

Try to select a location away from areas where the trees may be disturbed by children, animals or equipment.

6. Preparing Land Before Planting

Before an orchardist starts any type of planting, he must have his land ready. Too often scraping, hauling, plowing and such are left until later. It is much easier and more successful to set trees on a clean, well-prepared field, free of clods, weeds and holes.

Plow under cover crop

Many orchardists plan ahead far enough to have a cover crop plowed under before planting. This allows for good water-holding ability, as well as penetration, and holds down erosion from wind and water. Some just plow and disk the planting row and keep cover crop growing between rows.

If you plan on laying out the orchard with the button wire system, it is necessary to have a clean field.

Consider subsoiling

Using shanks to break up plow soles down the tree row to allow young roots to penetrate deeper is beneficial in many areas, especially if the soil has been in crops previously. This also makes for a soil easier to dig and tamp around trees. Depth of shanks depends on depth and thickness of plow sole. If hardpan is present, the same type of operation is needed, and in many cases, deeper and heavier equipment.

7. Selecting Proper Planting Time

Time of planting must be considered by area. Trees

do better in some areas with spring planting, and others prefer fall.

Spring plant in north

In most northern areas that have severe cold weather, trees are planted in the early spring, usually as soon as workers can get on the ground. Planting trees in the fall in cold areas causes frost injury and often death.

Select fall or winter planting in mild climate

In areas where winter temperatures are mild and there is little chance of deep soil frost, orchardists will plant trees in the fall or winter. Tests have shown that trees planted in fall or winter have more first season growth. This is possible because root growth can take place under cooler conditions than top growth.

Late spring planting a hazard

Trees planted when summer temperatures are beginning to get warm suffer to the extent of death. Often the plants fail to leaf out properly, sunburn flourishes and the trees may become stunted or die.

8. Planting the Young Trees

All of the plans you have made so far have been in preparation for this moment—planting your tree. Don't "throw care to the winds," especially now.

Keep trees moist

The tree roots, mainly, must be kept moist at all times—before and after planting. Do not spread trees out over the field, before planting, exposing them to the weather. Take them directly from under the canvas or sacks or from the water and put them into the prepared hole.

Use planting board

Orchardists like to have their rows straight. See chapter on cultural practices.

Dig large enough hole

The hole should be large enough to avoid any root crowding. It must be deep enough so roots won't push upwards, and the depth after tamping should be the same as it was in the nursery.

Care of tree at planting

Do not prune the roots. Cut off only damaged, dead or unusually long or crossed roots.

Set the bottom limb towards the prevailing wind and lean the tree slightly toward that side.

Setting aside top soil at time of digging is recommended, but with mechanical diggers this becomes impractical. Do not add fertilizer around plant roots.

Use care in tamping

Fill the hole with fine loose soil, and after every 6 inches or so of soil added, tamp ever so gently. If soil is dry, add water to help settle the soil close to the roots. Sprinkling of organic material around young trees is not practiced in most large commercial plantings.

Staking may be done if conditions make it essential. Do not tamp too hard.

Prune back young trees

Select your scaffold branches and trim off other undesired growth. Unless you cut back some limbs you will create an imbalance between limbs and roots because of loss of roots from transplanting. If you have only a whip and no side branches, tip it to about 40 inches.

9. Caring for trees after planting

If you have followed the approved practices to this point, your tree is ready to grow. Keep it growing vigorously during the first season.

Keep immediate area clean

Weeds or other crops should not compete with the young tree for moisture and nutrients. If trees are doing poorly, ⅓ pound of actual nitrogen may be applied 6 to 8 inches from the trunk, or in water after the young trees have become established. After three or four years, then sod and other cultures may begin.

Use tree protectors

Many types of tree protectors are on the market. Some are used in combination for sunburn and pest control. Check protectors to be sure they don't interfere with limb development.

Whitewash may be considered

Some orchardists still prefer using whitewash for protection against sunburn. It is a good practice and is successful.

Pinching back may be desirable

After a tree has become well established and vigorous new growth is in evidence, re-examine your planned framework. Pinch back shoots that you plan to remove later, and it will result in better growth to desired limbs.

Maintain good soil moisture

Don't guess about this practice. Never let your young trees suffer. Stunting from lack of water is your fault and trees do not respond properly to your "killing them with kindness" later.

10.   Managing the Developing Orchard

Choose fertilizer program carefully

Apple trees, like any other fruit, do their best when nutrients are available. Those nutrients deficient in the soil must be supplied. Nitrogen should be added if shoot growth is less than 6 to 10 inches. One pound of actual N for average trees is satisfactory, depending upon a number of circumstances, as discussed in the chapter on fertilizers. Cut or add amount for smaller or larger trees.

Boron deficiency will cause a cork-like area in apples, and a lack of magnesium may also be a problem. Symptoms of manganese and zinc deficiency should be watched for, also. Most orchardists use magnesium limestone if needed, borax in soil or spray and a complete fertilizer almost every year to supply nutrients. It may be advisable to "split application" of fertilizers—in the fall and early spring, about a month before bloom. Nitrogen in urea sprays can be added if heavy bloom occurs and it appears your tree is in for a good year.

Observe available moisture

Most new plantings are now using some form of irrigation. Even areas that have summer rainfall find higher profits from a more uniform application of water.

11. Pruning

Pruning should be done with training in mind. The procedure outlined in Chapter VI is applicable with slight variations, depending on variety and location. Generally, apples grow quite a few more laterals than are needed after a few years, and these must be removed.

Choose modified leader system

This system, often referred to as "spaced open head" is trained by many along the "delayed open center" method. The tree is allowed to develop as in the central leader type for a few years, then the central leader is cut back to a desired lateral. This could aid in larger selection of laterals.

Prune young trees carefully

Young trees can be slightly dwarfed by too much pruning. Trees need leaf surface to develop buds, healthy limbs and roots. Delay in production is also attributed to early heavy pruning. Confine your sharp pruning shears to keeping the tree in balance and save yourself some unpleasant results.

Fig. 17.2—Training apple trees. Occasionally growers will es-
palier apple trees for ease in picking and in landscaping.

Fig. 17.3—Young apple tree developing nicely.

Pruning young bearing and older bearing trees

Remove only dead, broken, crossing or competing limbs from bearing trees. Too often growers prune back trees to open them up. This is not a good practice in seven- or eight-year-old trees, because you cut down production area by eliminating fruit spurs.

Depending on your practice, trees can be headed back when they are about 15 years old without any material production loss. Older trees will need more attention. Severe cuts may be necessary to keep the trees to proper size and to encourage quality and color in fruit.

12. Selecting Preharvest Management Practices

Determine "thinning" practice for apples

Generally, an apple tree, especially Golden Delicious, sets more fruit than it can mature. Thinning then is necessary. Hand thinning apples 6 to 8 inches apart is still a good practice. Using chemicals is effective. Advice from a professional is recommended for any chemical thinning.

Consider preharvest sprays

Apples have a "habit" of dropping a few before and during maturity. Patterns are difficult to change, so growers use various chemicals to keep apples on the trees longer. It cuts down pickings and often encourages more growth and color. 10 p.p.m. of NAA (Naphthaleneacetic acid) does a good job (except on Winesap and McIntosh). Some concentration of 2,4-D also is effective.

Fig. 17.4—Apple limb displaying wooly apple aphis knots.

Determine disease and pest control program

Apples are not an orphan in the fruit industry when it comes to damage by diseases and pests. Codling moth, scab, cedar rust, apple maggot, scales, mites

Courtesy, Union Carbide Co.

Fig. 17.5—Apple aphid destroying young growth.

APPLE VARIETIES

Variety (In Approximate Order of Ripening)	Origin	Areas Where Grown	Harvest Season	Remarks on Pollination and Fruit	Fruit Color and Quality	Fruit Outlets
Red Astrachan	Russia introduced to U.S.A. in 1835.	California.	July.	Partly self-fruitful, poor shipper.	Green to entirely red, good.	Home use and local market.
White Astrachan	Russia introduced to U.S.A. about 1820.	California.	July to Aug.	Self-fruitful, easily bruised.	Greenish white, good.	Culinary and local market.
Gravenstein	Germany imported to U.S.A. by 1824.	California.	July to Aug.	Self-unfruitful, susceptible to bitter pit	Red stripes, very good.	Culinary, early dessert and canning.
Wealthy	Minn., approx. 1860.	N.Y., New Eng., Mich., Minn.	Aug. to Sept.	Self-fruitful	Medium red, fair to good.	Dessert and culinary.
McIntosh	Ontario, Canada, approx. 1870.	N.Y., New Eng., Mich., British Columbia, Ontario, Canada.	Aug. to Sept.	Self-unfruitful, tender flesh, apple scab, early drop.	Medium red, very good to best.	Home use and local market.
Jonathan	New York, approx. 1800.	Northwest, Midwest, Virginia, California.	Sept.	Partly self-fruitful, Jonathan spot.	Bright red all over, very good to best.	Dessert and culinary.
Cortland	New York (cross made in 1898).	New York, New England.	Sept.	Partly self-fruitful.	Medium red, good.	Dessert and culinary.
Delicious	Iowa, 1881.	All areas except South. Northwest, Midwest, Virginia, New Eng.	Sept.	Self-unfruitful, needs good color, tends to turn mealy, good prices.	Striped red to full red, good.	Dessert only.
Rhode Island Greening	Rhode Island approx. 1740.	N.Y., New Eng., Mich.	Sept. to Oct.	Triploid, self un-fruitful.	Green, good.	Drying and culinary.

(Continued)

APPLE VARIETIES (Continued)

Variety (In Approximate Order of Ripening)	Origin	Areas Where Grown	Harvest Season	Remarks on Pollination and Fruit	Fruit Color and Quality	Fruit Outlets
Golden Yellow Delicious	West Virginia, 1890.	Northwest, Midwest, Virginia, New York, Calif.	Sept. to Oct.	Partly self-fruitful, fruit needs high humidity to store.	Yellow, very good.	Dessert and culinary.
Yellow Newtown (Newtown pippin)	New York, Early 18th century.	Northwest, Oregon, Calif., Virginia.	Sept. to Oct.	Self-fruitful, good keeper, internal browning, russet on skin.	Green to yellow, good.	Best for drying and culinary.
Baldwin	Mass. 1740.	New Eng., New York, Mich.	Oct.	Self-fruitful.	Medium red, good.	Culinary.
White Pearmain	Unknown, date unknown.	California.	Oct.	Self-unfruitful.	Yellow, good.	Home use and local market.
Northern Spy	New York, approx. 1800.	New York, New Eng., Mich.	Oct. to Nov.	Self-unfruitful, late light bearing.	Bright striped red, very good.	Dessert and culinary.
Rome Beauty	Ohio, 1848.	Midwest, New Eng., Northwest Virginia, Calif.	Oct. to Nov.	Self-fruitful, late blooms.	Medium red stripes, fair.	Dessert and culinary, baking.
Stayman Winesap	Kansas, 1866.	Midwest, Virginia.	Oct. to Nov.	Triploid, self-unfruitful, needs careful handling.	Medium red, very good.	Dessert and culinary.
Winesap	Unknown, dates back to colonial period.	Northwest, Midwest, Calif.	Oct. to Nov.	Self-unfruitful, thin fruit on old trees.	Entirely red, very good.	Dessert and culinary.

and mildew are some of the important ones. Problems vary from area to area and controls change. Seek advice from local officials.

13. Determining Harvest Procedure

"Show me a man who hasn't looked at his harvest with pride and an inner feeling of accomplishment." Considerable care and planning are behind—but the important job at hand is what you have been waiting for. This, then, has been your objective.

Select workers with care

Careless handling by pickers, especially for fresh market, can cause waste. Picking should start with the lower branches, advancing to the top. Stems should remain attached to the apple and will remain so under good picking procedure.

Show pickers how

Place the thumb between the stem and spur, bend the apple toward the thumb with a quick motion and the stem will separate from the spur.—Well, try again! Do not twist too far or the stem may twist out. Fresh markets pay more for apples with stems because of higher grade and longer storage ability. Do not allow the "snap, crackle, and pop" routine, where the apple is snapped from the tree with a crackling sound and popped into the container. Place apple carefully in the container. Keep the fruit in the shade until it is picked up and prepared for its planned outlet.

XVIII

APRICOTS

History

China receives the credit as being the original
home of the apricot, which appeared later throughout
Europe. Writings show that the apricot was brought
into Rome about the time of Christ. England has history
of the "cot" in 1562 and it was recorded in Virginia
around 1720 and in the California Santa Clara Mission
about 1792. Seedlings were grown in many places in
America, but a congenial place in which to grow this
fruit commercially was not found until it was planted
in California and other local areas of the Pacific Coast
states.

Present Outlook and Trends

The apricot industry has had many fluctuations in
acreage, yield and price. Around 1930, California had
approximately 80,000 acres in apricots. 1959 statistics
show slightly less than 37,000 acres and 1972 records
34,000. The past five years new plantings have increased roughly 1,000 acres/year. Production has
ranged from 150,000 tons in the United States to

Fig. 18.1—Tilton apricot planted in 1902. This apricot is beyond maximum production, but has served its owner well. It is on peach rootstock.

250,000. The industry needs a good all around apricot variety.

Statistics of Interest

The average of 5 tons per acre varies from year to year because of alternate bearing habit and weather conditions. Over two-thirds of the crop goes into canning and this should increase. Dry cots will perhaps continue at about 20 per cent of the crop, mostly in California, where all of the commercial drying is done. Fresh sales will continue to show improvement as advertising, storage and packaging improve.

California produces around 40 per cent of the world apricot crop and over 90 per cent of the United States crop. The kernels of some of the sweet apricots grown in Palestine are eaten like almonds.

Major Apricot-producing Areas

With California producing such a large percentage, and mostly for canning, other states find a ready market for the fresh market fruit. Specific locations are in Washington (6 per cent), Colorado, Utah, Oregon, New York, Arizona and Idaho. Michigan has several varieties being considered for eastern areas.

Outside the United States, apricots are produced in Europe, Australia and Africa, and in Chile and Argentina in South America.

Activities Which Involve Approved Practices

1. Selecting a suitable location.
2. Deciding on varieties.
3. Planning orchard planting system.
4. Determining nursery supply.
5. Caring for delivered trees.

6. Preparing land before planting.
7. Selecting proper planting time.
8. Planting the young tree.
9. Caring for trees after planting.
10. Managing the developing orchard.
11. Pruning.
12. Choosing approved preharvest practices.
13. Determining harvest procedure.

1. Selecting a Suitable Location

Perhaps no fruit has been neglected by pomologists so much as has the apricot. Recently, however, an increasing number of research stations have taken up or rejuvenated their efforts to produce an apricot variety to fit locations other than California.

Choose a proper climate

Climate is probably the most important factor limiting commercial production. The early blooming habit of the apricot and its chilling requirements (to break the tree's winter rest) preclude commercial production in most fruit-growing regions of the nation. Apricots require less chilling than most peaches and Santa Rosa plums.

Select Clear, Dry Weather

The best climate for apricots is clear and dry weather, with fairly cold winters and only moderately high spring and summer temperatures before harvest. Continued cool, damp weather may cause fruit brown rot. Extremely high summer temperatures (of 100°F. to 105°F. or more) during fruit ripening may cause pit-burn and damage fruit quality.

Fig. 18.2—Inadequate chill. This apricot limb shows some delay
in leaf development from a warm winter. Notice bare spots
along limb.

Choose a good soil

Apricots grow well on a wide range of soils. The best soil for apricots is a deep, fertile well-drained loam or clay-loam soil. If lighter soils are selected, more fertilizer and frequent irrigation will be needed to produce high quality and yield. The apricot appears to do better than peach on poor soil. Ammonium sulfate is used by growers at 3 to 7 pounds per tree, depending on size, age and vigor. Avoid soils containing excess chloride or sodium.

Good water supply important

Normal rainfall may provide enough moisture to keep apricot trees alive and bearing some fruit. Inadequate water, however, results in weak growth, small trees and low yields. In California, the great bulk of the acreage is irrigated, and results have shown that nearly all new commercial plantings are under this system.

Three acre-feet of water where most commercial orchards are planted appears to be ample. A light application of water previous to harvest has aided in controlling pit-burn if high temperatures are present.

2.　Deciding on Varieties

Many varieties of apricots are known and the demand for the apricot varies with different localities. Choose the best variety adapted to your needs. One may choose a less popular variety to secure special benefits.

Blenheim and Royal

These two varieties have nearly lost their identity because of their similarity to each other. They constitute about 50 per cent of California's bearing acreage, a decline from previous years. The fruit is medium to large, oval, orange-fleshed and quite aromatic. The skin is yellow to orange, the flavor is sweet and sprightly and it is blessed with a firm texture. It is equally valuable for canning, or drying or fresh. It ripens from June 15 to June 30 in California.

Choose Tilton for later ripening

The Tilton makes up about 40 per cent of the California plantings. Most new plantings in California are Tilton. They out-produce Blenheim, ripen more uniformly and the tree is more vigorous. The Tilton is used for drying, shipping and canning.

Select varieties to fit your use

The Moorpark is not being planted in California. Mostly it is grown in New York and is good for canning. Other varieties include Early Montgament, grown in Washington and Utah; Kings Cot, a large early fruit; and Perfection, a large, early fruit that is self-unfruitful and good for fresh consumption. Modesto and Patterson show promise as new varieties in central California.

Seek market outlet

Before you venture into a large planting of apricots it would be advisable to talk to canners or dried fruit processors and make sure you are selecting a variety they will use.

Seldom need pollinators

All commercial varieties of importance grown in America are self-fertile and require no pollinator. Two varieties considered new, Perfection and Riland, are self-incompatible and will pollinate with Royal-Blenheim.

3. Planning Orchard Planting System

Planning the orchard planting system properly requires a well founded plan. Laying out the area for trees to meet your future plans of operation is indeed important. Depending on local conditions, trees are spaced from 20 to 30 feet apart on the square system; 25 feet is the distance most often used.

Choose square system for apricots

Most California orchards are planted by the square system, in which the trees and rows are the same distance apart. However, other plans which have some merit are the hexagonal system, by which approximately 15 per cent more trees are placed on a given area of land than is possible with the square system, and, in hilly, easily eroded locations, the contour system. Apricot trees on apricot roots become larger than those on plum roots.

Intercropping may be considered

Extreme caution must be used in intercropping apricots. Planting of tomatoes should be avoided because of occurrence of Verticillium wilt. Land previously in tomatoes should also be avoided. Cotton, melons, potatoes and strawberries carry a less damaging strain. Many of the vegetable and small fruit crops require frequent irrigation. This frequency of irrigation causes apricots to grow too vigorously and excess growth results. Proper management of intercrops can be profitable.

Consider filler trees

Filler trees in apricots have been used to advantage. However, the apricot is a vigorous growing tree and when planted 25 feet, more or less, it isn't long before fillers must be taken out. A sort of hedge row planting is being tried, where another tree is planted between two trees down a row, leaving one direction the same 25 feet for necessary management practices.

4. Determining Nursery Supply

Growers seldom grow their own nursery trees. The care and technique of raising young trees does not always fit your other management time. Ask a farm advisor, local agriculture instructor or professional grower in the area for advice.

Order trees by grade

Trees of medium size—about $\frac{1}{2}$ inch in diameter —usually makes the best growth in the orchard.

Trees purchased in California must conform to the agriculture code. For yearling trees, the minimum size is $\frac{1}{4}$-inch caliper 2 inches above the bud, and the trees not less than 8 inches tall. The grade sizes are in increments of $\frac{1}{8}$ inch up to $\frac{1}{2}$ inch, and then in $^3/_{16}$-inch series. The tree height may also be given, such as 4 to 6 feet, 3 to 5 feet and 2 to 3 feet. June-budded trees may have a minimum caliper of $^3/_{16}$ inch and may be graded in $\frac{1}{16}$-inch intervals up to $\frac{3}{8}$ inch. If the tops of such trees are over one year old, the age should be shown on the label. The trees should be healthy.

Select rootstock

The principal rootstocks used for apricot are seedlings of apricot, peach and plum. While disease and soil troubles appear to be most important in selecting a rootstock for apricots, many locations seem to be relatively free from serious problems in this respect. In such locations either peach or apricot rootstocks seem to give about equal results.

Use Apricot Root on Old Peach Soil

However, if apricots are planted to a site previously in orchard on peach root, the apricot root should be used. Apricots on peach roots sometimes grow less vigorously than those on apricot roots in such situations. Apricots are resistant to nematode.

Choose Marianna 2624 for Wet Areas

Excess moisture in amounts which will damage trees on apricot or peach rootstocks will usually not harm apricots on myrobalan seedlings or Marianna rootstocks. A small percentage of myrobalan seedlings make poor unions with apricot varieties; in these cases the trees either make poor growth or break at the union under the stress of winds or heavy fruit loads.

Bacterial canker will attack trees on myrobalan more readily than those on either peach or apricot.

Oak-root fungus (Armillaria) is less severe on Marianna. However, Marianna is quite shallow-rooted.

5. Caring for Delivered Trees

If your trees cannot be planted at delivery time, they must be taken care of properly until you can plant. Heel them in until needed.

Keep roots moist

It is of the utmost importance to keep the roots

moist. However, the soil should be well drained. If the trees appear to be dry when received, they may be soaked in water for 24 hours before heeling in; or they may be completely covered with moist earth for a few days.

6. Preparing Land Before Planting

Do all necessary heavy field work before planting. Subsoiling should be done well ahead to allow for a little settling and clod breakup. Scraping should also be complete.

Subsoil an approved practice

Growers seldom plant an orchard without considering some method of breaking up the soil to a depth of at least 4 feet. Young trees do better when their roots have freedom of movement.

Trees in cold storage

If it appears you are going to plant your trees later than March, keep trees dormant by putting them in cold storage. However, late planting is not a recommended practice.

7. Selecting Proper Planting Time

Nursery trees in California are delivered after the first of the year and can be planted any time after being received to well into March. Areas that have extreme winter frost select fall or spring planting, depending on their management practices. Fall plantings are preferred, generally. Under all circumstances, plant trees in moist soil or supply moisture.

Late planting not advisable

When planting of trees is practiced after March, the grower can expect poor results. Usually the temperature is becoming warm and the trees do not function properly with no root growth. Stunting often is the result, as well as trees dying.

8. Planting the Young Tree

Apricot trees are tough when mature, but tender when being transplanted. The future success of your orchard is in your hands—how will you deal with it? Following practices will help.

Keep trees moist

A few minutes of the bright sun beaming down on tender young roots dries them out and they die. These, then, must be replaced with new growth, resulting in time and growth lost because of carelessness. A wet canvas, sack, sawdust or other material will assure your trees of healthy roots all day.

Consider planting board

Growers like to have trees in a straight row. It is important to keep trees in line because much of our modern equipment is bulky and a tree out of line is quickly damaged.

Dig hole big, deep enough

Unless the soil is in poor physical condition, due to grading operations or other causes, the holes for planting the trees need be only large enough to receive the roots without bending or cutting. Unduly long roots may be shortened; broken ones should be removed.

Position of tree at planting

Growers conscious of a strong, well-balanced framework often point the largest, or lowest scaffold limb to the north, or into the prevailing wind. The tree is also tipped slightly towards the north, or wind. Wind and sun reactions tend to pull tree to upright position in later years.

Use care in tamping roots

The soil should be sifted between the roots and firmed, either by tamping gently or by settling with water. A well-planted tree with a normal root system is not easily pulled from the ground after being set.

Do not plant tree too deep

The trees should be planted at the same depth at which they grew in the nursery. This is usually determined easily by the position of the bud union and differences in bark color at the old ground line. Diseased or pest-damaged trees should be discarded. Do not add fertilizer to young roots.

Prune back young tree

Pruning at planting. As the tree is received from the nurseryman, the root area has been greatly reduced in proportion to the top by loss of roots in the digging operation. It may be also necessary to cut out or shorten intertwined or damaged roots.

Maintain balance between roots and top

After the tree is planted, the top is cut back. This

is mainly to reestablish the balance between roots and top, but also to regulate the height of the growth from the young tree because these new shoots will become the main framework branches, or primary scaf-

Fig. 18.3—Keep the center of the tree open.

folds. Therefore, trees are cut back to a height of about 24 inches at the time they are planted.

Can begin framework development

Apricot trees usually develop numerous branches in the nursery, in contrast to many other deciduous trees. Usually these branches are cut back to 6 inches (uppermost one) and others 4 or 5 inches and are the beginning of primary scaffolds. Cut off all other branches to stubs.

9. Caring for Trees After Planting

The important job of orchard management is now beginning. Young apricot trees need constant attention. Usually they will develop nicely with minimum attention if proper practices have been followed.

Keep area around tree clean

Weeds, cover crops or intercropping plants should be kept well away from young trees. Young trees should not have competition from other plants for moisture and nutrients.

Consider tree protection

Whitewash is used by many growers to protect young trees from sunburn. A good practice is to whitewash before the hole is completely filled, assuring the tree of full protection to the soil line.

Use tree protectors

Some forms of protection, cardboard, newspapers or commercial type, interfere with the normal growth of limbs, and should be moved if growth is desired in that location. However, protectors aid in controlling rabbits, as well as preventing sunburn.

Consider "pinching back" on vigorous young growth

Normal pruning practice delays selection of the main scaffold branches until the first dormant pruning, but in many locations the vigorous growth made in the first summer could be profitably directed to formation of permanent parts of the tree. This would result in fewer pruning problems at the time of the first dormant pruning, and would substantially reduce the amount of pruning needed.

USE VIGOROUS GROWTH TO ADVANCE

The apricot tends to develop many branches during the first summer in the orchard, some of which cannot be utilized for shaping the tree. Beginning when the young growth is 3 to 4 inches long, judicious pinching of some of these young shoots will throw most of the growth into unpruned branches and aid in shaping the tree.

DO NOT REMOVE ALL GROWTH

Pinching must be done with moderation. Do not remove the growth entirely. A few leaves should be left to protect and help nourish the tree. Properly performed and followed up, such summer pruning will materially reduce the amount of severity of the first dormant pruning, even though the tree makes less total growth as a result.

Proper soil moisture essential

Young apricots will not develop properly if the

roots are allowed to become dry. Stunting and dying are results. Overwatering later will not make up for the neglect.

10. Managing the Developing Orchard

Fertilize poor soil

In soils of low fertility, the trees may well repay small nitrogen applications, but only under most unusual conditions will other soil amendments be practical. Young trees should recieve only about $\frac{1}{4}$ pound of ammonium sulfate (or equivalent amounts of other nitrogenous fertilizers) scattered about 10 to 12 inches from the tree trunk. Apricots usually require less nitrogen than peaches. Heavy fertilization may be needed on mature trees in poor soils.

Minimum cultivation necessary

Apricots, if kept clean, will grow very well with little culture. However, weeds and other plants must be kept away. Do not till the soil just to be doing something.

Maintain proper soil moisture

Perhaps the most important operation to consider is proper soil moisture. Good growth is necessary for strong framework and early production. Water frequently enough for continued growth.

11. Pruning

The future of your orchard is based pretty well on the type of pruning procedure you follow. This is a very important operation.

Choose vase pruning

Most apricots are pruned to the vase form although the modified leader system is also quite popular. Training the young tree to the desired type is covered in the chapter on pruning.

Fig. 18.4—Well pruned apricot tree. This tree is big enough, and the grower is keeping it cut back to good height.

Continue shaping tree

After the third full season of growth in the orchard, the tree will start bearing considerable fruit. However, for one or two seasons longer the dormant pruning is as much concerned with the shaping of the tree as with fruiting.

Pruning at four or five years is essentially a matter of thinning out excess branches and cutting out those which tend to cross or interfere with more desirable branches.

There will probably be some strong watersprouts from the scaffolds near the points of previous cuts which will also need to be removed. It is important to admit light to the center of the tree for fruit spur development.

Keep tree at proper height

After the maximum height is attained (assuming there is a wise choice of scaffolds and branches) the shaping function of pruning is largely replaced by pruning to induce annual, heavy production of good-sized, high-quality fruit. Many growers are using mechanical pruners on the tops and hand cutting out the centers and sides.

12.   Choosing Approved Preharvest Practices

Determine if thinning is necessary

Apricots usually set too much fruit and must be thinned. In some cases over 5,000 fruits must be taken from a large mature tree. Overbearing trees seldom set a good crop the next year. However, some years the grower would like some system of "adding" fruit to the tree.

Hand thinning is accurate

Apricots are thinned in mid-April in California. Care should be taken that culls are removed in preference to good fruit. Hand thinning is expensive and slow. Fruits should be thinned 2 to 5 inches apart and never over two fruits per spur.

Chemical thinning shows promise

Growers who have experimented with chemical thinning report good results. Using the various chemicals on Royal and Tilton especially looks promising. Blossoms are sprayed when 65 per cent open in some areas to blossom time and one to two days after.

Pole thinning is used

A pole to suit your desired length with an 8- to 12-inch piece of sturdy rubber hose attached is a fast but less effective method of thinning. Some growers use a section of "V" belt, doubled over in a semicircle, to pull or hook the fruit.

Select effective pest control program

Some of the common diseases and pests of apricots can be controlled if done on time and properly. Brown rot develops readily in humid weather, attacking fruit and blossoms. Spring sprays are very effective.

A timely spray is also effective against shot-hole fungus, a fungus that mars the fruit and leaves shot-like holes in leaves.

The codling moth, twig borer and peach tree borer are a problem in some areas but can be controlled. Verticillium (Black heart) and bacterial gummosis cause problems in some areas. There are no controls

Fig. 18.5—Bacterial canker on apricot.

known, but good management should be practiced. Cytosporina Dieback, a canker forming disease is on the increase. The fungus invades the tree through bruises resulting in dead limbs. The local extension service and orchard salesman can be of tremendous help. Know what you have before applying a cure.

13.　Determining Harvest Procedure

The harvesting and handling of apricots will vary somewhat with the intended outlet. Usually the grower knows before harvest time the most probable outlet for his fruit. Certainly, if he intends to ship, such practices as thinning must be modified to give the most profitable sizes in relation to total tonnage. Production for the drying-yard or cannery, on the other hand, will usually call for less thinning and later harvest. In case of drying, some growers shake the fruit onto canvas or the ground, box them and haul them to the drying area.

Picking season varies

Experience has shown that the picking season for a given variety usually lasts about two to three weeks, and the fruit is harvested in two or three pickings.

Consider "spreading" harvest period

By a selection of varieties ripening at slightly different times, or because of differences due to local environment within the orchard, the fruit may be picked continually over the entire period, thereby keeping labor and equipment busy.

Know specifications in your state

The California Fruit, Nut, and Vegetable Standardization Act specifies the sizes and types of packages that may be used for shipping to the various markets and provides for the manner in which the packages shall be packed and marked. Defects, size of fruit and container weights are some of the regulations covered. Growers in other states should ascertain specifications to be met in their areas.

Fig. 18.6—Apricots in drying yard.

Grower can consider three markets

Canning, dried and fresh fruit outlets give the grower a diverse method for marketing his product. The economic outlook from year to year may determine his method of handling. Generally growers limit their outlet to one source, and regardless of source, they should make sure they are doing justice to the apricot industry by marketing good-quality fruit—in any form.

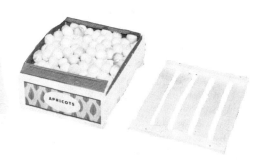

Courtesy, Wooden Box Institute

Fig. 18.7—Apricots ready for customer. Fruit displayed in this manner will find high favor with the merchant as well as the customer.

Chapter

XIX

CHERRIES

History

The original home of the cherry is lost in history. Primitive dwellers in all parts of the North Temperate Zone used cherries as part of their food. Pliny, in 70 A.D., described the cherry as being in Rome, Germany, England and France.

The cherry was one of the first fruits brought to America by early colonists. It was planted in the East and moved west with the settlers. Missions of California grew cherries, and the cultivation of cherries was known in Oregon in 1847. Some species are native to the United States. Cherries are grown in some form in every state in the United States proper.

Present Trend and Outlook

Good quality cherries now on the market have increased their popularity. The trend is for increased per capita consumption as cherry growers display and sell only high-quality products. Antitranspirant sprays used have increased size and appearance. Storage, transportation and advertising are bringing this usually unappreciated fruit into more homes in its various forms. Sales of processed cherries are expected to expand more rapidly than sales of fresh cherries.

Statistics of Interest

The cherry ranks third as a stone fruit in the United States. Cherries are divided into two main groups: Sweet-large, early-blooming trees susceptible to winter cold and the sour group—usually a smaller tree, heavy bearing and hardier than the sweet cherries. A third group, the Duke type, is a hybrid or cross between the sweet and sour cherries. The Duke is not too widely known. Its characteristics are rather intermediate. There are approximately 15 million cherry trees in the United States, consisting of about 1,200 cherry varieties, with only a few varieties grown commercially.

Cherry trees are a favorite for planting around the home and are used as such in many areas of the United States. The world production is around 1¼ million tons. Europe produces 1 million and North America, ¼ million. Germany is the leading producer with production paralleling that of the United States. Michigan produces 80,000 tons (over 95 per cent sour) and California 31,000 tons (all sweet). Sweet cherries are used mostly fresh, though canned, maraschino and frozen have shown an increase. Sour cherries have long dominated the field for use in pies. Other uses include preserves, ice cream, desserts and maraschino. Sixty per cent of the cherry crop is of the sour type and 40 per cent is sweet. Nearly all sweet cherries are produced in the West, and sour cherries are produced in the Midwest and East.

Major Cherry-producing Areas
of the United States

Locations of commercial plantings are pretty well

located around the Great Lakes area, Northeastern Coast and the West Coast areas. The southern part of the United States does not supply any great amount of the market. Michigan is the leading state, followed by California, New York, Oregon, Washington and Wisconsin. Pennsylvania, Utah and Idaho also produce cherries of commercial significance.

Activities Which Involve Approved Practices

1. Selecting a suitable location.
2. Deciding on varieties.
3. Planning orchard planting system.
4. Determining nursery supply.
5. Caring for delivered trees.
6. Preparing land before planting.
7. Selecting proper planting time.
8. Planting the young cherry trees.
9. Caring for trees after planting.
10. Managing the developing orchard.
11. Pruning.
12. Choosing approved preharvest practices.
13. Determining harvest procedure.

1. Selecting a Suitable Location

The cherry is very sensitive and exacting in its climatic requirements. It is not adapted to most locations in the great interior valleys of California, probably because of the high temperatures and low humidities there. Where it does thrive in the interior, the climatic conditions are usually modified by coastal influences.

Warm winters cause blossom delay

Following the moderately warm winters common

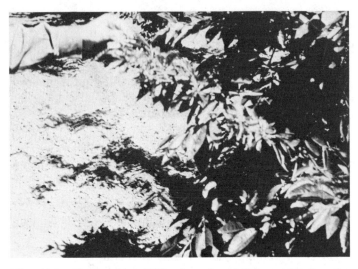

Fig. 19.1—Cherry tree displaying zinc deficiency. Notice the light-colored, small, curly leaves in clusters. Cherries planted on sandy soils often show these symptoms of zinc deficiency, resulting in reduced yield.

where sweet cherries are commercially grown, the blossoms are delayed a little in coming out. In the East the sweet cherry tree blossoms as early as, or a little earlier than, the peach, while in most places in the West it tends to blossom later than most peaches.

Varieties of sweet cherries vary in the amount of cold required to break the rest. Unusually warm winters will result in no fruit. Areas of sour cherry production do not have any great lack of chill problem, although sour cherries have a long chill requirement. Because varieties differ in rest requirement one should seek local advice.

Select proper soil

Cherries do best on light, well-drained loamy soils.

Trees do not do well on heavy, water-logged soils, although sour cherries do better on marginal soils than the sweet. A deep soil is desirable.

Air drainage can be an advantage

Although most cherries are not in areas of late frosts, good movement of air is desirable. Sites near foothills or large bodies of water aid in air circulation.

Dry, cool spring weather desirable

Cherries do better in areas that are cool and dry in the spring, since this cuts down the spread of brown rot. Cherries also do better in cool summers, as they develop better flavor.

2. Deciding on Varieties

Although many varieties can be grown, only a few are selected as commercial plantings. In selecting varieties a grower must be aware of his outlet. Seldom do successful growers go into cherry production without knowing something about their possible market. Local canneries, packers and receivers can give advice.

Choose popular varieties

About 90 per cent of the 14,500 acres of cherries grown in California consist of three varieties: 10,000 acres of Bings; 2,300 acres of Royal Anns; and 1,600 acres of various other varieties. Lambert makes up nearly one-half of Washington's cherry crop.

Varieties differ in many respects

The varieties named differ—sometimes markedly

—in appearance, maturity date, eating quality, suitability for processing, tree growth and in other respects. Such differences influence the marketability and profitability of different varieties and should be included among the factors considered when growers choose the varieties they wish to grow.

Select proper sour cherry varieties

Three varieties of sour cherries make up the majority of plantings. Montmorency, the outstanding variety, is used in canning and freezing, mostly. English Morello and Early Richmond are two other important varieties.

Consider Duke type

This cross between sweet and sour cherries is quite limited in growth at present. Most varieties of this type have the word Duke in their name, such as May, Late and Royal Duke.

Provide for pollination

This becomes a problem, as all three types mentioned differ in their requirements. Care must be taken to select pollinators that bloom about the same time.

Choose proper pollinator for sweet cherries

Research shows that all sweet cherry varieties will not produce crops when self-pollinated. Some, such as Bing, Lambert and Napoleon are inter-unfruitful with each other. As a rule, Black Tartarian and Republican strains do well with Napoleon. Pollinizers for Bing include Black Tartarian, Morean, Von, Lambert,

Montmorency and English Morello. Careful selection of pollinators is important. Pollinator trees should not be over three or four rows away. Double rows of pollinators may be planted, then four rows of the selected variety. This is repeated throughout the orchard.

Plant sour varieties in solid block

The important sour cherry varieties produce good commercial crops when they are planted in a solid block pattern. However, more satisfactory pollination results with bees or other insects that aid in pollen transfer.

Select pollinators for Duke

The Duke needs help! Cross pollination is necessary for this type to produce a satisfactory commercial cherry crop. Sweet cherries are used for the early type and sour for the late varieties.

3. Planning Orchard Planting System

Great care should be given to laying out the orchard before planting. Although trees will grow as well in crooked rows as in straight, tillage and use of other machines will be more difficult. Moreover, growers take pride in having the rows straight.

Choose square system

Most orchards are planted by the square system, though some are laid out by the alternate or diagonal system.

Consider planting distance for sweet cherries

The proper distance apart for planting cherry

trees is important in the West. Probably no sweet cherries should be planted closer than 24 feet (dwarf trees on Stockton Morello root 18 to 20 feet) ; and for good growing conditions, 28 to 35 feet would be desirable. Many old cherry trees have a spread of 35 to 40 feet. Michigan plants some varieties such as English Morello and semidwarfs at 15' x 15', and 20' x 20' for some sour and Duke types.

Select pollinator arrangement

After the planting plan thas been selected, the arrangement of the varieties from a pollination standpoint is important. At least every fourth row, and preferably every second row, should be a pollinizing variety. For convenience in harvesting, it is best to plant two rows of one kind, then two rows of the pollinizing variety, and repeat; or, if one variety is preferable to another, four rows of the favored sort, then two rows of the pollinizer, and so on. Where it is desirable to have only a minimum number of pollinizers, one tree of the pollinizer to eight of the favored variety is recommended, planted as every third tree in every third row.

Don't plant too close

Cherries, if given good care, will spread wide and produce heavily. Close planting will force growth upward and crowd out fruiting wood. Don't let this happen.

Intercrop for cash

Often the grower wishes to plant intercrops in the young cherry orchard. With good soil and plenty of moisture, there probably is no objection to this plan, provided the grower remembers that cherries are the main crop and that the intercrop must not be grown at the expense of the trees.

It is questionable whether fertilizers are necessary in a newly planted cherry orchard, especially if the right kind of soil has been selected.

Filler trees not a usual practice

Because of the pollination problem, most young cherry orchards are not interplanted with any other trees.

4. Determining Nursery Supply

Ordering cherry trees in any great amounts should be done well ahead of planting time. In order to be assured of varieties and pollinators selected a grower should contact the potential nursery from 8 to 10 months ahead. Usually a financial adjustment is made in your favor by a reliable nursery company.

Choose rootstock for the area

Cherries are propagated primarily on two main rootstocks. One may have the advantage over another in a particular area.

SELECT MAZZARD FOR LARGER TREES

Mazzard is the seed of the sweet cherry and is compatible with all varieties. It is a very vigorous grower, being slightly more resistant to excess soil moisture than Mahaleb. It gives larger trees and is generally believed to produce larger cherries than other understocks.

MAHALEB TENDS TO DEVELOP SMALLER TREES

Mahaleb is more able to withstand drought, makes a somewhat smaller tree than Mazzard, but is not completely compatible with Black Tartarian. Some varieties tend to overbear on Mahaleb understock.

Stockton Morello was developed for the heavy, wet soils of the Delta area in California and has been satisfactory. This dwarfing stock brings cherry trees into bearing early.

Order young trees

The trend in planting cherry trees has changed somewhat. Many growers a few years back planted two-year-old trees. Now it is recognized that one-year-old trees do better. Mortality of trees is higher than for most other fruit. Sour and Duke cherries are planted in many areas on two-year-old trees.

5. Caring for Delivered Trees

Young cherries are especially injured by improper care between nursery and planting. Keep the trees in good shape.

Consider heeling in trees

Trees that must sit around over a day or so should be put in the ground temporarily. Heeling them in by use of a trench and keeping them moist is necessary.

Keeps trees moist during field planting

Often the grower takes his trees from a trench and carelessly puts them on a trailer or truck to haul to the field. This should be done carefully, and they should be covered with sacks, canvas or straw to protect young roots from the sun or wind. Keep them moist. Extreme care should be taken not to injure the cherry buds. Cold storage of trees may be necessary if planting is to be delayed very long.

6. Preparing Land Before Planting

The proper preparation of land before planting is important in giving the trees a satisfactory start. As a rule, land planted to cherries has been previously worked, so that preparation is mainly a question of deep plowing or subsoiling to break up any plowpan present. Where irrigation is practiced, the land should be properly prepared. In some few sites the question of drainage may be important, though cherries in general are not adapted to conditions of soil where drainage is unsatisfactory.

Fig. 19.2—Holes dug using a backhoe in preparation for fumigation before planting. This is a very desirable practice in new orchards located on old orchard sites.

Not necessary to prefertilize

It is doubtful whether any good cherry soil requires fertilization before planting, though the use of a green manure crop the year previous may be desirable, primarily to improve soil tilth.

Young trees need water

In most of the cherry districts, irrigation is at least desirable for young orchards and necessary for bearing ones. It is, therefore, unwise to start a new orchard without irrigation facilities, especially in areas of no summer rainfall.

7. Selecting Proper Planting Time

All areas of cherry production cannot be planted at the same time, so local conditions must be taken into consideration.

Consider spring planting

California and parts of Oregon and Washington plant cherries from January to March. Sections of the Middle West and East plant in the spring as soon as the ground can be worked without injury. Late spring plantings should be avoided as this results in a high per cent of loss. It might be mentioned that the top of the cherry usually grows before the roots, and this tends to dry them out.

Fall planting may be necessary

Some areas in the West, Northeast and Great Lakes area prefer fall planting as they appear to get earlier spring growth. However, in areas of cold winters frost damage may occur.

8. Planting the Young Cherry Trees

Planting young cherry trees is similar to that of all others. The important moment for all your preparations is now at hand. Use extreme care and the approved practices mentioned for other fruit plantings.

Identify pollinators

Planting of cherries becomes a particular problem because of close plantings of pollinators to the selected variety. Planters must be sure they do not mix them up.

Cut back young tree

Because the cherry has a tendency to be a central leader, cutting back at planting is necessary for development of vase or open-center training system. Sweet cherries are cut about 35 inches; sour, 26 inches.

9. Caring for Trees After Planting

After the orchard is set out, the trees should be kept growing vigorously. The recommended practice of clean cultivation for young orchards is probably desirable for most locations, especially where irrigation is not possible. However, as with other orchards, growers are increasingly using a type of ground cover and keeping it cut close to the ground.

Consider tree protectors

Young cherry trees are subject to all sorts of pests, from deer to rabbits. Rabbits can be controlled by tree protectors and deer by repellents or a wire cage. Sunburn can be controlled by whitewash or tree protectors of a paper material. Care should be taken with young limbs.

Maintain soil moisture

Perhaps no deciduous trees react more drastically to dryness than sweet cherries. In areas of hot summers and good soil they should be watered every three weeks, more or less, the first two years. Sour cherry trees are not quite so susceptible to dryness, but the Duke responds like the sweet type. It should be kept in mind that the sour cherries react favorably to proper soil moisture also.

Keep area close to tree free of competition

Young cherry trees slow down when plants such as cover crops, weeds or intercrops are too close. Other plant roots compete for soil moisture and nutrients at the expense of the tree.

Pinch back only when necessary

Growers often make the mistake of pinching back young tree growth even when it is not doing too well. Pinch back only when the tree produces unusual vigorous growth.

10. Managing the Developing Orchard

Cherries react very favorably when proper amounts of nitrogen are applied. If the young trees are making 12 to 30 inches of growth and the thickness is satisfactory, then they are growing satisfactorily. As trees mature, the growth for a good fertilizer program is about a foot.

Fig. 19.3—Cherry tree showing results of poor management. Improper pruning and incompatible grafts result in this deformity.

Check sour cherries for lateral growth

Sour cherries often produce straight terminal growth with no side branches cutting down on fruiting area, so plan for at least 12 inches of growth. A 1-1-1 NPK fertilizer is used in many areas in sandy soil. Growers apply from 100 to 700 pounds of ammonium sulfate per acre depending on variety, soil and size of tree. Some areas do not apply any if they show good growth. Sour cherries use more nitrogen than sweet cherries.

Additional elements needed

In many areas of the West, iron, zinc, potassium and manganese must be applied. Deficiencies in any one can affect the total growth and crop.

Maintain proper moisture level

Irrigation is practiced in most areas of the West.

However, in areas of high rainfall (16 inches) cherries are grown with success with no irrigation to producing trees. The interior valleys of California require from one to six irrigations, depending on soil, temperature and maturity of trees. Sweet cherries are sensitive to high or low moisture conditions.

Consider clean culture

Generally speaking, clean culture is practiced with cherries, although areas where erosion is a factor do use a cover crop or sod.

11. Pruning

Proper pruning is a skill that must be learned, and it is necessary that you know the bearing habit of your chosen variety.

Train to vase or open center

Most cherry trees are trained as vase, or open-center, trees. At the time of planting the tree should be cut back to balance the top with the root system and also to form the head at a desirable height (24 to 30 inches). During the first summer, lateral branches will develop. These will form the primary framework of the tree, three to five being selected for this purpose —preferably three. If the trees start growth vigorously, the framework branches may be chosen in May of the first growing season. Where this is done, one should subdue the undesirable branches by cutting them back, and should allow the framework branches to grow undisturbed.

Summer-pinch with moderation

In orchards making only moderate growth, the

trees should not be summer-pinched, but should grow undisturbed until time for dormant pruning, when the framework is selected. In choosing the framework branches, one should leave only those that will make a symmetrical head.

Select well-spaced primary scaffolds

The branches should be properly balanced around the trunk and should be spaced, both up and down, as far apart as possible (6 to 8 inches). One should not select two branches which are opposite each other on the main trunk, particularly if the open-center type of tree is planned; otherwise the center branch will be choked out. These primary scaffolds should be headed at 15 to 30 inches or more from their junction with the trunk.

Special training may be needed

Since young, vigorous cherry shoots tend to branch only near the tip, usually the desirable practice is to head the new growth moderately for the first three or four years and to thin out undesirable branches.

Where vigorous growth is obtained in the second and third summer, one may save a year or more of training by summer-pinching the vigorous shoots in May. This practice will force lateral branching and will also give spread.

Watch for unusual growth pattern

An unbalanced tree often results if a vigorously growing limb is not subdued. Occasionally one limb will quickly outgrow another. Head it back severely, or if it is in a good position, use it to advantage as framework.

Treat large cuts

In areas of high humidity, the orchardist should treat large pruning wounds with a disinfectant to control rot. Bordeaux paste is used, as well as commercial products. Keep material applied until wound is healed.

Prune the bearing tree very little

The purpose of pruning bearing trees is to remove dead and interfering branches and also to renew the fruiting wood. The sweet cherry produces its fruit laterally on long-lived spurs, which are economically productive for 10 years or longer. It therefore needs less renewal wood than almost any other deciduous fruit tree. Most cherry growers do very little pruning on bearing trees.

Do a little summer work

The general practice is to remove dead wood in the early summer after harvest, at which time it is more easily distinguished than in winter, when the trees are dormant. In addition to the removal of dead wood, crossed and interfering branches are cut out from time to time. In pruning, no stubs should be left, and large cuts should be protected against wood rots.

12. Choosing Approved Preharvest Practices

Thinning not as yet practical

A number of experiment stations are trying chemical thinning of sweet cherries with dinitro, a chemical now "outlawed" in some states. Hand thinning is

Fig. 19.4—Splits in cherries can be caused by late rain or improper irrigation.

considered too expensive, and the chemicals do not remove deformed fruit, so neither is practiced commercially. Sour cherries usually are not thinned because the size of the fruit is not a major factor. Research has shown there is not much improvement in size from thinning.

Choose effective pest control program

Because cherries are attacked in different areas by a long list of pests and diseases, it is difficult to make recommendations.

Bacterial gummosis is perhaps the most troublesome, and no adequate control is known. Buckskin, a virus-like disease, is a serious problem in California. However, control is possible with a type of antibiotic. Brown rot is often damaging but can be controlled. Others include virus diseases, stem pit, cherry fly, peach tree borer, aphid, slug and scale and root rot.

13. Determining Harvest Procedure

The time to pick depends upon the type, variety and the fruit outlet.

Determine maturity

California has state maturity standards that demand at least certain colors for red or black cherries. At the time of picking they must attain a solid-light color. Some of the varieties considered soft, such as Chapman and Black Tartarian, are picked by light color for shipment. For local markets they are allowed to darken.

Sampling a method of determining when to pick

Selecting according to overall flavor and color perhaps is one of the most often used methods of determining when to pick.

Cherries increase in size and weight

Some growers that produce the firm-fleshed sweet cherries harvest early, expecting a market advantage. This is not considered a good practice, because these cherries do not have good flavor and are usually small and have poor color. Customers who buy these seldom come back.

Let cherries ripen on tree for fresh-local markets

A cherry picked half-ripe will remain so. They do not ripen if picked before they are mature, especially sour cherries. Sweets may crack so must be watched carefully. Early-picked fruit may shrink when processed, and since cherries continually gain in size until mature, they should be harvested at the proper time.

Selecting harvesting procedure

Tree shakers are being used in some areas harvesting sour cherries. Michigan growers, with the aid of Michigan State University and U.S.D.A., have made good progress to nearly complete mechanization of some sour cherries, using shakers and bulk bins for specific market outlet. Sweet cherries are more difficult to harvest mechanically.

Hand picking sweet cherries

Cherries to be shipped fresh must have stems attached; otherwise the skin will be broken, and the fruit will not hold up during shipment. In removing the fruit from the spur, the picker grasps the stem firmly between the thumb and forefinger, giving it an upward twist. Care must be taken not to break the fruit spur.

Normally fruit for canning or processing should be picked with stems. If, however, the fruit will be delivered to the cannery or processing plant immediately, it may be picked without stems—a practice used in some quick-freezing plants. To prevent bruising, the fruit should always be placed carefully in the picking receptacle and should never be thrown or dropped.

A machine has been devised for separating sweet cherry clusters and still leaving stems.

Storage a problem

One of the most difficult fruits to store, and still maintain the same delicious fruit, is the cherry. A system of adding 25 per cent carbon dioxide at 45° F. to the storage area looks promising for good market cherries.

Chapter

PEACHES—QUEEN OF FRUITS— AND NECTARINES

A. Peaches

With the apple considered king of fruits, it is only proper that the peach be considered the queen. It is a pity "the two shall never meet" and produce a "Peapple" or maybe "Appeach."

History

The peach, as we know it in the cultivated sense, came from China. References to the peach in Chinese writings are traced back 2000 B.C. Theophrastus, in 330 B.C., wrote of the peach in Greece.

The Spanish explorers received credit for the peach in America. The peach was widely grown in Mexico during the era of Cortez. The Indians traveling far and wide spread it through their countries and into southern United States areas. Peaches for brandy were grown by Virginia colonists.

Peaches are grown commercially in Turkey, Persia, Africa, France, Australia, New Zealand, Japan, China, England and Buenos Aires. The latter boasts of thousands of acres of the fruit. In England, peaches are grown under glass.

Major Peach-producing Areas of the United States

The West Coast area, including California, Washington, Oregon, Nevada and Idaho, leads in peach production.

Present Outlook and Trends

The Elberta peach is the leading variety in the United States, but other varieties with more desirable characteristics are being planted. The Elberta does not have a low temperature resistance, and quality is a problem. Also, late ripening varieties usually produce heavier than early ripening varieties, such as the Elberta.

Peaches, the second ranked deciduous tree fruit in the United States, has serious competition from other produce. However, the industry is fairly constant with around 8 pounds per capita. New varieties are constantly being developed, some proving to be superior to older varieties. Transportation, storage, processing and advertising all are contributing to the increasing demand for this popular food. Often there are more peaches than markets, however, the various organizations within the industry keep a sharp eye on developments and make their voices heard.

Colorado leads in the Southwest with Texas, Oklahoma, New Mexico and Missouri increasing their plantings.

Peaches in the south Atlantic area of Georgia, South Carolina and nearby states add a tremendous amount of value to the local economy.

Michigan, Ohio, Illinois and Indiana take care of most of the markets in the Midwest.

States in the Northeastern Coastal area, with Pennsylvania, New Jersey and New York leading the way, are increasing their plantings each year.

Peaches are grown for one reason or another in 38 of the United States and to some extent in Canada.

Activities Which Involve Approved Practices

1. Selecting a suitable location.
2. Deciding on varieties.
3. Planning orchard planting system.
4. Determining nursery.
5. Preparing land before planting.
6. Planting the young tree.
7. Caring for trees after planting.
8. Managing the developing orchard.
9. Pruning.
10. Selecting approved preharvest practices.
11. Determining harvest procedure.

1. Selecting a Suitable Location

Most locations for peach growing have been selected as mentioned previously. One contemplating going into the peach business would be wise to grow only in areas showing a history of successful orchard operations.

Choose location for advantages

The workers that live in locations where peaches are grown usually have a working knowledge of what to do in an orchard. Repairs to equipment, and supplies needed, may be secured more easily.

Choose site of low humidity

High humidity hinders bloom growth and invites disease.

During bloom the peach orchard needs good weather for proper pollination and disease control. Fogs, long rainy spells and low temperatures interfere with pollination and encourage blossom rots such as brown rot—a highly destructive fungus disease.

The best weather for the trees and fruit during the growing season is a good balance of rather high temperatures (80° F. to 95° F.), abundant sunlight and low humidity. Peaches do not do their best in cool,

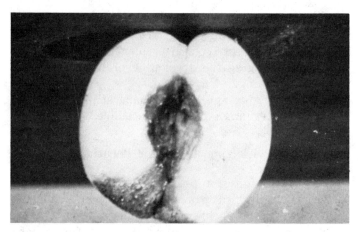

Fig. 20.1—Brown rot on a peach. This disease causes tremendous losses to growers. High humidity aids in its growth.

damp and foggy areas. They lack proper quality and suitable color.

Determine if site temperature is too high

Continuous summer temperatures over 100° F.

ripen the fruit too quickly and may shorten the life of the trees. Sizing peaches in very hot weather is difficult. Temperatures above 70° F. during rest period are considered to offset the accumulating rest hours.

Choose location for "winter chill"

Peaches, depending on variety, need varying amounts of cold weather to break the rest period—1,000 to 1,500 hours below 45° F. for most clings and 400 to 1,500 hours for freestones. Winter temperatures below 0° F. are dangerous although trees in late dormancy have stood 10° below 0° for a short time. Elberta needs from 750 to 800 hours to break rest in fresh buds, and leaf buds need closer to 1,000 hours. Fort Valley, Georgia, reports that an application of dinitro and oil in February will take the place of around 200 hours of chilling requirement.

Warm winters may have harmful effect

If the winters are not cold enough, peach trees leaf out slowly and erratically, the bloom is spread out longer and orchard operations become difficult to time. Perhaps most damage is from loss of buds that deteriorate and drop off in the prebloom stage.

Select frost-free site

Frost damage reduces peach yields.

Crop-damaging frosts usually occur during bloom or just shortly after bloom. A good orchard site has to be reasonably free from the danger of spring frost. If the orchard needs to be heated frequently, it cannot compete economically with frost-free areas protected by cultural means.

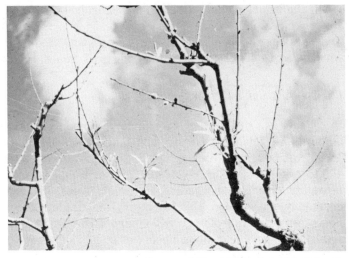

Courtesy, California Polytechnic State University

Fig. 20.2—Peach showing results of inadequate winter chilling. Note the peaches set on its limb and tree still blooming with erratic leaf growth.

Choose the best soil

The best soil for peaches is one of medium texture such as deep, sandy loam, at least four feet deep. However, peaches produce profitably on a great range of soil types. Avoid water-logged soils. Good soil drainage is a must. Tree sizes and production decrease as the soil becomes heavier, since heavy soils hold more water and drain poorly.

Avoid poor soils for peaches

Peaches do not thrive on deep-seated salt soils either. They may soon show the leaf scorch and dieback typical of too much salt. The excess salts may be caused by a high water table. Row crops, however, grow well on such soils.

Fig. 20.3—The young tree planted in this oak-root fungus-infested soil will never develop properly, as evidenced by the trees in the background.

Soils high in boron rarely set commercial peach crops. Trees on these soils have had to be pulled out in spite of otherwise favorable growth characteristics.

Avoid locations infested with oak-root fungus; none of the present peach rootstocks is resistant to it. The more recently formed soils along rivers and streambeds often are heavily infested with this disease.

A second or third planting of peaches does not grow well in some locations and, as yet, there is no satisfactory answer to the problem. Consult your farm advisor to find out if there are replant problems in your area.

Choose good water supply

With a good soaking from winter rains or snow, peaches need two to four acre-feet of water during the growing season. On hot days an average acre of mature trees will use up to 0.3 acre-inches daily.

DETERMINE IF SUPPLY IS CONSTANT

Plenty of water is a must for growth. A good water supply is also necessary to size growing fruit properly. A tree which exhausts its soil moisture checks fruit growth. The fruit will grow again when the tree is reirrigated but it may be undersized.

2. Deciding on Varieties

The production of peaches is divided into two industries—clingstone peaches, those that have the characteristic of the flesh adhering to the pit, and freestones, those in which the flesh breaks freely from the pit. The clings go into canning, while less than one-half of the freestones are used fresh, the rest being processed.

Selection of variety important

Successful peach growing depends on a wise selection of varieties. Decision on varieties is important in the establishment and management of a peach orchard. A variety should yield satisfactorily; it should have an appropriate rest period for the locality in which it is to be grown; the time of blooming and initiation of growth in the spring should be after the customary date of freezes and killing frost; the trees and fruit should be resistant to diseases encountered; and finally, the trees should be vigorous and adaptable to the area. The variety also should sell well. Size, color, flavor and degree of ripening are factors that influence sales.

CONSIDER NEW VARIETIES

Many new varieties have been introduced in recent years as a result of intensive breeding programs conducted by state and Federal research agencies and interested plant breeders. Characteristics of these new early varieties, such as skin color, firmness, flavor and disease-resistance are superior. By selecting the proper combination of varieties to provide for a succession of ripening dates, fruit will mature throughout late spring

Fig. 20.4—This peach orchard is being converted by grafting the trees to a more profitable variety.

and summer. The market outlet used and the length of the favorable marketing season determine the combination of varieties that provide the best succession of ripening periods.

Evaluation studies conducted over past years show that varieties vary widely in adaptation. New varieties, therefore, should be planted on a trial basis until they are fully tested and recommended by qualified personnel.

ELBERTA STILL FAVORED VARIETY OF FREESTONE IN NATION

Because of its wide adaptability, this variety still makes up a large per cent of the commercial plantings in many of the peach-producing areas. However, Elberta is losing in popularity as more desirable varieties for specific locations are being developed. Elberta is a large, golden-yellow-skinned peach that shows a red blush when it is exposed to the sun. Fay Elberta is the leading freestone in California with over one-fifth of all new plantings.

A number of states in the Midwest and South report an increase in plantings of Redhaven. Its fruits are of medium size, freestone and with highly colored dark red tough skin. The flesh is yellow, of good quality, nonbrowning and exceptionally firm for its season. It ripens about a month before Elberta. Trees are vigorous and productive and require careful, early thinning for good fruit size.

Other important freestones in order of ripening include Jersey Lord, Redhaven, Sullivan, J. H. Hale (which is more popular in the Pacific Northwest than Elberta) and Rio-Oso-Gem. Babcock and Ramona are important in areas, such as southern California, that have a short chilling climate.

Choose Freestones for Drying and Fresh Market

Lovell, Muir and Elberta are the popular varieties in California for drying. The peaches must be ripe and of good quality. As markets for one variety over another is not a major concern, a high drying ratio often determines the selection. Muir dries at 5 pounds fresh to 1 pound dry, Elberta 7 pounds fresh to 1 pound dry.

Regular Elbertas and Fay Elbertas are used in canning as well as the fresh market. The major freezing variety is the Rio-Oso-Gem.

Select Clingstones for Most Processing

A large, yellow-fleshed, heavy producer of excellent quality are some reasons the Halford is the number one peach in California. However, new plantings of Carolyn, Loadel, Carson, Starn and Peak are also being planted in increasing numbers.

Seek professional help

Because of the many areas of peach growing and the everchanging demand for one variety or another, as well as newly developed varieties, you should not plan a large planting without contacting the farm advisors, local nurseries or other market outlets for advice—and one better—listen, not just hear.

For example, some varieties once a favorite have not even been planted in the past two to eight years, and the remaining trees have been removed—Cortez, Sowell and McKnight (clings) and Babcock, J. H. Hale, July Elberta and Redgloble (freestones).

Pollination

With the J. H. Hale not being planted, there is no

problem left as far as peaches needing a cross-pollinator. However, it is still important to have bee activity for pollination.

3. Planning Orchard Planting System

An experienced grower knows the importance of establishing a peach orchard correctly. It is the first step in insuring the successful, efficient operations that must follow. Most peach orchards don't show a profit after 25 years, so plan for that time.

Choose proper tree spacing

Tree spacing depends on the land to be planted. Fertile soil calls for regular planting distances to fit your locality; less fertile soil means planting trees closer together. Why? On less fertile soil the trees will be smaller and more trees per acre will be needed for maximum production.

Texas uses 20' x 25' in the eastern part and 25' x 30' in North Central; Ohio, 20' x 25'; and California, mostly 20' x 20'. Local conditions are an important factor and one should seek local advice.

Hedgerow planting in experimental stage

Some new orchards are being planted hedgerow style experimentally: 14' x 28', 16' x 24' or 16' x 22'. In the latter planting, the drive rows are 26 feet apart. Sunlight strikes both sides of the trees equally when the rows are run north to south, or slightly to the southwest. Hedgerow plantings are allowed to grow together, with movement through the rows restricted. It has some advantages for mechanical harvesting when the picking platforms are being used.

Square system popular for peaches

The square system, as mentioned previously, means each tree is an equal distance from adjoining trees and 20' x 20' is often used for medium-size trees on good soil or 18' x 18' on less fertile soil on the square system. As larger equipment is introduced, the rectangular system may be your choice.

Choose intercrops carefully

Remember, peaches are the main crop. Grow intercrops only where there is plenty of water.

Choose intercrops which do not interfere with normal irrigation practices. Do not plant crops which cause trees or soil to be attacked or infested with detrimental insects, nematodes, diseases or weeds.

Filler trees not recommended

Because the peach is a fast grower and needs a lot of water, using filler trees between plantings is not a common practice. Using peaches as fillers for others such as walnut is done; however, it is not recommended. The frequent irrigation required by peaches causes crown rot in walnuts.

4. Determining Nursery

Good nursery stock and a reliable nurseryman are essentials of a successful orchard venture. Your farm advisor or agriculture instructors are men that can supply you with reliable names and information on nurseries.

Order trees by grade

Peach trees should be ordered by grade. Sizes

Fig. 20.5—Peaches interplanted with citrus. This grower's citrus will have a good start if the peaches are removed. Not crowding yet.

Fig. 20.6—Peach trees bought from unreliable nursery. These three trees were all supposed to be the same variety. Tree with no leaves in foreground is actually a nectarine.

recommended for plantings range between ⁵⁄₁₆ inch to ¹¹⁄₁₆ inch in diameter. A tree in the medium range is generally more satisfactory and easy to manage. Large-sized trees such as ¾ inch or more may be tempting, but small trees are easier to handle, and the mortality rate is less. Medium-sized trees will be the same size at the end of several years anyway. Trees two to three years old should not be considered for commercial plantings.

An example of an order blank follows.

JUNE BUDDED FRUIT TREES—ACRE BASIS

(10% Discount for Prebudding Orders Placed Before May 31)

Size (Caliper)	³⁄₁₆–¼	¼–⁵⁄₁₆	⁵⁄₁₆–³⁄₈	³⁄₈–½	½–⁵⁄₈	⁵⁄₈–Up
– – – – – – – – Price per Tree – – – – – – – – –						
PEACHES FREESTONE ON S-37	.50	.65	.75	.80	.85	.90
Alamar (Add 10¢) (P. P. No. 930)						
Elberta						

A typical order might read: 100 Peaches, Free-stone, Elberta. ⁵⁄₁₆-³⁄₈ caliper. 3"-4" ht. on R.S. (S-37) root. Delivery Jan. 25. No substitute.

Select rootstock for local area

Over 95 per cent of the peach trees in the United States are budded on some form of peach seedling roots.

Horticulturists are constantly seeking to improve the resistance-ability of a rootstock for peaches. A grower must evaluate his conditions. U.S.D.A. and experiment stations have imported stock for breeding and some show promise.

SELECT NEMAGUARD FOR JAVANICA
AND ROOT-KNOT NEMATODE

Nemaguard peach rootstock, introduced by the U.S.D.A. in 1960, shows excellent promise as a nematode-resistant rootstock for peaches, almonds and nectarines, especially where the javanica nematode is present in the soil. However, it is a problem on wet soils.

The Lovell peach rootstock is cheap and used quite successfully with growers who do their own propagating. Lovell is not resistant to nematode. Both these two peach rootstocks can be obtained as virus-free, a recommended procedure.

Plum, almond and apricot have been used in some areas but have not been too satisfactory.

Once the trees are delivered to you, they become your responsibility. The nurseryman has taken great pains to deliver to you trees worth planting. Heel them in immediately.

Consider putting trees in cold storage

If weather conditions make it impossible for you to plant you can put the trees in cold storage, and they can be planted as late as the middle of May. However, the later the planting, the poorer the results. Trees planted by this method should be watered as soon as they are planted. Treat the roots the same as for heeling in. Storage conditions range from 32° F. to 38° F. Do not place in cold storage after growth starts.

5. Preparing Land Before Planting

Do not wait until after your trees are planted to

Fig. 20.7—The soil was not properly prepared before planting in this orchard. The replanted area did not receive enough water.

do your leveling, scraping, subsoiling and plowing. There is no substitute for well-prepared land for the new orchard.

Consider "subsoiling"

It is important to give young peach roots plenty of room to grow—down as well as out. Breaking up clods, subsoil, plow sole or hardpan is using good judgment. Many growers subsoil without the mentioned conditions to assure roots of a soft, loose soil in which to grow.

Select proper planting time

In many areas of the South, trees are planted in the fall. However, most peach areas plant any time after the trees shed their leaves. Areas such as California don't receive their trees until January, and growers plant from then to March. Local conditions such as frost, winter crops and damage from rodents or animals must be considered.

HAZARDOUS TO PLANT TOO LATE

Often an orchardist puts planting off too long or he couldn't get on his field. It must be kept in mind that the later you plant after spring, the poorer the results obtained.

6. Planting the Young Tree

Planting the young tree is the beginning of an interesting experience in fruit production. Now you are ready to test your ability in bending nature to your plans. The following approved practices will aid you in success.

Keep trees moist

Young peach roots will dry in a few minutes if they are exposed to the sun, air or wind. Keep them moist or covered by use of sacks, canvas, soil or sawdust. Keep rows as straight as possible.

Dig holes right size

Dig holes just large enough to hold the roots. If the holes are too large, the trees will usually sink in too deeply with the first irrigation.

Soil must be firm

If blasting was done before digging, the trees will

settle unless the soil is thoroughly wet from winter rains or irrigation. Settle the soil in the bottom of each hole before planting the trees. Blasting can also compact soil, which is undesirable.

Plant trees at the same depth that they were grown in the nursery. Make sure the bud faces the afternoon sun; this reduces sunburn injury and cuts down on the chances of flat-headed borers entering the trunk.

Trim roots properly

Remove damaged roots and shorten any others that seem extra long. Spread the roots enough to prevent any crowding. Then work the soil well in around the roots and make sure there are no air pockets. Watering after planting will help eliminate air pockets and provide adequate moisture.

Fill holes carefully

Use care in filling the holes. Soil should never be packed too tightly, especially in the heavier soils. A number 12 boot stomping unmercifully on tender young roots should be avoided.

Prune back young tree

Experienced peach growers prune back young peach trees at planting. The young bare-root tree often has a number of small limbs branching. These are cut off and the central stem cut off at about 30 inches.

Leaving the tree unpruned at planting has been tried in some California orchards. The tree tends to develop a better root system and more total growth the second year. But pruning must be done sometime and growers believe the more severe pruning later tends to set the tree back. The increased leaf surface resulting from no pruning at planting appears to be advantageous to its vigor. First-year pruning has an advantage in producing a better form and should be practiced.

7. Caring for Trees After Planting

A well-planned operation for taking care of your trees after planting is most important. The job has just begun. Your young peach trees need constant attention, and their future success will depend on your care.

Select proper tree protectors

Because of the various types of protectors available, no particular one can be recommended. Cardboard and milk cartons are commonly used around the lower part of the tree. Do not let the protector interfere with limb development. Whitewash is used effectively against sunburn.

Consider "pinching back" on vigorous growth

If your young peach trees are pushing too fast, you should consider pinching or cutting back 4 to 6 inches of the tips to encourage lateral growth below the pinch or elsewhere on the tree. Often the selected or desirable limb is not developing so fast as the vigorous shoots, and clipping the ends of these shoots will cause more growth in others.

Maintain proper soil moisture

Making sure the young trees have ample available water is one practice you must not neglect. "Flooding

it with devotion" later will not make up for the dry
condition earlier. Stunting from lack of water takes
place quickly.

8. Managing the Developing Orchard

Selecting fertilizer program carefully

Peach trees, like others, do their best when all
nutrients are available. Nitrogen seems to be the most
important need. When the tree comes into bearing, the
grower must consider a 1-1-1 ratio on sandy soils and
perhaps a 2-2-1 for heavier soils. Potassium has been
found to give good response, and phosphorus is used
in large amounts by the plant. Apply a complete fertilizer often enough to give you satifactory results. If
manure is available, it should be applied at about 6
tons per acre in the fall.

Amount of fertilizer varies

No definite fertilizer recommendation can be made
for all peach orchards. Soil type, fertility, amount of
erosion and the age and condition of the trees all enter
into one of the more perplexing problems of orcharding.
Results of research indicate the effect of the rootstock, and behavior of the individual tree is more likely
to determine the rate of tree growth and its productive
ability than any variation of plant nutrients.

CONSIDER ONE APPLICATION

Some growers consider that one application of
nitrogen during each of the first three years is sufficient
to secure the desired tree growth. Usually the required
nitrogen is obtained from an addition of $\frac{1}{2}$ to 1 pound
of ammonium nitrate to the tree during each season.

Fig. 20.8—K deficiency on peaches. A healthy crop of peaches cannot be expected if this condition prevails.

New varieties create problem

The introduction of the new early-ripening varieties of peaches further complicates fertilizer recommendations. Recent results of an extensive fertilizer

Fig. 20.9—Peach leaf curl.

test with Dixired peaches in Texas show that a spring fertilizer application delays ripening from one to two weeks.

The problem becomes less critical as the season advances, but the grower should be careful in the fertilization of bearing trees in the drier areas of the country. Frequently, a heavy application of fertilizer will delay the maturity of the fruit until a dry period occurs, resulting in total or partial loss of the crop. A fertilizer test with the Halehaven variety showed that it was affected by this condition approximately one year in three. A balanced fertilizer of a 1-2-1 ratio is suggested where the moisture supply is likely to become deficient during midsummer. This provides trees with essential plant food elements without promoting excessive vegetative growth.

Consider spraying

Experiments have proven that nutrient sprays such as zinc can be applied very efficiently and successfully. Local conditions must be considered before others can be applied.

Plan cultivation practice

New implements have caused changes in cultivation practices. Weed knives, brush choppers, rotary mowers and various types of rototillers have eliminated much of the disking.

Don't till the soil for pleasure

Make sure cultivation is absolutely necessary for proper orchard operation before disking the soil. A weed-free orchard is not worth the cost if it must be at the expense of the soil.

Certain orchard operations do justify soil cultivation—removing noxious weeds; incorporating cover crops, prunings or manure; providing loose soil for making levees or furrows; making a smooth surface for harvest crews; or preparing a seedbed for cover crops.

9. Pruning

Pruning and training peach trees are not for an inexperienced grower. Seek out advice and have a local grower or farm advisor show you how, then have him watch you do it until you completely understand the skill. Training the tree the first year has been discussed.

Second year: Select the "open vase" system (open center)

During the winter, or dormant season, all limbs along the main trunk are cut off except the three selected for the framework. Each of the three or four main scaffold limbs is cut back, preferably about 12

Fig. 20.10—Aerial crown gall on peach tree.

inches above the juncture of the branches with the main trunk. This stimulates the growth of lateral branches. Two limbs growing in opposite directions and rising at different points are selected from these lateral branches and encouraged to produce the tertiary scaffold limbs of the permanent framework. Limbs that grow into the center of the tree should be cut out to produce an open center.

Third year pruning: Still training

Each of the secondary scaffold limbs is pruned back, if necessary, to produce additional framework limbs around the perimeter of the tree. Center limbs and low-hanging outside limbs should be removed. Some thinning of smaller limbs and twigs along the main branches is necessary, and tips of leading branches should be cut back to preserve the uniform shape of the tree and maintain it at the desired height.

Fourth year and over: Tree has its framework

With the scaffold limbs and framework of the tree well established, future pruning should keep the fruiting area at the desired height, maintain the open-center feature of the tree and discourage overbearing by judicious thinning of potential fruit-bearing limbs. Thinning is accomplished by removing limbs along the main framework, leaving relatively short fruiting limbs spaced about 8 inches apart, and by heading back most of the vigorous growing limbs that tend to give the tree excessive height.

Peach pruning facts

Peaches are pruned more heavily than any other deciduous tree, especially when developing the open-center type. They produce fruit on shoots of the past season's growth, and it is necessary to replace nearly all the fruiting wood each season. About one-third of the last year's growth should be left on bearing trees.

10. Selecting Approved Preharvest Practices

Determine if thinning is necessary

Thinning is necessary for the production of quality peaches although growers of back yard orchards do not often make a practice of it. Some cannery outlets and fresh markets will not accept fruit under certain sizes (2⅜ inches in diameter for grade 1 canning in California).

Thinning practices change

The demand for larger fruit has created a need for exact thinning, namely the early-ripening varieties that tend to be small. Some require even wider spacing than the older varieties that attained good marketable size with little thinning. Six to 8 inches is recommended on many to reach size and up to 12 inches on early varieties.

Large size fruit profitable

Many growers cannot see the advantage of removing fruit. It seems fairly clear that if a harvest of X pounds of large fruit brings top prices and twice as

PEACH THINNING

Diameter of Peach	Number in 10 Pounds
(inches)	
2	76
2⅛	63
2¼	53
2⅜	45
2½	38
2⅝	33
2¾	29
3	22

many pounds of small fruit bring bottom prices, if sold at all, thinning for large fruit is profitable.

Time to thin

There is no one best time for thinning all varieties or in all seasons. Timing also affects the cost and quality of thinning. Where there are no other considerations, the largest harvest size follows the earliest thinning.

However, early thinning can cause an increased number of split pits and gummy fruits. It is more difficult to remove fruit early in the season than later. Early thinning does not let the thinner detect cull fruit as well as later thinning. By delaying thinning, a number of fruits fall off in the normal drop.

Select thinning method

Fruit usually is thinned by hand-pulling, by knocking with a looped section of a V-belt or rubber hose attached to a short pole and by shaking. Chemicals are being used experimentally. Hand-pulling is slow, tedious and expensive but is most practical for varieties which must be thinned early when the fruit is small. Thinning with a belt or hose is effective for removing fruit that has attained $\frac{1}{2}$ inch in diameter. Shaking involves the use of mechanical shakers or knockers. This rapid method should be followed with more careful hand-thinning.

CHEMICAL THINNING

A number of chemicals have been introduced for the thinning of peaches as more interest develops concerning the expense of the methods mentioned. Variable results are obtained when used on different varieties. Some varieties are thinned too much and others show little response. Standard concentrations do not produce the same degree of thinning during different years. Hormone-type chemicals such as NPA at 150 to 300 p.p.m. have shown promise on some varieties. From $3\frac{1}{2}$ to 5 gallons per tree are used. Chemical thinning obviously requires less labor; however, results have been inconclusive, and additional research is needed before chemical thinning can be recommended.

Select disease and pest control program

Peaches are subject to many troubles. They will require some annual sprays. Fruit and foliage diseases most likely to be troublesome are peach-leaf curl, mildew, rust and blight (shot hole).

Several virus diseases attack peaches and are noticeable usually by leaf distortion or spotting. The peach is susceptible to wet soils, crown rot and oak-root fungus, which do not show leaf symptoms. The trees usually fail in the spring or early summer.

Insect pests most likely to cause damage are those attacking the ripening fruits, among which are the peach twig borer, the codling moth and the major fruit injuring insect in California—the Oriental fruit moth. Serious damage is done in some years in California by the stink bug. Grubs of various wood-boring insects are also likely to be present, though they often do no extensive damage, and may escape unnoticed. Trees growing vigorously are usually less likely to be attacked by insects than those that are weak or sunburned.

Consult your local farm advisor for advice on diseases and insects of the peach and for pest control recommendations.

11. Determining Harvest Procedure

The commercial peach producer must realize the harvest is his ultimate objective. Profitable sales depend on his harvest procedure.

Select mature fruit

The development of sweetness and other taste factors ceases when a peach fruit is harvested from a tree. It is important, therefore, that the fruit remain on the tree until it is ripe enough to insure good eating quality, at least for the fresh fruit market. Several ways may be used to determine ripeness.

Color is a measure of ripeness. Growers learn to associate various shades of ground color with maturity. A change in ground color from whitish-green to yellowish-green is a basis for determining maturity of most varieties. All fruit on a tree does not mature at the same time.

Skin Color Not Always Reliable Guide

Color cannot be relied on entirely as an accurate index for peach varieties that develop extensive red pigmentation well before maturity. Yellow ground color, particularly at the stem end, is a good indication. The best color index is the absence of green color at the shaded area where the fruit-bearing twig has been in contact with the fruit. This area has been shaded by the twig and the interfering red pigments do not form here. Yellowness of this area and peach maturity are directly related. Experienced pickers become adept at selecting fruits that are mature by their general appearance, except those varieties that are all red.

Firmness of Flesh Also Being Used as Test

Firmness of flesh is another way of determining maturity. Hand pressure has been used and more recently accurate fruit pressure testers have been used for this purpose. This has been proved to be the most accurate means of measuring maturity and maintaining the desired level of fruit quality going to market. Fully ripened fruit has a pressure test of less than four pounds as determined by the Magnuss-Taylor pressure tester. This is too ripe. The ideal stage of maturity by pressure test is in the 4- to 7-pound range. This fruit ships well and ripens sufficiently during the short holding periods in the market system to be of prime quality when offered for sale. Pressure testers may be obtained from most orchard supply houses.

Market outlets determine maturity

The actual degree of desired ripeness is deter-

Fig. 20.11—Size of peach not a "maturity factor." These three Rio-Oso-Gem peaches were picked at maturity. The center peach is the normal size for this variety.

Courtesy, Ugo Cavaiani and Sons

Fig. 20.12—These 90 boxes of regular Elberta peaches represent the first picking of six sample trees. The orchard produced 37 tons per acre. Production like this is not an accident.

mined by the market outlet. Peaches should be full-ripe for use in ice cream, firm-ripe for canning or freezing, firm-ripe to full-ripe for sale at roadside markets and hard-to-firm-ripe for distant shipment.

Hydro-cooling

Valuable fruit will remain so if it is taken care of properly. Peach hydro-cooling is used when the fruit is to be held in cold storage for short periods. Storage is recommended when an even or orderly flow of fruit into marketing channels is desired. Hydro-cooling is a way of rapidly removing field heat from the fruit. This heat can be harmful in that rates of maturation and breakdown are directly related to heat. Cooled fruit has a longer storage and market life.

The process of removing heat by hydro-cooling involves flooding or spraying the fruit with ice water. Commercial hydro-cooling units are available, or small capacity units can be built.

Postharvest ripening and storage

Peaches which are not fully mature can be held at room temperature one to two days in the early summer; however, when day temperatures are high and the relative humidity is low, excessive shriveling and weight loss occur. When this condition exists, ripening should be carried out under cool temperatures.

Firm-ripe peaches of standard market size can be held in cold storage for three to six weeks at temperatures of 30°F. to 32°F. with humidity at close to 85 per cent.

Canning peaches must be No. 1

California produces over 90 per cent of the canning peaches. They must be at least 2⅜ inches in diameter, firm, clean, ripe and free from any insect-type damage.

Drying peaches a profitable outlet

Peaches for drying are allowed to mature on the tree, but must be firm. Fruit is cut in half, laid on a tray with exposed flesh up, treated with sulfur fumes for four or five hours and then dried in the sun or other heat. It usually takes from 8 to 10 days to dry the halves. The drying ratio averages about six to one— some varieties less, some more. An exceptional crop would be 2 tons of saleable dried fruit per acre.

A more thorough job needs to be done to acquaint the consumers with this tasty, healthful fruit.

Fig. 20.13—This 4 x 5 pack of Rio-Oso-Gems in the popular L.A. lug is ready for the customer.

B. Nectarines

Perhaps one of the most interesting, yet mysterious fruits of all time is the nectarine. Most say it is a fuzzless peach. Genetically, the missing fuzz is the only apparent difference between the peach and nectarine.

There are freestone and clingstone nectarines; like the peach, both may have white, red or yellow flesh, and the flowers follow the same pattern as the peach.

Leaves of the nectarine show similar variations, and one cannot distinguish between peach and nectarine pits. The fruits are the same, but generally the nectarine is a little smaller, has a stronger aroma, has a more pronounced flavor and is slightly firmer-fleshed. The tree itself cannot be distinguished from the peach by most growers as their form, growing habits and development are identical.

History

Much has been written about the history of this fruit. Evidence of the nectarine dates back over 2,000 years where it is lost or merges with the peach.

Writers believe that nectar, described in Greek mythology as the drink of the Gods, came from the nectarine, or that nectarine was named from it.

The Romans knew the peach as the "Persian Apple." The nectarine resembles an apple more closely than a peach does. Could that have been a nectarine rather than a peach?

In 1741, Collinson recorded an incident where a peach tree bore nectarines. This is not unusual, under certain conditions.

Various Peach-Nectarine Variations Possible

Pomologists have added some interesting crossings of the peach and nectarine. A white nectarine on a yellow peach resulted in a number of white peaches and yellow nectarines. A growing peach or nectarine tree may suddenly produce a limb or two of the other. You may plant the pit from a peach and grow a plant developed with one-half of the individual fruit having the characteristic fuzz and the other half resembling the fuzzless nectarine. Scientists report the absence of fuzz on the nectarine basically is due to a single gene for smooth skin.

The nectarine is a good example of "bud variation." However, nearly all peach trees pollinated with peach produce true, likewise nectarines.

Present Outlook and Trends

Research stations are looking for a better nectarine—namely, for canning and drying. A number of new varieties look most promising. Also there is a need for growing larger nectarines, and this is being done by crossing them with peaches. Of the 15,000 acres of nectarines in California, Sun Grand, Early Sun Grand and late Le Grande are the most popular varieties grown.

Many customers, when properly acquainted with the aromatic flavor of the nectarine, will select a nectarine over a peach—quality being equal. It will pay growers to advertise and popularize this excellent fruit. Plantings throughout the growing areas are on the increase, and most markets do not have enough high-quality fruit consistently.

Statistics of Interest

California has most of the commercial orchards of nectarines in the United States. Most of the crop is used for fresh fruit and is packed carefully with dividers for shipping. A number of research stations in the eastern and southern United States are doing work to improve the nectarine. Tonnage is usually low because the best are used for fresh market. Production ranges from 2 to 7 tons per acre, depending on year and location. A few nectarines are dried and frozen, but not many are canned.

Activities Which Involve Approved Practices

Choose all approved practices for the nectarine that have been selected for peaches with just a few exceptions that are listed as follows.

1. In areas where the plum curculio is a pest, spraying may not be so effective on nectarines as on peaches. The fuzz on peaches holds on a good layer of

the desired spray material whereas the latter may slide off of the slick-skinned nectarine. Therefore, nectarines may have more wormy fruit.

2.   Nectarine with its smooth skin will need more attention from attacks of fungus diseases in humid areas, especially brown rot. Thrips also may attack nectarines more severely.

3.   Some research stations report the nectarine is a little more susceptible to cold than peaches.

Chapter

XXI

PEARS

History

The pear, like the apple, is a pome fruit. Writers agree that it was native to North Persia and the Northwestern Himalaya Mountain range. Several varieties were cultivated as early as 1000 B.C. Around 300 B.C. Theophrastus mentioned them. In the period from 1780 to 1850 a number of plant breeders were growing many seedlings in the hope of growing better varieties.

Pear growing in the United States dates back to the earliest white settlers—on both the east and west coasts. However, the first recorded pear was the Endicott, in Salem, Massachusetts, about 1830.

Present Outlook and Trends

The Bartlett continues to be the most important pear variety. As an example of California's 44,000 acres of pears, 42,000 are Bartlett. Surveys indicate pears are considered more of a "special occasion" fruit than most others. The total outlook seems promising as per-capita consumption has gained. Transportation, storage and advertising will also increase the demand. The trend is for a better quality, added amounts of pears in fruit cocktail and higher sales of fresh marketing fruit. Some increase has been noted in canning halves and drying. Many growers have shown an interest in several new rootstocks that result in smaller trees.

Statistics of Interest

Pear varieties run to about 2,600 named and classified. Of this total perhaps 100 are considered important. In the western areas, that produce 85 per cent of the total United States crop, not over 20 varieties are grown commercially, and California, the top producer, records six.

Pears rank third in importance for deciduous trees in the world and fourth among all fruits together.

France leads in production, and the United States is second, followed by Germany. Total income, acrewise, is much higher in this country because a large part of the European product goes to "perry"—which is cider. Most United States production is canned for fruit consumption. About 3 per cent of the pears are dried. The rest are sold for fresh market.

Major Pear-Producing Areas of the United States

Most expansion, as well as existing orchards, is in specific areas of the Rocky Mountains.

California, Oregon and Washington are considered the most highly commercialized pear growing sections in the world; and well they should be, with 85 per cent of the United States' supply produced there.

The Great Lakes region produces some pears, but mostly for local or home use, or canneries. Several eastern states, principally New York and Pennsylvania, also produce small commercial amounts. Other states do produce pears, but not to any great extent.

Activities Which Involve Approved Practices

1. Selecting a suitable location.
2. Deciding on varieties.
3. Planning orchard planting system.
4. Determining nursery supply.
5. Caring for delivered trees.
6. Preparing land before planting.
7. Selecting proper planting time.
8. Planting the young tree.
9. Caring for trees after planting.
10. Managing the developing orchard.
11. Pruning.
12. Selecting preharvest practices.
13. Determining harvest procedure.

1. Selecting a Suitable Location

Since most of the pears in the United States are produced in the West, it seems reasonable that one could recommend a "western-type" location. However, the pears are grown in quite "special" locations—east or west.

Choose proper "winter chill" area

Pears require about the same amount of chilling as the average apple. Pears need around 1,000 hours below 45°F. in the winter. Most pear varieties will endure relatively low winter temperatures.

Inadequate winter chill results in uneven blossoming and foliation, which makes an effective spray program for blight and codling moth control difficult.

Cross-pollination, in areas where it is necessary, also may not be complete.

Select frost-free site

Pear buds open a little earlier than apples, and later than almonds or some of the stone fruits. Selection of an area free of frosts during blossoming is a major consideration as artificial frost control is questionable. Locate a good site for pears and plant them there.

"The pear is jeopardized for its diversity"

The rolling slopes of many Pacific coast areas have good air drainage—ideal for pears. But in many places they are planted to earlier-blooming fruits—so to the lower frost area goes the pear. The slopes offer a natural soil drainage, also a condition excellent for this fruit. But because they can tolerate considerable moisture, and do pretty well on shallow soils, pears are planted on soils of second or even third choice.

High summer temperatures aid pear perfection

Pears can be grown in areas of higher summer heat than apples. Actually a Bartlett will reach a higher degree of perfection in such areas. It is also known that the Bartlett ripens unevenly and the core tissue is affected if summers are too cool. The latter are used for canning or drying, while those produced in hot summer areas are shipped for fresh market—and more money per pound.

Choose a productive soil

Plant pears on a clay-loam, well drained, deep

soil. The pear will tolerate a wider range of soil conditions than other fruits. Plant it in a heavy, sticky clay soil or adobe and it will surprise you with a good crop. However, the pear, as other fruits, performs majestically on deep, fertile loams—and most are planted on such soils.

Good water supply important

Special attention to proper watering, irrigation or drainage will result in a profitable venture.

Pears continue to amaze pomologists by their toughness in drought and their equally great determination to survive prolonged excess moisture conditions.

2. Deciding on Varieties

The important pear varieties in the United States are of the European species. Garber, Kieffer and LeConte are hybrids which are crosses between European and Japanese varieties.

Choose reliable, popular varieties

No one can foretell the market in 10 or 20 years so the orchardist must go by modern trends. Pears, as other fruits, differ in their performance from area to area; often these areas are just a few miles apart.

Select varieties to fit the market

Pear varieties come in a number of sizes, shapes, colors, flavors and textures. Regardless of this, all somewhere have some type of market.

Bartlett Is Most Popular Pear
(Called Williams Outside of America)

Three-fourths of the pear production is the Bartlett. It is well-suited for a variety of uses such as

Courtesy, Wooden Box Institute

Fig. 21.1—Lug of Bartlett pears ready for the consumer.

drying, canning, local sales and shipment. California produces nearly all Bartletts while Washington's production is about half Bartletts.

Anjou Is Increasing in Northwest Area

Washington has shown an increase in Anjou plantings and is now the most important winter shipper from that state.

Oregon looks to Anjou as a more important variety than Bartlett because of its shipping ability, size, quality and desirable appearance, and because it stores well. Anjou, however, is slow at coming into bearing.

Comice does very well on the West Coast and is used mostly for gift packages. This outlet shows good promise. The Max-red Bartlett, a bud mutation of Bartlett, is worthy of attention. Its skin color has proven quite attractive to markets and its quality is good.

SELECT KIEFFER FOR SOME EASTERN AREAS

A heavy producer with inferior quality, this variety is still popular. The fruit is attractive, and the tree is adaptable to a variety of soil conditions as well as being quite blight-resistant.

Check local authorities for varieties

Because of the different behavior of pears in specific locations, seek out the farm advisor or others who are familiar with production requirements.

Note: Consult the table "Pear Varieties" at the end of this chapter.

Provide for pollination

The pears, like some apples, can't seem to get along without help. Most pears are partially self-incompatible. Some need a cross-pollinator and a few are cross-incompatible. However, most varieties have viable pollen, overlap in bloom, and are compatible, so usually two varieties will pollinate satisfactorily.

Bartlett and Sekel will not pollinate each other. The Bartlett will set fruit "parthenocorpic" (without fertilization) but does better with a pollinator.

Encourage bee activity

Bees are reluctant to visit pear blossoms so it

may be necessary to eliminate weeds and other flowers that compete for their attention. Addition of bee colonies will help.

3. Planning Orchard System

Again the pear, like the apple, is a long-term investment. Keeping that pencil sharp at this time is time and money saved.

Select square system for pears

The most common planting is on the square corner plan. Distances vary in areas and for varieties. The most common distance is 25′ x 25′ although a number of orchardists report 20′ x 20′ has been satisfactory. Eastern areas should have pollinators not over 50 feet from another variety. Western states can use less pollinators for certain varieties. See Chapter V for other planting systems. Some growers have shown interest in hedgerow planting.

Intercropping is practiced in the west

Small fruits and vegetables are planted between young trees, and this has proved profitable. However, it must be kept in mind that the practice must conform to the approved orchard management plan or it should not be attempted. Any type of injury to trees from excess water, sprays or machinery will result in ultimate loss.

Most pear growers in the East question the use of interplanting because of the influence of fire blight.

Consider filler trees

A number of growers have been experimenting

with a modified dwarf pear tree to help defray the first few years' expenses. Dwarf trees come into bearing earlier and then can be taken out when crowding starts from the permanent trees. A number of orchards have all modified dwarfs and report success.

4. Determining Nursery Supply

When you have made up your mind concerning what variety of tree you want, the rootstock needed and the number of trees to order, check for a reliable nurseryman. If you order about a year ahead of time, many nurseries make financial adjustments in your favor.

Choose a reliable nursery

Chances are a "busy nursery" is a dependable one. A dependable one will know the trees it sells you are exactly what you ordered. It isn't completely unusual to order a particular variety and end up with one slightly off-character. Make sure trees are healthy before accepting delivery.

Order trees by grade

Young pear trees do better than older trees at planting and are less expensive to buy. Because of the shock to the older trees, young one-year-olds usually come into bearing about the same time anyway.

$5/16$ to $3/8$ inch diameter	2 to 3 feet
$3/8$ to $1/2$ inch diameter	3 to 4 feet
$1/2$ to $5/8$ inch diameter	4 to 5 feet
$3/4$ to 1 inch diameter	6 to 8 feet

Select rootstock for the area

Pear rootstocks vary greatly in their disease and

insect resistance, as well as in other plant characteristics. To date the ideal rootstock is non-existent. The best stock for propagation has received a great deal of study. Selecting rootstocks appears to be a matter of growing areas.

USE FRENCH (*P. Comunis*) FOR CALIFORNIA COAST

High and low yielding orchards are found on all of the commonly used stock such as French, Old Home, Domestic French and Imported French. The University of California Research Committee suggested that the French roots mentioned above will maintain higher production over a longer period of time.

CHOOSE STOCK RESISTANT TO FIRE BLIGHT

Chandler recommends grafting or budding seedling trees to a variety such as Old Home, which is resistant to blight, establishing the framework, then top-working this to the desired variety after a few years. Old Home x Farmingdale will likely replace some of its old faithful stock, particularly in cold climates. This rootstock has high blight and decline resistance, good anchorage, vigor and uniform growth habits. Several Quince rootstocks are also used. However, trees get too large, sucker badly and take longer to come into production.

5. Caring for Delivered Trees

Your reliable nurseryman will deliver your trees in top condition. If you want them to remain so, plans must be made. If you plan on planting them in a few days, do not let them dry out. Heel them in.

Fig. 21.2—Dormant fire blight canker on pear.

6. Preparing Land Before Planting

A clean, well-prepared field will do much to eliminate crooked rows and unnecessary work. Do not wait until after your trees are planted to disk, plow, scrape or harrow. Occasionally, if early planting is planned, and a grain crop is already growing, a disk is run down the row only, and the cover crop is left for a while between rows.

Subsoiling an approved practice

Pear roots like to go deep with little interference. Breaking up the plow sole or hardpan is a recommended practice. The shanks can be single, double or more and penetrate the soil below the hard areas, allowing roots to go deeper.

7. Selecting Proper Planting Time

The earlier in the winter the trees can be planted, the better they do, provided there is no danger from winter cold.

Selecting spring planning

Areas of cold winters plant in the spring because of winter damage. Planting can be done as early as one can get on the field.

Choose fall or winter planting in some areas

In mild winter areas, trees do better when planted in fall or winter. Growth starts earlier and the tree develops more quickly.

Hazardous to plant too late

Where temperatures are high in the spring, planting in late March or April can be harmful. The tree may be stunted or die from sunburn and drying out.

8. Planting the Young Tree

Now you are ready for a big day. You have quite an investment already. Proceed with caution as you have the life of the tree in your hands.

Keep trees moist

Tree roots are quickly dried out. One-half hour in the sun or wind will cause young roots to dry out and these must be replaced at the expense of tree growth. Keep them under a wet sack or canvas. Do not lay them out where they are to be planted, then dig the hole.

Use planting board

If your field has been laid out with stakes, a planting board will help you keep your trees in good alignment.

Dig hole big and deep enough

Do not dig a hole so small that the roots crowd and bend when you put the tree in. Tree should be planted the same depth it was in the nursery as indicated by a soil ring.

Care for tree at planting

Roots should only be cut if they are broken, too

long or crossing. The bottom limb, planned for a primary should face into the prevailing wind and lean slighty in the same direction. Do not add any fertilizer or organic matter to roots of tree other than good topsoil.

Use care in tamping

Carefully put in some fine, loose topsoil and tamp with the fingers first. Then add more soil, tamping every now and then, gently, to firm the soil. If conditions are too dry, a few gallons of water will help settle the soil around the roots. Do not tamp vigorously—roots may be broken.

Prune back young tree

Young pears are often cut back from 25 to 30 inches to force lower branches out for future framework. If growth has started, remove all but those desired for primary fromework.

9. Caring for Trees After Planting

Often orchardists believe the job is over when the trees are planted and pretty well leave them on their own. Trees need constant attention and should be kept growing vigorously during the first season.

Use tree protectors

Many types of tree protectors are in use. Whitewash can be used for sunburn, and cardboard protectors protect part of the tree from sunburn and pests. Make sure the developing limbs are not interfered with.

Pinching back may be needed

A young established pear tree often makes too much growth after becoming established. Orchardists find clipping or pinching off the ends of those to be cut later forces growth to the desired limbs.

Maintain proper soil moisture

Never allow young trees to get too dry. Stunting takes place quickly and your most devoted attention later will be largely in vain. Moisture must be available at all times.

10. Managing the Developing Orchard

Select fertilization program carefully

Pear trees do their best when all nutrients are available. Some deep, fertile alluvial soils, however, have not shown appreciable response to a fertilizer program. Application of nitrogenous forms gives most response. Young non-bearing pears need little fertilizer when planted on good soil, and fertilizer should be applied on bearing trees only if needed.

Choose cultivation practice

Young pears can be grown to quick maturity with proper, timely cultivation practices. Available moisture must be maintained.

11. Pruning

Pruning is considered a very important cultural operation in the production of regular crops of large-sized pears. Proper pruning will produce a consistent crop that is typical for its specific variety.

Select pruning system that fits variety

A careful study of varietal characteristics and local influences determines to a great extent your pruning program. Varietal growth patterns differ in many localities, and an orchardist should seek local advice.

Choose pruning system similar to apples

Nearly all that has been written about apples applies to pears, with a few exceptions. Heavy pruning of pears can produce undesirable, excess, vigorous growth. Most pear varieties fruit primarily on spurs, and the apple, at least for the most part, fruits on both shoots and spurs.

Important to "spread" growth habit

Pears tend to grow upright and orchardists should make efforts to use a spreading practice. Braces, cutting to the outside buds and tying down laterals are helpful. When the tree is mature, the weight of the fruit will help spread the branches.

Prune out infected limbs, crowding growth

In all sections where pear blight is a problem the danger of inducing a vigorous growth that will be susceptible to blight must be considered. Head back only enough for thinning out enough wood to allow tree to make moderate growth.

Avoid heavy cutting

Generally speaking, pears can stand abuse and endure neglect at pruning time with less injury than most other fruit trees, but it creates areas of entry for infections.

Treat fire blight cuts

When blight is removd, cut well below infected area 6 to 10 inches and disinfect with a solution of lysol or bichloride of mercury (1 to 500). Use on shears and pruning cuts. Cyanide of mercury (1-500) is also used, mixed with equal amounts of bichloride of mercury.

12. Selecting Preharvest Practices

The orchard should be in a condition that will facilitate your planned operations, especially at harvest.

Determine if thinning is necessary

Many varieties of pears tend to set heavy crops of fruit which the tree is unable to develop to good marketable size. This is particularly likely to occur with such varieties as Winter Nelis, Bosc, Bartlett and occasionally with Anjou. If medium- to large-sized fruit is desired, it is necessary to thin part of the crop from such trees, in order to have a larger leaf area per fruit. In California, Bartlett thinning is seldom necessary.

Many pear varieties, such as Bartlett, Hardy and Bosc, tend to set the fruit in clusters, often three to five fruits setting on a single spur. If the set of fruit on the tree as a whole is excessive, these clusters should be reduced to one or two fruits each. On the other hand, if the set of fruit on the tree as a whole is not excessive, fruit on these clusters will reach satisfactory size and quality without thinning.

Fig. 21.3—Pear limb displaying fire blight and a poor supply of fruit wood because of previous blight removal.

No set of rules for thinning

It is impossible to lay down hard and fast rules for the thinning of pears. The number of fruits a tree will carry and develop to good marketable size will vary with the vigor of the tree and with the growing conditions. Experiments indicate that, with nearly all varieties, from 30 to 40 good leaves per fruit are essential for the building of the materials that go to make them. These leaves, however, need not be directly adjacent to the fruit. With extremely heavy sets, thinning to reduce the amount of fruit in proportion to the leaf system is essential if fruit of best size and quality is to be obtained.

Under present standards larger-sized fruit is required for canning than for fresh market purposes. If the crop is intended primarily for cannery use it is particularly essential that fruit of good size be secured.

Control pear drop

Bartletts in some areas tend to drop fruit before they can be picked. Bosc will do the same. Applied a week before normal harvest, 2,4-D and NAA hormone sprays are used effectively.

Drop may be caused from improper management practices such as boron, magnesium or moisture deficiencies. An oversupply of nitrogen may also cause early drop.

Determine disease and pest control program

A number of insects and diseases cause serious losses, often total crop failure in commercial orchards. Fire blight, scab and dead end are considered diseases that need constant attention.

13. Determining Harvest Procedure

Picking fruit in the "green" stage may seem silly,

Fig. 21.4—Pear psylla ready to begin damage.

but with pears it is necessary for high quality. Pears are often picked three to five times, depending on outlet.

Handling and storage

Since pears, both for fresh shipment and for canning, are harvested prior to becoming tree-ripe, the question of the state of maturity at which they are to be picked is very important. If they are harvested too early, the quality is poor; if they are allowed to become too mature on the tree, the storage life is shortened, and many varieties tend to break down at the core while still sound at the surface. Numerous investigations to determine the proper picking maturity of pears and the best methods of handling following harvest have been conducted. Check with local farm advisor.

Decide on time to pick

An important and difficult task is deciding when to pick. The orchardist must be alert to increase in sugar content, size, softness and gradual change in color. Color of seeds, color change from green to yellow of skin (using color charts) and pressure testing give ample basis for determining time to pick. Again pressure test varies in areas, varieties and use of fruit. For example, the Bartlett in California ranges from 20 to 23 pounds pressure and in Washington 15 to 23 pounds pressure on the pressure tester.

Select workers with skill

Pears bruise easily and must be picked and handled with utmost caution. Never allow a worker to drop the pear into a container. Pears should be cooled

Fig. 21.5—Blight of pear twig.

PEAR VARIETIES

Variety	Origin	Tree Characteristics	Relative Yield	Picking Date	Size	Shape	Quality	Outlet	Remarks
Bartlett	Chance seedling intro. to U.S. 1797	Upright, medium size	Heavy	Late June to middle of Sept.	Medium to large	Oblong pyriform	Good	Shipping, canning	Widely adapted, very susceptible to blight
Hardy	France 1820	Sturdy and vigorous, med. size, upright	Heavy	About same as Bartlett	Large	Obtuse pyriform	Very good	Shipping, fruit cocktail	Pollinizer for Bartlett, intermediate stock for Bartlett on quince
Bosc	Belgium; intro. to U.S. 1832	Med. to large, upright, spreading	Regular	Aug. 15	Large	Pyriform, long tapering neck	Very good	Shipping	Susceptible to blight
Anjou	France; intro. to U.S. 1842	Large, vigorous, spreading	Uneven bearer	Aug. 10	Medium	Roundish pyriform, short, thick stem	Good	Shipping	Comes into bearing early
Comice	France 1849	Upright, weak	Light	Aug. 10	Large	Roundish to obovate	Considered best of pears	Shipping, holiday trade	Exacting in soil and climate requirements
Winter Nelis	Belgium; intro. to U.S. 1823	Strong grower, hard to train, med. to small, spreading	Very productive	Sept. 1	Small	Roundish obovate	Good	Shipping	Somewhat resistant to fire blight, pollinizer for Bartlett
Seckel	Chance seedling 1800	Blight resistant, mod. vigorous	Heavy	Month after Bartlett	Small	Obovate	Very good	Home orchard	
Wilder	N.Y. 1884	Large, vigorous, upright	Very productive	June 10	Large	Oblong pyriform	Good	Shipping	

Fig. 21.6—Lug box of pears in polyethylene liner ready for shipment.

as quickly as possible and down to 34°F. or lower within two days. Pears must be taken out of storage and ripened at about 65°F. with humidity at 83 per cent. A properly ripened pear is always in demand. It is up to each commercial producer to see to it that his product is of high quality.

Chapter

XXII

PLUMS AND PRUNES

"The prune is always a plum—but the plum is not always a prune."

A prune is a variety of plum that can be dried successfully without removing the pit. Desirable drying varieties are also sold as fresh fruit or for canning.

Plums are usually grown primarily for uses other than drying.

History

The history of plums is quite complicated. Some pomologists believe the cultivated plum did not exist in a wild state. Writings mention the plum in Greece in the Sixth Century, B.C. It was found grown in many areas and described in various forms. The plum and prune were known to be an important staple for the Turks, Huns and Mongols.

Plum varieties were brought to the United States by colonists in the form of seeds and grafting scions. Choice plums were selected and the pits planted, which resulted in many varieties in local areas. Outstanding varieties were quickly distributed and carried to many parts of the country by western migration. Most native plums of America are not of any commercial importance except for experimentation.

Outlook and Trends

The present outlook is promising. Increased production will be partially offset by increased per capita consumption. The buying power of the consumer will increase and result in the buying of fruit, otherwise considered extra. The trend is for larger fruit, and with better varieties, storage, advertising and organization, the plum industry has become secure. Each year for the past 10 years, California growers have planted over 1,000 acres each of plums and prune type plums.

Statistics of Interest

Plums rank close to first in importance as a deciduous fruit in Europe but are edged out by apples, peaches and pears in the United States. European plums grow best in West Coast areas of this country. Over 2,000 varieties of plums have been grown and used to some extent. Commercial plantings, however, are limited pretty much to three main species— European, Japanese and hybrids of Japanese. Plums in some form are grown throughout the North Temperate Zone around the world. However, the prune, a dried high-sugar plum, is grown less widely. United States leads, with Yugoslavia, France and Australia growing considerable quantities along with Chile, Argentina and South Africa. Prunes are produced in greater quantities than plums in the United States.

Of California's plum crop 95 per cent is sold fresh, with over 80 per cent being shipped out of state. Four major varieties make up over 65 per cent of the sales. Canning and freezing are done in small quantities. Plums account for 25 to 30 per cent of the deciduous

Fig. 22.1—A healthy prune orchard resulting from proper management and use of approved practices.

fruit shipped from California, depending on markets, set, etc.

Yields per acre vary. Marketable plums yield 6 to 10 tons (15 exceptional), whereas prunes produce 6 to 8 tons as fruit and less as cured, as they dry at the ratio of 2½ or 3 to 1.

Major Producing Areas in the United States

Of the over 160,000 acres in plums and prunes in the United States, 125,000 acres are in California. Prunes make up 96,000 acres, and various plum varieties total 28,000 acres. Oregon has 12,000 acres, Michigan 8,500 acres, and Idaho and Washington total 3,500 acres each. Other areas around the Great Lakes and Texas have increased plantings.

California produces over 82 per cent of the prunes in the United States, followed by Washington, Oregon and Idaho. Eastern Washington and Oregon grow prune varieties for fresh, freezing and canning, and Idaho's crop goes mostly as fresh fruit.

Activities Which Involve Approved Practices

1. Selecting a suitable location.
2. Deciding on varieties.
3. Planning orchard planting system.
4. Determining nursery supply.
5. Caring for delivered trees.
6. Preparing land before planting.
7. Selecting proper planting time.
8. Planting the young tree.
9. Caring for trees after planting.
10. Managing the developing orchard.
11. Pruning.
12. Selecting preharvest practices.
13. Determining harvest procedure.

1. Selecting a Suitable Location

Plums are adapted to many locations, but specific types do better in particular locations. Before continuing with this subject it will be necessary to explain the three main types, as reference will be made to them.

European type (Domestica) which includes the prune

This is the most important type grown. Such varieties as French and Italian fall in this group.

Japanese type

This is mostly used for shipping and fresh

market. This type of plum is never blue. Santa Rosa, Kelsey, Beauty and Satsuma are some varieties.

American type

There is a large number of plum species native to America, but few of commercial importance. Cheney, Blackhawk and Craig are some varieties.

Choose proper "winter chill" area

Most plums need a substantial amount of winter chill to satisfy the rest period. Most prune varieties are not planted in mild winter climates, like that in Southern California, for instance. Some varieties, such as the President, require more chill than apples. Tragedy, however, performs quite well in a mild winter area. Improper chilling can cause total crop loss. Because plums react differently to particular locations, it is most important to seek local advice.

Select proper soil

Plums are grown on a wide variety of soils, although a deep, well-drained, medium-textured soil is generally the best. Some good-producing orchards are on light, sandy soils but require special soil management programs.

Choose proper water drainage

Plum rootstocks such as Myrobalan or Marianna can tolerate some wet soils but eventually require water drainage. Prolonged wet feet are damaging.

Frost a problem in marginal areas

A poor selection of a location can result in late

frost injuring blossoms or even young fruits. Air drainage will help, and some growers use orchard heaters. However, it is best to avoid such areas.

Select proper drying temperature
for prunes

Prunes require a moderately long season of clear, warm weather for maturity and ultimate drying. Some fog occurs in a number of prune-producing areas, but it usually clears early enough for adequate heat.

2. Deciding on Varieties

The grower must decide on his market outlet before he selects his variety or varieties. Many popular plum varieties also need a pollinator.

Plum varieties show differences, sometimes quite marked, in appearance, palatability, marketability, tree growth and productiveness.

Select for fresh shipment

California plums grown for fresh shipment are primarily either of the European group (Prunus domestica) or of the Japanese group (Prunus salicina). In addition, there are hybrids of the latter with other species.

Japanese varieties can be profitable

Japanese varieties (including hybrids) typically are medium to large; flat, round, or heart-shaped; red or crimson, never blue or purple; and very juicy. Many ripen early and can be marketed before the main avalanche of summer fruits arrives. They must be handled carefully and promptly between harvest

in the orchards and delivery at retail stores because
they tend to bruise easily.

Selecting European type

European varieties generally are smaller; oval
or roundish; and blue or purple. Compared to Japanese
varieties, most European plums are milder, especially
those shipped late in the season, and have a firmer
texture. They may be allowed to nearly ripen on the
tree and still arrive at distant markets in good condition.

Avoid other fruit competition

European varieties bloom later in the season when
danger from frost damage is less, but they ripen when
competition from other deciduous fruits is greater.

Provide for pollination

Many Japanese varieties are self-unfruitful. Sometimes self-fruitful varieties are cross-pollinated to increase yields. Usually European varieties are self-
fertile and do not require cross-pollination for securing
good crops. However, they are less productive than
Japanese varieties. They start bearing and reach
full maturity at a later age.

Because some plums react differently to pollination in local areas, professional advice should be obtained.

3. Planning Orchard Planting System

Plums and prunes need specific orchard operations,
therefore it is necessary to plan your system well.

Select square system of tree location

Most California orchards, old and new, are planted somewhere between 22 to 25 feet on the square system. Some areas of deep fertile soil extend this distance to allow for greater growth in such fertile soil. With modern mechanization it becomes necessary to plan for machinery that does nearly all the harvest work.

Avoid close planting

Even on poor soils, one should use caution when planting trees 15 to 18 feet on the square system. Some growers have added a tree down one row but are quick to remove it. Any arrangement other than an approved practice should be given serious negative consideration.

Intercrop for cash

Young plum and prune orchards with small trees, and large distances between the trees, present the grower with a temptation to grow intercrops as a source of income before the orchard starts to bear well. This may be done, but it should be kept in mind that the development of the orchard is the primary aim and the intercrop should be handled in such a way that the growth of the trees is not materially decreased.

Keep tree area clear

Reasonable space must be left between the trees and the intercrop, and adequate water and soil nutrients must be available to both at all times.

No intercrop should be grown that will introduce diseases or insects into the orchard. For example, tomatoes are not recommended as an intercrop because of the danger of introducing the fungus *verticillium albo-atrum,* causing verticillium wilt in the tomatoes and blackheart in the prune trees.

4. Determining Nursery Supply

It is important to contact a reliable nursery. Order trees well ahead of time to assure your selected stock. Often nurseries have discounts for trees ordered from eight months to one year ahead.

Select rootstock for local conditions

The plum has less problems with rootstock than most deciduous trees, although a number grow successfully.

CHOOSE MARIANNA 2624 ROOTSTOCK

Marianna 2624 plum rootstock is the best all around rootstock for plums, prunes and apricots. It seems to be able to do what the other plum rootstocks can do, plus having the advantage of being resistant to oak-root fungus—a serious problem in some plum and prune areas. Marianna is a cutting grown rootstock and is relatively shallow-rooted. This is an advantage in heavy, wet soils or soils of poor drainage. It is also immune to soil nematodes and is resistant to crown gall. Myrobalan seedlings and Myrobalan 29C cutting plum rootstocks are other rootstocks that are used in place of Marianna 2624, but are generally used under specific conditions and do not have the overall versatility that Marianna 2624 has. Marianna 2623 is no longer being used as a rootstock since it does not have the resistance to oak-root fungus that 2624 has.

CONSIDER OTHER ROOTSTOCK FOR SPECIFIC AREAS

Peach rootstock is of some use in sandy areas. About 50 per cent of Idaho's Italian prunes are on peach root. All Japanese varieties appear to do well on it but some European varieties do not. Apricot can be used in slight alkali or nematode areas. However, there are some unsuccessful graft unions. Almond should not be considered.

Order trees by grade

The nurseryman must know exactly what you want. He will know if you order right. Plum and prune trees are graded by the diameter of the trunk at a point 2 inches above the center of the bud union. Height of tree may also be given.

Examples of grades:

¼ to ⅜ inch diameter	2 to 3 feet
⅜ to ½ inch diameter	3 to 4 feet
½ to $1\frac{1}{16}$ inch diameter	4 to 6 feet

Trees should not be less than ¼ inch in diameter or less than 8 inches high. June-budded trees may be an exception. Select a medium-sized tree.

Plant young trees

There are times when a grower is tempted to plant trees over one year old. This is not a good practice as mortality is high, a larger hole is required and more care is needed. Young trees will catch up, anyway.

5. Caring for Delivered Trees

The nursery takes good care of its trees and once

delivered, the responsibility for continued care is up to you.

Heel in trees

If you cannot plant at once, dig a trench deep enough to hold the roots, remove trees from package and put roots in the trench. Cover roots with fine, moist soil. Lean tops towards south so trunks will not get too much direct sunlight, resulting in sunburn.

Trees should be heeled into well-drained soil; excess moisture should not be allowed to collect around the roots.

6. Preparing Land Before Planting

A better job of planting can be done if the land is prepared properly.

Irrigation system will aid in determining preparation

Land preparation is dependent on the type of irrigation system, if any, that will be used. If irrigation is practiced, the land should be properly graded and the irrigation system installed before the trees are planted.

Avoid deep grading

In grading, care must be taken to avoid scraping too deep, so that infertile subsoil is exposed. Establishing grades is a job for an engineering service, of which many are available throughout fruit-growing sections.

Sub-soiling a recommended practice

Young roots need room to grow and this is helped

by breaking up the plow sole or hardpan by subsoiling. Planting is also made easier by this practice. Growers should do this under almost all conditions.

7. Selecting Proper Planting Time

Planting time of trees varies from area to area. However, as most plum trees are in the western area, these will be considered.

Plant in early spring

Trees will usually be received from the nurseryman early in January. They should be set out in the orchard as soon after that time as possible—preferably in January or February. Plum trees have been planted successfully as late as the first of April, but such a procedure is not recommended.

Avoid late planting

Late-planted trees are often injured or even killed, because they may send out leaves which require water, before the root system becomes well enough established to absorb an adequate amount of moisture from the soil.

Spring plant in North and East

Consideration should be given to spring planting in areas of severe winters. Some fall planting is done in areas of mild winters.

8. Planting the Young Tree

Planting the young tree is not the time to be guessing. Use every possible means at your command to do the best job.

Keep trees in good condition

Young tree roots should never be allowed to dry out. Keep them moist at all times. A few minutes in the sun or wind can result in great damage to them and cause a setback.

Planting board may be used

Growers still like to keep their rows straight. With modern machinery to dig holes, markers are destroyed. Using a planting board will put trees in line.

Dig hole big enough

Dig a hole large enough to hold the roots conveniently. Root pruning is done only when the roots are broken, twisted around each other or too long. Many trees have been injured by too deep planting, so it is recommended that they be placed at the same depth at which they grew in the nursery.

Use care in tamping

The soil should be brought into close contact with the roots, either by tamping, or by settling the soil with water, as soon as the trees are planted.

Apply water generously

Water should be applied to newly planted trees if the soil is dry at the time of planting, or if they are planted late in the spring. When the trees are planted without watering, it is well to leave the top 2 or 3 inches of soil loose to facilitate the penetration of rainwater.

Consider pruning young trees

Most young prune trees as received from the nursery consist of a straight whip, without lateral branches. Thus, pruning at planting usually consists merely of cutting this whip back to 24 to 30 inches from the ground.

Side branches at planting used to advantage

The occasional side branches that occur on some nursery trees may be utilized in starting the main branches if they are properly located. Those branches that are saved, however, should be cut back to 6 inches or less. Unsuitable branches should be cut back to a ½-inch stub, or a single bud.

Some growers are of the opinion that young trees should be allowed to grow a few months, then summer pruned. Work done along this line at the California Polytechnic State University showed better selection of scaffold branches and eventual growth. However, more severe pruning is necessary as scaffolds grow rapidly. Generally the timing is such that other management practices must be done.

9. Caring for Trees After Planting

Generally young trees don't need too much attention, provided a few approved practices are followed.

Keep tree area clean

Weeds, cover crop or intercrops must be kept well away from the young tree. Competition for moisture and nutrients is a detriment to young roots striving for food.

Consider tree protection

Protecting the top of young trees with tree protectors or whitewash is necessary. The plum and prune are sunburned easily when young.

Tree protectors, made of paper or some other material, are satisfactory if they are placed on the trees in such a way that they will not be moved later in the season and thus expose tender bark that has previously been shaded.

Pinch back vigorous growth

Some varieties of plums grow vigorously the first year and pinching off 6 or 8 inches of the terminal growth tends to direct growth to the desired areas. De-shooting is also a practice to be considered as many young trees push one or two shoots more rapidly than others.

Maintain proper soil moisture

This is one practice that is essential. Young trees die quickly when they become dry. Regardless of how you do it, keep enough available moisture in the root area to keep the tree growing vigorously.

Fertilization may be necessary

In poor soils, where trees are doing poorly, applying about ¼ pound of ammonium sulfate, or its equivalent, to a tree in a band about a foot from the tree will help. Manure may also be used.

10. Managing the Developing Orchard

Choose fertilizer program carefully

European plums require less fertilizer than Japanese varieties. If Japanese varieties show 4 to 6 feet of growth from water sprouts, the trees are normal and the fertilizer program is all right. Between 100 and 300 pounds per acre of nitrogen is used on bearing trees (2 to 3 pounds per tree), but must be cut to about $\frac{1}{2}$ pound per tree for two- to three-year-old trees. Growth may be satisfactory without any fertilizer. Potassium deficiency may be a problem with European plums, resulting in branch dieback. Adding 20 pounds, more or less, of potassium sulfate per tree, or a substitute, will help. Zinc deficiency is also a problem in some areas and must be corrected.

Maintain proper moisture

Plum rootstocks are not easily injured by too much water but are quick to show signs of stress when dry. Vigorous growth must be maintained to give tree early and subsequent bearing area. From 2 to 3 acre-feet are used in areas where irrigation is necessary.

11. Pruning

During the first few years in the orchard, the pruning of trees is aimed primarily at the development of a shape that will lend itself to economical culture, and at getting strong crotches.

Select "open center" for some growth habits

Choice of training system is pretty well determined by the tree's growth pattern. Most plums are trained to open center, such as some Japanese varieties and Burbank, because they display a spreading habit of growth.

Consider "modified leader" for
upright growth pattern

Santa Rosa, Stanley, Wickson and most of the European varieties tend to grow to a tight, upright pattern, consequently they perform better with the modified leader system. The pruning of European plums requires a little more attention than the pruning of other varieties.

Pruning bearing trees

Plums are pruned less severely than apricots and peaches; and prunes, if they are to be dried, are pruned even less than plums. Japanese plums tend to overbear, so they need heavier pruning than others. Pruning is quite similar to apples—thinning out growth, opening up the tree and maintaining proper balance and fruiting wood. Avoid heavy pruning.

12. Selecting Preharvest Practices

Determine if thinning is to be done

Thinning of plums is necessary for good-sized, well colored fruit. Hand thinning is done, as well as clipping, pole thinning and using chemical practices.

Hand thinning is expensive

Hand thinning, though dependable, becomes an expensive management practice. Usually the grower waits until after the June drop to determine his hand-thinning procedure. Usually fruit is thinned 2 to 4 inches apart.

Pole thinning is effective

Pole thinning is faster than hand thinning but not

so accurate. Often pole thinning results in the destruction of many young fruit spurs and buds. However, it is fast, and easily done.

Chemical thinning an "approved practice"

Chemical thinning of plums such as Santa Rosa, Wickson and Beauty has proven successful at the California Polytechnic State University orchard using Elgetol and Dinitro. Growers throughout the state have used chemical thinning successfully.

SPRAY AT 75 PER CENT BLOOM

Elgetol 30 and 318 are used at 3 pints per 200 gallons of water. Dinitro 289 is also used at 3 pints per 200 gallons of water. Do not overthin.

Select approved pest control program

An effective pest control program is necessary as plums are subject to a number of problems. European plums are especially subject to damage from mites and thrips, and in humid areas, aphids. Other pests are controlled very effectively with up-to-date sprays and equipment. Red spider, scale and borers are other pests that need attention in some areas.

13. Determining Harvest Procedure

The outlet of plums determines the type of harvest procedure. Plums, being exceptionally perishable, undergo changes after harvest: as the fruit ripens, its flesh softens and ultimately becomes overripe. Mature plums have a better flavor but require more careful handling to avoid bruising, and are not profitable.

PRUNE VARIETIES

Variety	Tree Characteristics	Pollination	Yield	Size	Drying Characteristics	Fresh Quality	Skin Color	Season	Flesh Color	Remarks
French (Agen)	Strong, vigorous tree	Self-fruitful	Good	Small to med.	Excellent, high quality	Good, sweet	Purple	Late Aug.	Golden yellow	
Imperial	Buds clustered on spurs, slow growth	Self-unfruitful	Light in some years	Large	Difficult to dry, high quality	Shipping plum	Purplish red	1 wk. earlier than French	Yellow with greenish tinge	Tender skin
Sugar	Wood brittle, pruned heavily	Self-fruitful	Alternate bearer	Med.	Fruit tends to be coarse and stringy	Shipping plum	Purplish red	2 wks. earlier than French	Golden yellow	Large pit
Robe de Sergeant	Glossy green foliage	Self-unfruitful	Good	Similar to French	Similar to French in appearance	Good	Purple	Same as French	Greenish yellow	
Burton		Self-unfruitful	Good	Large and elongated	Difficult to dry, high quality	Good	Purple	Same as French	Yellow	Tender skin
Coates	Similar to French	Self-fertile	Good	Med.	Similar to French	Good	Purple	Same as French	Golden yellow	Pit large and rough
Italian (Fellenberg)	Med.-sized tree	Self-unfruitful in Cal.	Good where grown	Med.	Not dried in Cal.	Shipping plum	Purple	Same as French	Similar to Imperial	Suffer in dry or hot climate, grown in N. W.

EUROPEAN SHIPPING PLUM

Variety	Origin	Tree Characteristics	Pollination	Approx. Shipping Dates	Size	Shape	Skin Color	Flesh Color	Quality	Remarks
Earliana		Average vigor		2nd wk. June	Small	Oblong	Purple	Light amber	Fair	
Tragedy	Chance seedling, 1820	Vigorous, productive	Self-unfruitful	1st wk. July	Med.	Oval	Dark purple	Greenish yellow	Good	
Diamond	England	Large, vigorous	Self-unfruitful	Last wk. July	Large	Oblong	Purple	Yellow	Poor	
President	England, intro. by Millard Sharpe 1909	Weak	Self-unfruitful	Last wk. July	Med. to large	Oval	Purple	Yellow	Poor	
Emilie		Vigorous	Self-unfruitful	Last wk. July	Large	Oval	Purplish	Greenish yellow to amber	Good	Replacement for President
Rayburn Tragedy (Late Tragedy)		Vigorous	Self-unfruitful	Last wk. July	Med.	Oval	Dark Purple	Greenish yellow	Good	
Giant	Burbank 1894	Moderate vigor	Self-unfruitful	1st wk. Aug.	Large	Oval, slim-necked	Purplish red	Amber	Fair	
Standard	Burbank 1914		Self-unfruitful	1st wk. Aug.	Large		Purple	Amber		
Grand Duke	England	Moderate vigor		2nd wk. Aug.	Large	Oval	Purple	Greenish yellow	Fair	
Pond (Hungarian)	England, intro. 1856	Moderate vigor		3rd wk. Aug.	Large	Oval	Purplish red	Amber	Poor	

JAPANESE AND JAPANESE-HYBRID SHIPPING PLUMS

Variety	Origin	Tree Characteristics	Pollination	Approx. Shipping Dates	Size	Shape	Skin Color	Flesh Color	Quality	Remarks
Beauty	Burbank 1911	Vigorous and brushy	Partially self-fruitful	Last wk. May	Small to med.	Heart	Crimson	Amber	Good	Very heavy set
Burmosa	Cal. Exp. Sta. 1951	Spreading, vigorous	Self-unfruitful	1st wk. June	Med.	Round	Greenish, red blush	Light amber	Good	Promising intro. tree stone
Santa Rosa	Burbank 1906	Vigorous	Partially self-fruitful	2nd wk. June	Med.	Heart	Purplish red dots	Amber to red at skin	Excellent	Fruit not clustered
Formosa	Burbank 1907	Mod. vig., short thick spurs	Self-unfruitful	2nd wk. June	Large	Heart	Yellow, red blush	Pale yellow	Good	Tends to have light crop
Climax	Burbank 1899	Mod. vig., short thick spurs	Partially self-fruitful	2nd wk. June	Large	Heart	Red	Yellow	Good	Subject to pit-splitting
Redheart	Cal. Exp. Sta. 1951	Very vigorous	Self-unfruitful	3rd wk. June	Med.	Heart	Dull red, brown spots	Dark red	Good	Promising intro.
Wickson	Burbank 1892	Narrow, upright	Self-unfruitful	1st wk. July	Large	Heart	Greenish yellow to light red	Amber	Good	Freestone
Gaviota	Burbank 1900?	Weak	Self-unfruitful	1st wk. July	Med.	Oval	Yellow to red	Amber	Good	
Burbank	Burbank 1888	Spreading	Self-unfruitful	1st wk. July	Med.	Round	Yellow, red blush	Yellow	Good	Small fruit size

(Continued)

JAPANESE AND JAPANESE-HYBRID SHIPPING PLUMS (Continued)

Variety	Origin	Tree Characteristics	Pollination	Approx. Shipping Dates	Size	Shape	Skin Color	Flesh Color	Quality	Remarks
Duarte	Burbank 1900	Vigorous	Self-unfruitful	1st wk. July	Med.	Heart	Dull red, brown spots	Dark red	Good	
Satsuma	Burbank 1886	Vigorous	Self-unfruitful	2nd wk. July	Med.	Round oval	Purple, red-brown spots	Dark red	Good	Good for processing
Becky Smith	Millard Sharpe 1920	Vigorous	Self-unfruitful	3rd wk. July	Med.	Round	Yellow, red blush	Yellow	Fair	Attractive fruit
Late Santa Rosa	Bud sport of Santa Rosa	Vigorous	Partially self-fruitful	3rd wk. July	Med.	Heart	Purplish red dots	Amber to red at skin	Excellent	Fruit not clustered
Kelsey	Intro. from Japan 1870	Mod. vigorous	Self-unfruitful	Last wk. July	Large	Heart	Green to purplish red	Greenish yellow	Good	
Red Ace	Burbank 1931	Like Burbank	Self-unfruitful	Last wk. July	Med.	Round oval	Dull red	Red	Good	Better size than Satsuma
Sharkey	Millard Sharpe	Upright, spreading	Self-unfruitful	Last wk. July	Med.	Round	Yellow, red blush	Amber	Good	
Mariposa	Armstrong Nurs. 1935	Vigorous	Self-unfruitful	1st wk. Aug.	Med.	Oval	Purple red dots	Dark red	Good	Promising new intro.
Late Duarte	Bud sport of Duarte	Vigorous	Self-unfruitful	1st wk. Aug.	Med.	Heart	Dull red dots	Dark red	Good	
Elephant Heart	Burbank intro. by Stark Bros. 1929	Vigorous	Self-unfruitful	Last wk. Aug.	Large	Heart	Purplish red	Red	Very good	Often shipped greener

Select proper maturity

Wholesalers and retailers prefer firmer, "greener" plums which hold up better during numerous handlings.

It is necessary to determine when the fruit should be picked to combine suitable carrying and handling character with good dessert quality. Then plums must be packed properly, handled carefully and precooled promptly.

Packing sheds used for packing

Field packing has been largely replaced by central packing houses, which are equipped to handle and cool the fruit rapidly. These shipping agencies collect the plums from various producers, pack them, assemble the cars and make shipments and sales.

Harvesting prunes

Nearly all prunes are harvested mechanically. Shakers, mechanical catchers or pickups and lifting equipment in the orchard eliminate nearly all hand labor.

Chapter

XXIII

WALNUTS (PERSIAN)

History

Walnut history goes back to earliest times, and although the actual date isn't known, most authorities agree that the English walnut originally came from ancient Persia. From the Middle East walnuts spread to Greece and Rome, whence they were carried to England. Records show that they have been grown there since 1562.

In Roman times, walnuts were used for medicinal purposes and for dyeing, as well as for a food. In Germany, for instance, young farmers proved their fitness for marriage by showing proof that they had grown a certain number of walnut trees. And in many countries walnuts were an important form of barter.

The Franciscan Fathers are credited with bringing English walnuts to California. They planted the trees beside their missions, where they flourished. The first planting of commercial importance in Southern California was at Goleta, near Santa Barbara, in 1867. In Northern and Central California, walnuts were pioneered by Felix Gillet of Nevada City, who introduced the famous Franquette variety.

In botanical terms, the walnut we're concerned with is called "Juglans Regia"—meaning the Persian or, more currently, the English walnut.

Many still call "Juglans Regia" the English walnut, but that's a misnomer, since it only became known as English because it was transported all over the world in British trading ships. However, the black walnut, "Juglans Nigra," is a native of America.

Present outlook and trends

Walnut production in California is shifting from the southern districts to the northern and central areas. In 1936, 65 per cent of the bearing acreage was in the southern counties. Today, less than 5 per cent is there. Over 13,000 acres of the non-bearing acreage is planted to the Hartley variety. Payne is second, with over 8,000 acres planted. Franquette is third in total acreage, but fourth in new acreage. Ashly is becoming popular with 6,500 new acres. Seventy per cent of the crop is controlled by the Diamond Walnut Growers, made up of over 1,100 grower-owners.

Statistics of interest

Over 90 per cent of the walnuts produced in the United States are grown in California. Turkey and the United States produce over 60 per cent of the world's supply. California produces about 168,000 tons per year; Oregon, 17,000. Both states will increase production, as California alone has 49,000 acres not yet in production. France has had a decline in production of about one-third, but Italy's has increased. Iran, Yugoslavia, Rumania, China and India also produce substantial quantities.

California has around 207,000 acres in walnuts— about 49,000 non-bearing. The best commercial varieties produce up to 2 tons per acre, although the average per year ranges from $\frac{1}{2}$ to 1 ton. There are approximately 8,000 acres of black walnuts in California.

Some growers estimate a minimum of $400 per acre as the cost of establishing a young orchard in addition to the cost of land.

Activities Which Involve Approved Practices

1. Selecting a suitable location.
2. Deciding on varieties and pollinators.
3. Determining orchard planting system.
4. Preparing land before planting.
5. Planting the young trees.
6. Caring for trees after planting.
7. Training young walnut trees.
8. Managing the developing orchard.
9. Pruning.
10. Selecting preharvest practices.
11. Determining harvest procedure.

1. Selecting a Suitable Location

Choose proper chill area

Insufficient winter chilling can be a serious problem with some walnut varieties, especially in some southern California areas. Leaves tend to come out late, and bloom is also delayed. More severe cases result in the nuts being small and the crop being small, also. The walnut chart in this chapter gives more details.

Select frost-free site

Spring frosts below 30°F. in the spring are a serious threat to new walnut shoots. Catkins (flower of walnut) and young fruits are injured by late-spring frosts.

Hot summers may be harmful

Sunburning occurs on walnuts exposed to the sun when summer temperatures go above 100°F., accompanied by low humidity. Early extreme heat produces a "walnut blank," or no kernel inside. High mid-summer temperatures result in shriveled kernels, dark color and stain on the shell, resulting in culls. White-wash sprays help in controlling sunburn.

Choose a productive soil

Silt loam, 5 to 6 feet deep, with good drainage, is considered an ideal soil.

Good drainage helps to control crown gall

Coarse, sandy soil or adobe layered with clay is a good choice. Water tables of 9 feet or more, free of alkali, are desired. Lack of sufficient boron can also be detrimental to walnuts.

Good water supply important

Irrigation: Most walnut trees need to be irrigated at least three times during the growing season. It may take from 1½ to 2½ acre-feet of water for the three irrigations to wet down to the full depth of the feeding roots. If the rains are deficient, some late winter irrigation before growth starts will also be needed. Actual experience is necessary to anticipate irrigation needs fully, especially when considering cover crops.

Fig. 23.1—Irrigating walnuts. These walnuts will not suffer from lack of good irrigation.

2. Deciding on Varieties and Pollinators

Joseph Sexton, in 1867 near Santa Barbara, planted some walnuts he obtained from Chile. Through selection, we now have what is known as the "Santa Barbara" soft-shell types. Most of the soft-shell types in the industry are traced to these early plantings. A grower should bear in mind that whereas a walnut can provide its own pollen, generally if proper pollenizers in addition are present, crop size can increase. The reason is that certain conditions, such as weather, can cause the pollen from the male flower to fall before the female flowers from the same tree are receptive. There is no one walnut variety suited for planting throughout the walnut districts.

Select Placentia for Southern California

The Placentia does very well in the cool coastal

areas of Southern California. The trees are large and bear quite heavily. The kernels crack out at around 45 per cent, and the harvest is early. The kernels darken in areas of high summer temperatures. Placentia has a short chilling requirement. However, any sizeable plantings are not anticipated.

Hartley plantings increasing in northern and central areas

This good producer, with a good kernel quality (45 per cent crack-out), is becoming a popular variety. It is replacing the Franquette variety in the northern areas. Hartley has a medium chilling requirement. It comes into bearing at an earlier age than most other varieties.

Plant Payne in central and southern California

The Payne produces heavy when trees are quite young. The chilling requirement is quite short. The Ashley variety is nearly the same as Payne. However, for one reason or another, the Ashley and Payne have both increased their plantings over 6,000 acres each. Ashley does come into bearing at an earlier age. Kernel yield is somewhat higher, and a more light-colored kernel is apparent on this variety.

Franquette popular in Oregon

This variety blooms late and escapes the spring frosts. It cracks out at nearly 50 per cent, has long chilling requirements and is harvested quite late. Yields are often poor in central valleys of California.

3. Determining Orchard Planting System

Planting walnuts is a long-time investment. Considerable planning is neeeded in determining the planting system. From 12 to 27 walnut trees to an acre are found in the mature orchards. General observation and the opinions of many walnut growers agree that in the past the trees have been planted too close together.

Plant trees 60 feet apart

Mature orchards with the trees 60 feet apart each way (square system) are among the most productive in the state. With this spacing the individual trees have room to develop fully. A large proportion of the nuts are produced on the side branches, and the trees maintain a healthy, vigorous growth of new fruiting wood for many years. Orchards are generally planted 50' x 50' (17 trees/acre) and 30' x 30' (48 trees/acre).

CLOSE PLANTINGS NOT ADVISABLE

In the close plantings, where the trees are only 25 to 30 feet apart, the side branches are shaded most of the day, the fruit spurs on the lower branches soon die and the crop is borne mainly in the tops of the trees, resulting in reduced yield.

Use filler trees

A favored system is to plant the orchard 30' x 30'. The trees may be all of one variety, but often the variety to be removed in 10 to 12 years is Payne, leaving the selected variety on the 60' x 60'. Payne bears early, grows slowly and produces quite heavily when young.

Consider top working in orchard

Some growers like to plant the black walnut seeds

or the trees in the orchard and top work them (to English varieties) when they are ready. When seeds are planted, two or three seeds are used in one place, and the best growing shoot is selected for stock, but generally, using seeds is not recommended. Budding to desired variety is usually done when planting by seeds is practiced. Using young seedling trees grown in a nursery should be preferred over using seeds.

Choose right rootstock

NORTHERN CALIFORNIA BLACK WALNUT ROOTSTOCK

Walnuts are propagated and grown on the northern California black walnut rootstock primarily because of its tolerance to oak-root fungus. Since this rootstock is susceptible to crown rot, irrigation must be handled carefully to discourage development of the crown-rot organism.

HYBRIDS ARE BECOMING POPULAR

Selected paradox hybrid rootstocks may offer some resistance in areas where the lesion nematode has become a problem in walnut orchards. These are first generation hybrids resulting from crossing the Northern California black walnut and a Persian variety.

The paradox hybrid is also quite resistant to crown rot and has been used in areas where soil moisture conditions are not suitable to the northern California black walnut. It is very susceptible to oak-root fungus, however, and should not be used in areas where the fungus is known to be present.

4. Preparing Land Before Planting

Because of the 30- to 60-foot distances between

most walnut trees, exacting land preparation is not so necessary as for closer plantings. Walnuts are often planted around farm perimeters, along roadways and lanes and do well with little pre-land preparation. However, it must be remembered that the orchard will be there a long time, and one should make plans accordingly.

Prepare planting row

Walnuts are planted from January to March when the cover crop, if planted, is still growing. Many orchardists disk or plow a 5- to 8-foot swath down the planting row and leave the soil between undisturbed. The cover crop is then allowed to grow until the proper time for turning it under.

Subsoiling is recommended

Because the walnut likes to push its roots deep and quickly, subsoiling is done. Hardpans and plow soles caused many growers growth problems before the practice of subsoiling was used extensively.

5. Planting the Young Trees

The future success of your long-range investment will depend to a large extent upon your skill in planting your trees.

Order trees early

Walnut trees sell according to size: a medium-sized tree, about 8 feet high, may do better than one larger, and it usually costs less. Nurseries advise early ordering to assure delivery on time as well as right varieties. Heel in trees immediately.

Plant trees early

Walnut trees should be planted during January or February so that the soil may be thoroughly settled around the roots and growth may start with the beginning of the normal growing season, which is usually March in southern California. Holes should be dug deep enough to allow room for the full length of the taproot, which may be from 18 to 30 inches. The lateral roots may be 6 or 8 inches long, and the hole should be wide enough to accommodate them.

Dig hole big enough

Walnut roots are usually larger than other tree roots being transplanted. Prepare the hole properly so the roots are in deep enough and not crowded on the sides. A planting board should be used because of the large hole usually dug.

Care of trees at planting

Prune off only damaged, broken, crossed or twisted roots, and then with caution. Fit the hole to the roots. Any extremely long roots can be trimmed back. The bottom limb, if in a good location, should be placed into the prevailing wind and the tree leaned slightly in the same direction. *Do not add fertilizer to the roots.*

Use care in tamping

Sift loose soil around the roots carefully. Some planters like to sift in loose soil to about a 6-inch-depth, then pull up on the tree slightly. This tends to straighten the roots and give them a downward direction. Settling soil with water is desirable. Do not tamp after trees have been watered.

Use top soil for tamping

In filling in the soil around the roots, the top soil should be used. It should be tamped thoroughly without bruising the roots. A better stand of trees may be expected, and a prompter growth in the spring, if the young trees are thoroughly irrigated as soon as they are planted. This can be accomplished by running a single furrow along the row and cutting the water in at the basin left around each tree when it was planted.

Watering planted trees not always necessary

Irrigation at this time may not be essential from the point of view of available soil moisture, but it will be well worth the extra care, as a means of thoroughly settling the soil around the roots to prevent their drying out.

Head young trees

Young walnut transplants are headed 5 to 6 feet above the ground at planting. Buds are destroyed at the lower portions of the tree as growth begins. Side branches may be left, especially in areas where sunburn is a threat.

6. Caring for Trees After Planting

A considerable amount of investment has gone into preparing and planting the trees. A grower must continue taking good care of his trees so he will realize financial returns as early as possible.

Consider cover crop

Cover crops help maintain or improve the physical

Fig. 23.2—This young walnut orchard shows the results of using approved practices such as land preparation, irrigation and training. These trees were planted four months ago. A cover crop will be planted in the fall.

texture of the soil, and thus maintain or increase the rate of water penetration. Cover crops are also important in preventing soil erosion in orchards planted on even moderately sloping land.

Cover crops are well worth growing for the sake of maintaining a soil with good water penetration, even though the fertility and water-holding capacity are slightly affected.

Protect young trees

Whitewashing young trees has been a practice for many years and gives good results against sunburn. Special tree wrappers or protectors are used as control against sunburn, rodents, rabbits and the like.

Staking walnuts soon after or during planting may be desirable.

7. Training Young Walnut Trees

De-bud early for top growth

Soon after planting, shoots start growing all along the tree. Buds or shoots within 2 feet of the ground should be destroyed. This will force upper growth that will eventually be main limbs. If this is not done, upper part of the tree may not develop limbs or portions may die outright.

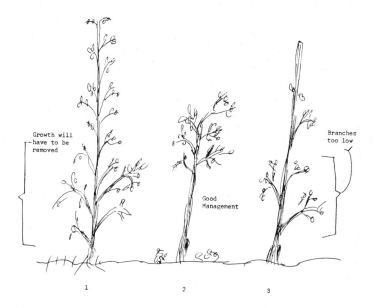

Fig. 23.3—No. 1: Young trees send off shoots all along stem. If bottom limbs were rubbed off at an earlier time, it would look like No. 2, desirable tree. No. 3 displays what often happens if bottom shoots are not removed.

Develop desired tree shape

Most walnut growers follow one of two training systems: modified leader and vase or open center.

Choose modified leader

Walnut trees grow big and carry a lot of weight in their branches. Mechanized harvest operations demand a strong framework. The modified training system is known for its strong branches.

Maintain good soil moisture

Soil moisture is a key factor in developing young trees to early maturity with good growth. They must have available water at all times. However do not flood them, resulting in water standing, as this is as serious as being too dry.

8. Managing the Developing Orchard

Most walnut orchards need some type of fertilizer.

Nitrogen is essential

Successful walnut growers add nitrogen, in one form or another, to their soil. Winter legumes do not add enough, in themselves, to satisfy the need, so most growers supplement with manures or commercial mixes.

Choose economical fertilizer

A fertilizer that provides the most nitrogen for the least amount of money should be considered, provided it does not have an undesirable effect on the soil. A once-a-year application of 100 to 150 pounds of actual nitrogen per acre should be considered.

Trees display neglect

Extreme nitrogen deficiency in walnut trees is marked by sparse, small, yellow leaves and many dead twigs in the top of the tree. Two other characteristics of a nitrogen-deficient soil are failure to produce good cover crops—especially non-legumes such as mustard —and a slow but steady decline in yield and in nut size. When either or both of these symptoms are apparent, apply nitrogen as a trial in part of the orchard.

Lack of zinc often a problem

Zinc deficiency occurs in many orchards planted on sandy soils or old corral spots.

USE GLAZIER POINTS

Limbs or trunks 2 inches in diameter or so benefit from driving pure zinc glazier points well into the sapwood and parallel with the grain of the English portion of the tree. Space them about 1 inch apart.

TREAT LARGER TREES WITH GALVANIZED IRON

Rectangular pieces 2 inches long of about 22 gauge galvanized iron are driven into the trunks or branches not more than 10 inches in diameter. Space these about 2 inches apart in a staggered pattern. Three pieces are used for every inch in diameter. Treatment lasts several years.

ZINC SULFATE CAN BE USED

Treating the soil with 36 per cent zinc sulfate in

one gallon of water in early winter has given some results in sandy soil. Place sulfate in a trench 4 to 6 inches below cultivation depth, 6 to 8 feet from the tree. Small trees need 5 to 10 pounds per tree, and larger ones up to 35 or 40. Zinc sprays for walnuts shortly after leafing out have been satisfactory. Some experiments indicate that sprays consisting of 1 pound of 36 per cent zinc sulfate in 100 gallons of water (or 2 pounds chelated zinc) have been effective.

Manganese and copper may be deficient

Some coastal counties and a few in the central areas suffer from these shortages. Manganese affects the leaves directly, whereas iron deficiency causes shriveling of the walnut kernel. Seek local advice for treatment before it is undertaken.

Boron may be deficient or toxic

Boron deficiency, referred to as die-back, is occasionally a serious problem. Shoots become elongated and leafless or may have misshapen leaves. Late winter application of from 3 to 6 pounds of borax, or equivalent, to a tree 10 years old or older is effective. Broadcast borax under the tree. Do this about every three or four years.

Boron toxicity has been observed in areas with water high in boron.

Select irrigation practice

The manner in which water is applied must be adapted to soil conditions, grade of the land, size of water supply and other local factors. On fairly flat lands, walnut trees are usually irrigated by means of furrows, contour checks, strip checks, square checks

Fig. 23.4—Die-back on young walnut trees. Boron toxicity produces these serious results.

or a combination check-and-furrow system. The check systems are better adapted to the use of relatively large heads of water. On steep slopes the contour furrow or ordinary furrow system or sprinklers may be used. In any orchard, choose the irrigation method best suited to the orchard and water supply conditions. Walnuts especially need adequate water for five to six weeks immediately after bloom.

Consider intercropping

Intercropping of young walnut orchards is a general practice. It has usually proved successful in making the land support the orchard until the walnuts come into bearing.

SELECT INTERCROP CAREFULLY

The crop to be grown depends upon various con-

Fig. 23.5—Walnut tree after removal of dead wood caused from die-backs.

ditions. Beans are an ideal intercrop in bean-growing districts and may be grown in the walnut orchard until the trees are 8 to 10 years of age. Several other vegetables can be grown in young walnut orchards without harm to the trees. These include tomatoes, peppers, melons, cabbage, lettuce, etc.

CORN, MILO AND ALFALFA ARE POOR INVESTMENTS

Do not grow intercrops of corn or milo because they may have a harmful effect upon the trees when the soil is permitted to become dry before harvesting the milo or corn. Although alfalfa is occasionally grown as an intercrop, its use is not recommended because of extreme competition for water and nutrients.

FRUIT TREES MAY BE USED

Peaches, apricots, prunes and other walnut trees are often interplanted. Usually the young walnut trees do not develop so fast with other trees, but the added income from fruit-producing trees offsets it. Tree interplants must be removed when tree limbs are 5 or 6 feet apart.

9. Pruning

Satisfactory walnut yields are associated with maintenance of good vigor in mature groves. In interior districts an average growth of at least 8 to 12 inches on upright shoots over the top of the tree seems desirable. In coastal districts 4 to 6 inches may be the desirable minimum.

Select one of two systems

There are two general purposes and methods for pruning walnut trees. In one method, the pruning consists of cutting off lower limbs that interfere with cultural operations and removing large limbs throughout the tops of the trees. In the other, the trees are pruned by removing small wood up to $1\frac{1}{4}$ inches in diameter to encourage and stimulate growth of new wood to replace the old fruiting wood.

Encourage open centers

Few walnuts are produced in the centers of old trees because of shade. Sunlight is essential to the production and maintenance of fruit spurs. Almost the entire crop will be produced on the outside twigs in the top or on the sides of the tree unless there is some thinning out of branches. A moderate thinning each year will promote more uniform production throughout the tree.

Do not leave stubs

In all pruning operations, the limbs are cut off without leaving any stub. It has been a common practice to paint all the wounds larger than 3 inches in diameter with a disinfectant. A thin bordeaux paste is used. However, in many areas growers have been able to grow walnut trees without this precaution.

10. Selecting Preharvest Practices

Choose effective pest control program

The codling moth, walnut aphid and navel orange worm are the major insect pests of Persian walnuts, from the point of view of widespread distribution, total acreage treated and probability of losses where control measures are neglected. The walnut husk fly is potentially a major pest, should it become generally distributed in the areas where susceptible varieties are growing. The red spider is controlled quite easily but becomes a serious pest if left alone. Local farm advisors have up-to-date control programs and should be consulted.

Fig. 23.6—Pruning a big walnut tree is a good practice. Keeping the center open is essential for top production.

CONTROL THE CODLING MOTH

Controlling this insect is a must in some early blooming varieties. The insect passes the winter as a caterpillar or larva within a silken cocoon, in crevices of the bark, in pruning scars, in debris on the soil or actually in the soil itself. It is also found in drying trays, in dehydrators and buildings where walnuts have been temporarily housed and in burlap sacks that have been used in harvesting and storage. The larvae transform into pupae in the spring, from which adults issue 18 to 30 days later. Emergence is prolonged over a period of from 6 to 8 weeks. The adults do not necessarily begin to emerge at the same time each year, therefore, a knowledge of when emergence begins and when the major peak or peaks occur is important from the point of view of satisfactory control. The moths are active at dusk, and females deposit eggs at this time, provided the temperature is approximately 60°F. or higher with little or no air movement.

Larvae thrive on walnut kernels: The first eggs of the season are laid on the green twigs and leaves, but later they are deposited on the fruits. Upon hatching, the larvae usually burrow into the nut and feed on the kernel. The earlier larvae of the season usually enter through the stigma or calyx, causing most of the nuts so infested to drop before they reach maturity. Later, entrance usually is made where nuts in clusters are in contact. When the shell becomes hardened, the larvae cannot penetrate it directly and hence must gain entry to the kernel through the fiber at the stem end.

Larva feeds for 35 to 45 days: The young worm must eat to mature, and it works at it over a month. When fully developed, it usually leaves the nut and spins a cocoon. Most areas have at least one full generation, some two, and others a partial third.

Walnut Aphid

This pest can reduce the crop up to 50 per cent, depending upon variety and situations for the year. Leaf stunting that affects nut size the current year also reduces tonnage the following year. Honeydew, a sticky by-product of aphids, can be observed on the leaves.

Disease control program important

Walnut blight, canker, crown gall, crown rot, San Jose Scale, branch wilt and dieback should be watched for constantly and taken care of properly. Farm advisors and local chemical representatives are excellent sources of information.

Control limb breakage

A heavy crop requires bracing. Braces can eliminate much of the weight from the limbs.

Fig. 23.7—Bracing walnut limbs to prevent tree damage.

Fig. 23.8—Walnuts hauled immediately to huller.

11. Determining Harvest Procedure

Most commercial orchards are harvested mechanically. Various systems are used, but as yet most are knocked onto smooth ground by mechanical knockers and picked up by machines.

Smooth ground early

Walnuts drop naturally over a long period (four weeks), and the ground should be ready. Growers in some areas like to run water lightly to firm the soil as close to harvest as possible.

Hull nuts immediately

Gather, hull and dry the nuts (6 to 8 per cent moisture) as soon as possible. Rain, fog and rodents

WALNUT VARIETIES

Variety	Origin	Chilling Requirements	Tree Size in Average Good Soil	Yield Mature Trees	Nut Size Mature Trees	Kernel a)Crackout b)Color c)Seal	Harvest Season	Remarks
Franquette	France	Long	Large	Light to Medium	Med./Sm. Lg./Med.	a) 48-50 b) Light c) Good	Late	Yields often poor in central valleys. Late leafing desirable for frosty mountain districts and nut size larger there.
Payne	Santa Clara County, Calif.	Short	Moderate	Med. to heavy, bears quite heavily early	Medium	a) 48-50 b) Med. c) Good	Early	Frost, blight, and sunburn loss sometimes serious. Needs good nitrogen supply. Good in central and So. Calif. Some increase in plantings.
Placentia	Orange Co., Calif.	Short	Large	Med. to heavy	Medium	a) 46-48 b) Med. minus c) Fair	Early	Good only in cool coastal areas of So. Calif. Kernels dark in hot interior districts.
Eureka	Orange Co., Calif.	Long	Large	Medium	Medium	a) 48-50 b) Med. minus c) Excellent	Mid.	Best quality in semicoastal districts of central Calif. Kernels shrivel in hot districts. Sometimes blight losses severe.
Hartley	Napa Co., Calif. (Fr. seedling)	Medium	Moderate	Med. to heavy	Large	a) 46-48 b) Light plus c) Fair	Late-mid.	Good throughout Central and No. Calif. Replacing Franquette except in districts subject to very late spring frosts. Large increase in plantings.
Concord	Contra Costa Co., Calif.	Medium	Large	Medium	Medium	a) 47-49 b) Med. c) Fair	Early	Extensive acreage only near S. F. Bay. Being replaced there by Payne.
San Jose Mayette	Fr. seedling grown in Santa Clara Co., Calif.	Long	Large	Light	Large	a) 42-46 b) Med. minus c) Poor	Late-mid	Poor yields and poor seal causing replacement by Hartley and other varieties.
Drummond	—	Medium	Large	Medium	Medium	a) 45-50 b) Light c) Good	Mid	Bark of light color which gives it sunburn protection.
Marchetti	U. Calif.	Medium	Moderate	Medium	Medium	a) 45-50 b) Light c) Good	Late	Nuts grow in clusters. Large leaves protect nuts.

can cause damage. Hulls often will dry to the nut and must be run through several times. These often end up as culls.

Store safely

Walnuts are a very valuable crop per pound and can easily be transported and stored for long periods without loss from spoilage. For these reasons, thievery is a problem, so nuts should not be left overnight in the field but gathered and stored securely.

Green hulls must be removed

With mechanical shaking, many nuts fall that are green. Most of these go through the huller unhulled. Water-sweating can be used, but the use of ethylene gas has proven more effective.

Customers prefer the "blonde" look

Most walnuts are bleached by using sodium hypochlorite solution for two to three minutes. It removes dirt and stains, leaving them with an attractive appearance.

Cellophane bags have increased sales

One- to 2-pound cellophane bags of walnuts have proven very popular with customers. Over 80 per cent of the in-shell nuts are sold this way.

Chapter

XXIV

SMALL FRUITS AND NUTS

Kiwi

History

Kiwis originally grew wild along the banks of the river flowing through the Yangtze valley of China. An Englishman in 1847 noticed the Kiwi while plant-collecting in China. Years later, about 1900, seeds were sent to England.

In the first decade of the twentieth century the first Kiwi seeds were introduced into New Zealand and California. At first the plants were grown in back-yards for ornamental purposes. After World War II, New Zealand planted large acreages of Kiwis and were exporting the fruit all over the world. Today California is planting acreage in Kiwis and even developing a marketing system for this relatively new-comer in tropical fruit.

How the name came about

Botanically it is known as *Actinidia Chinensis* Planch, but more commonly the Chinese gooseberry, the Yangtao vine or just Kiwi. The fruit was named

"Kiwi" after the kiwi bird, the national bird of New Zealand and the nickname of the New Zealanders.

There are approximately 20 species in the genera, all of East Asian origin. Only three produce edible fruits, the Chinese gooseberry being the best. The main varieties presently being grown commercially are Abbott, Bruno, Monty, Hayward and Chico.

Plant description

The Kiwi is a deciduous vine having reddish hairs on the stems and leaves. The heart-shaped leaves are 5 to 8 inches long. The flowers, borne only from the first three to five buds of new spring growth, are first white then turn a buff yellow color. The plant is dioecious, i.e., male and female flowers on different vines. Flowers on the male vine have a vestigial ovary, surrounded by numerous stamen. On fruiting female vines the ovary is surrounded by numerous stamen, but the pollen from these stamens has never been found to be viable, making pollen from a male Kiwi necessary.

It usually takes four to five years for a Chinese gooseberry vine to start bearing worthwhile crops, but about seven to eight years are required for it to reach full production.

Fruit characteristics

The fruit of the Kiwi vine matures between the first part of November and the first few days of December. When mature, the fruit is similar in size to a lemon or a lime. It is an ugly looking, brown-red fruit with a thin, tough, fuzzy skin and with no pit. When peeled or cut it reveals a moist, glistening fleshy fruit that is completely edible, right down to and including the small seeds which resemble strawberry seeds in size and texture. The flesh of the fruit ranges in color from a light lime green to a pale cream. In cross-section there is exhibited a pattern of light colored rays that are interspersed with a multitude of dark seeds in a

Fig. 24.1—A sketch showing fruiting and growth characteristics of a Kiwi vine.

pattern radiating from the center.

After the fuzz has been removed, the fruit can be eaten whole, sliced or cut-up. The taste has been

described as a sweet combination of cherries, canta-
loupes and strawberries with a touch of the tartness
of citrus fruit. It tastes like nothing you have ever
had before. It tastes like a Kiwi.

Cultivation practices

Methods of propagation are similar to those used
for the grape. Grafting or budding of the desired variety to seedling rootstocks is the general commercial
practice, but cuttings can also be taken and rooted.
Older vines can be topworked if a more desirable variety is desired. Seedlings are so highly variable in
character that they generally are undesirable for use
by the commercial grower. Also, because the seedlings
are dioecious, the grower may have to wait up to seven
years to discover the sex of the vine he has planted.
There is no reliable way to distinguish male vines from
female vines.

The growing conditions for Kiwis are few and
simple.

1.   A well drained soil is desirable. A friable
sandy loam is considered the best, although they will
grow in the wide range of soils from adobe to sandy.

2.   The weather conditions are of some importance. The vine, when mature, can withstand a hard
frost; the young, tender shoots and fruits are readily
susceptible to frost damage. It is generally considered
common practice to say that the temperature range
is 0° to 115°F. Frost and cooling precautions should
be used during the periods of either extreme.

3.   The growing season is about 210 days, depending usually on the temperature and other weather
conditions.

The Kiwi vine has cultivation practices similar to
grape vines in that they must be trellised, trained and

Fig. 24.2—A two-year-old Kiwi vine interplanted in an almond orchard.

pruned. Once properly trellised a few vines can provide a heavily shaded arbor and a rewarding fruit supply.

Pests and diseases

The plant is quite unique in that there are only a few pests or diseases that attack it. The diseases that affect it are: oak-root fungus, sclerotic twig blight and crown gall. Pests such as mites, thrips, root eelworm, greedy scale and the leaf roller caterpillar are of some importance. The nematode, however, will attack and kill the plant.

The use of the fruit, etc.

In the United States, Washington, Oregon and

California are growing Kiwis, with California having the most plantings (over 2,000 acres). The fruit can be used as a fresh fruit, for an ice cream topping, jam, jelly, pie, milk shake, cake topping and anything else the mind can dream up. It can even be used as a meat tenderizer as the fruit contains an enzyme called actinidin. Placing slices of a Kiwi on the meat and leaving them there for a short while will tenderize the meat.

The Chinese gooseberry also contains more vitamin C than citrus fruits.

The future for the funny little fruit from China seems to be rosy and bright.

Bushberries

Raspberries, loganberries, dewberries, blueberries, gooseberries, blackberries, olallieberries and boysenberries are called "bushberries" simply because they are the cultivated descendants of the wild briar patch. They typically grow best in the temperate and cool regions, with very little or poor growth in the warmer regions, deserts and plains.

Raspberries

Red Raspberries

Red raspberries were introduced into Europe over 400 years ago and into the United States about 1800. Ever since that time commercial raspberry plantings have been an agricultural product of this country. This bushberry produces a berry superior to the black raspberry and is possibly the best for home gardens. This berry has upright canes, generally non-branching. The plant sends out suckers and shoots from the root areas, and new canes are produced in areas away from the original plant. The plant is a perennial with the wood and canes being biennial, ie., one season the canes will grow, and the next season this cane will bear fruit and then die, while the roots live on.

The new canes, growing from the roots, emerge during the early spring, which is the fruiting period of those canes that grew the previous year. Because of this continual replacement of canes from year to year, there is an almost regular yearly production of berries.

BLACK RASPBERRIES

The black raspberry has a different growth pattern than does the red raspberry, in that the new canes come up from the crown of the original plant, thus making the plant rather bushy. The canes are considered to be more vigorous, often making considerable growth under favorable conditions.

The easiest way to tell the red raspberry plant from the black raspberry plant is by thorniness. The red has soft thorns while the black has very stiff spines that are sharp and firm, making the black raspberry uncomfortable to handle barehanded.

RASPBERRY VARIETIES

Red raspberries: Latham is probably the best known. It is relatively widely ranged, but not in the south, except in the cooler, high elevations.

Black raspberries (black caps): Cumberland and Logan are probably the two oldest and best known varieties. They are grown in a wide range of climates, in fields and clearings of many eastern and western states, although warm weather and diseases are not overly favorable to their development in the southern states.

Purple raspberries: A cross between the black raspberry and the red raspberry, it is not a commercially raised berry. Varieties include: Sodus, Marion and Columbia.

Everbearing raspberries: These berries produce a little fruit all summer long and are considered a good berry for the home gardner. Varieties include: Durham, September and Indian Summer.

Blackberries

The blackberry is adapted to a broader range of growing conditions and is grown over a wider area than are raspberries. The growth habit is very like that of the black raspberry in that the new cane comes up from the crown of the plant. Some varieties have a tendency to sucker and develop new canes from the areas surrounding the original planting location. It is distinguished from the black raspberry by the presence of the conical receptacle or bloom on the stem of the raspberry and the absence of it on the blackberry. The fruit of the blackberry is also a plumper and larger berry than the raspberry. Varieties: Eldorado is the best known erect variety. Trailing varieties are Logan, Young and Boysen. Blackberries are grown throughout the United States.

Boysenberries: The boysenberry, a variety of the blackberry, was originally introduced by Walter Knott and is thought to have been a chance seedling in the garden of Rudolph Boysen, for whom it is named. Because of its similarity to the youngberry, it could also have been Luther Burbank's Phenomenal.

The boysenberry produces a soft, high quality black fruit.

Dewberries, loganberries and olallieberries: All

are varieties of the blackberry. The dewberry is adapted to the same growing range as the blackberry, and it is also found in some of the southern states where the blackberry is not grown. Lucretia is the oldest variety, with Carolina just a little superior to it in quality.

Loganberries are very similar to boysenberries in fruit size and color.

Olallieberries are a cross between the blackberry, loganberry and youngberry.

Filbert, Hickory, Macadamia, Pecan and Pistachio Nuts

A nut is any dry fruit whose kernel or seed is encased in an indehiscent (not opening by splitting along regular lines or not opening at all), hard, woody shell or rind. The term "nut" often refers to the meat inside the shell, the shell or the seed of a fruit, as in the almond.

Nuts are generally high in protein (15 to 30 per cent) and rich in fat and oil (50 to 70 per cent). They also conain starch, vitamin C and the B vitamins, thiamine, riboflavin and niacin. Some nuts (walnuts and pecans) contain vitamin A.

In North America the most widely eaten nuts are peanuts, walnuts, almonds, cashews, pecans, piñons and pistachios. The leading nut growing states are: Georgia, 504,000 tons; California, 225,000 tons; and Texas, 216,000 tons.

In tropical regions the most popular nuts are coconuts, Java almonds, paradise nuts, pili nuts and breadnuts.

Filberts

The filbert, technically a hazelnut, is grown in

Oregon and Washington. In California three varieties can be grown in the foothills.

Hickory nuts

The hickory nut is native to North America. The trees grow 90 to 170 feet tall, the younger ones having gray bark, and the older ones rough and scaly gray bark. The nut (fruit) is round or oblong, having a husk that separates into four segments. The meat is hard and may be brown, white, gray or possibly another color. Types of hickory nuts include: shagbark, shellbark (kingnut) and pecan.

Macadamia nuts

The macadamia nut (Queensland nut or Australian nut) is native to Australia and was introduced into Hawaii and California about 1889. It was only in Hawaii that commercial production was extensive, until just recently. The tree grows up to 50 feet tall, having 1-foot oval- or lance-shaped leaves. The nuts are 1 inch in diameter with white kernels. The kernels contain an oil that is used in soaps and medicine. There are two commercial species.

Pecan nuts

The pecan nut is really a hickory nut native to India and the area southward from Texas and Mexico. The tree grows from 70 to 100 feet tall with deeply ridged, brown-gray bark. The leaves are yellowish-green with finely toothed leaflets. The deep brown fruit is encapsulated in a thin and brittle shell and husk. The nut is sweet to the taste.

Pistachio nuts

The pistachio nut (green almond) is grown predominately in the Eastern Mediterranean, Southwest Asia and to some extent in California and the Southern United States. The tree grows well in warm, dry regions, seldom reaching 30 feet in height. The nut is ¾ to 1 inch with a smooth, thin, dark gray shell that will open at its edge like an oyster shell. Under the shell the nut is covered with a thin, purple skin. The nuts are dried and eaten or ground and used as a food coloring and flavoring for ice cream. The kernels are often processed for their oil. Before the nuts are sold for commercial use, the shell is either bleached white or dyed red.

Chapter

THE GRAPE INDUSTRY

The giant grape industry, long asleep in the United States, has been awakened. Evident now is new life not only in the so-called non-wine grape segment of the industry but also, and to a greater degree, in the often slumbering wine grape segment. The consumer populace too has been awakened, increasing consumption of the low alcohol, fruit flavored pop wines and champagnes as well as the fine premium sweet and dry wines.

Grape growers have responded in kind by planting grape varieties that satisfy these demands. But all may not be well for premium wine, as the grape must be grown under proper cultural conditions and in the proper climate that will result in the grape's developing into an excellent varietal character that fits the winemaker's needs. For without a dependable, delivered, quality grape of true varietal character, a great premium wine cannot be made. Growers, winemakers and marketers all must work together to keep the proverbial giant awake. Some old adages, such as "Premium wines can be made only in small quantities" and "Sugar alone is the criterion for quality," have fallen and should be left lying. Good wines can and are being made in large quantities. As far as quality is concerned, wine is only as good as the grape, and that for the most part is up to the grower.

However, there cannot be a single-best wine, nor can there be a best soil, a best climate, the exact amount of sun and the perfect cultural practice, because opinions differ widely.

At no time in history has the grape and wine industry reached so far and touched the lives of so many people as today, and at no time before has the industry faced greater problems and greater challenges. Nor has the industry been so closely connected with expanding its own markets, sharing in contributing to the upsurge in developing scientific methods of growing grapes, making wine, processing raisins and fresh grapes and taking an ever-larger role in mankind's long struggle for numerous freedoms and peace of mind.

Grape production throughout the world exceeds that of all deciduous tree fruits. Most of the world's grapes—80 per cent—are grown for wine; table grapes account for 8 to 10 per cent; and raisins account for about 6 per cent. Some table and raisin grapes not only are eaten fresh but are also made into wine, unfermented juice and jelly. Wine grapes go into unfermented juices and jellies, too.

The growing of all types of grapes for the many outlets is a fascinating industry to be involved in. Each segment is a challenge and opportunity—for there will never be the ideal cultural practice in growing grapes or an all-perfect method in making wine. However, phenomenal markets for wines are being created, and at the same time our cultural methods are gaining on some of the most versatile elements of nature man has ever known. Who today would think that in the near future the United States would consume 5 gallons of wine per capita per year (France and Italy consume 25 to 30 gallons per capita per year) or that the growing demands of fine wine grape varieties would be partially adapted to what are now undesirable weather conditions? Both statements are well on their way to becoming realities. They reflect a tremendous future for a well planned coordinated industry. Be enterprising, become involved in this awakening.

However, this chapter will relate primarily to growing grapes (viticulture).

Distribution

Some type of grape is grown in every state of the United States and also in some areas of Canada and Mexico. South America is no newcomer to the grape industry; Argentina alone has more acres in grapes than California (over 500,000), and Chile has over half as many. Totally, South America has approximately 1 million acres in grapes and Africa has over 1½ million acres. As might be expected, Europe is the leader by far with about 17 million acres, and Asia has over 2 million acres.

Most grapes are grown in temperate zones, 30 to 50 degrees north latitude and 30 to 40 degrees south longitude. However, some grapes are grown in limited acreages outside these general areas.

It would seem there are well over 20 million acres of grapes in the world. This large acreage is impressive and will likely supply present needs. However, unless a high percentage is grown properly, in the proper location, resulting in a quality product, the world's appetite for a good wine, raisin or fresh product could stand still, and when that occurs the industry is going backward.

The grape industry often refers to grapes according to their use or market, and one must bear in mind that some varieties have several markets. Also any grape can make a wine of sorts and any grape can be eaten fresh.

A. *Wine grapes*: Usually grapes that can produce a satisfactory dessert (sweet) or table (dry) wine. The production of wine grapes is the major

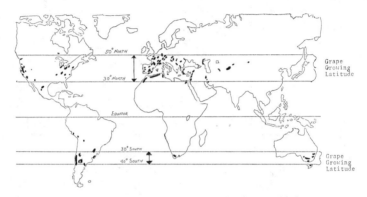

Fig. 25.1—Map of grape growing climates. Wine grapes grow best in the world's temperate zones, between latitudes that are shown on this map. Only a few regions with important vineyards lie outside these belts, as indicated by black dots.

acreage of growers in such important areas as South America, North and South Africa, Europe, approximately half of Australia and about one-third of the United States. Generally the fine wines are made from grapes that develop specific varietal characteristics when grown in the proper climate and location and under good cultural practices. A wine may have 100 per cent of a particular variety, while another may have 51 per cent or less depending on the label and where bottled.

B. *Table grapes*: Certain grape varieties that are grown for fresh market. In some cases they also are used as decorations, particularly during festive occasions, and also as a source of brandy and other wine blends. For example, the Tokay grape, generally grown as a table grape, can be used also in dry wine, champagne, dessert wine and brandy.

The good table grape for fresh market is readily edible and has attractive varietal characteristics such as color, large uniform berries and compact clusters. Many table grapes require special cultural practices such as girdling, thinning, filling leaves or the use of plant growth regulator sprays to increase size, sugar content, etc. The Thompson seedless is an example of growth regulators if the fresh market is its outlet and the Emperor, where pulling leaves for color and thinning for quality and bunch size are necessary.

C. *Raisin grapes*: Grapes, usually seedless, that when dried must have a pleasing flavor and maintain soft textures such as the Thompson, when grown, dried and prepared properly.

D. *Sweet juice grapes*: Grapes that when processed retain the varietal characteristic of fresh flavor. The Concord grape is the major variety. It is also used in making jelly, as well as wine and wine flavors.

E. *Canning grapes*: Seedless grapes that are processed and used with other fruit combinations. Thompson is the major variety.

The three general grape regions by species grown in the United States are:

1. Western States (California, Washington, Oregon, Arizona and Idaho)

European grape (*vitis vinifera*) varieties. There are over 8,000 named varieties, 60 of importance in California.

Varieties used for wine, table (fresh) raisins and

processing. Some varieties, i.e., Thompson seedless, when grown properly, can be used for all markets. European varieties have no serious rival for fine wines. They require a mild climate and a longer growing season than American varieties, although this also varies with varieties. *Vinifera* is also grown throughout warm areas of Europe, Australia, North and South Africa and South America. Some vinifera and vinifera crosses are also planted in other areas of the United States and Canada.

The pulp and skin stick together, and the fruit is sweet throughout.

2. Northeast, Great Lakes and Canada
American grape (*vitis labrusca*) varieties

These are native to this area. They are fresh market (table) varieties and are also used for making wine and jelly and juice for unfermented products. Some of the larger plantings are around the Great Lakes, New York and Pennsylvania. Washington, Oregon and California have commercial plantings also. These types are grown in many parts of the United States.

The grape is thin-skinned, more acid toward its center and around its seeds. The skin slips easily from the pulp, which clings tenuously to the seeds. Concord is the major variety. *Labrusca* withstands more severe winter temperatures than *vinifera* and requires 150 to 170 days from spring frost to fall frost.

3. Southern and Gulf States
Muscadine (*vitis rotundifolia*) Scuppernong variety

Used in this area for limited wine making, cooking and local fresh markets. Muscadine varieties tolerate mild winters, and some are used as rootstock as they are resistant to phylloxera.

The bunches are small and loose, and the grapes

have a noticeable musky odor. The seeds are quite large, and the vines are very vigorous.

Climate

There are some grape varieties for all climates suitable for grape production but no best climate for all grapes. Therefore it is necessary to evaluate well ahead of going into the grape growing business what the planned end product is intended to be. For example, there are areas, locations, and even sites within a few square miles, a section or a 40-acre plot that could produce one variety to a better quality than another variety using the same cultural practice. Reference is to soil changes and conditions, slope, wind, certain rock material influences and water drainage. For the most part the majority of California grapes are grown on soils of a sandy nature at least 4 to 5 feet deep. However, the deep fertile (loam) soils produce heavy crops, whereas the sandy gravel under similar practices produces a lighter crop. Tonnage from the lighter soils can be increased by using rootstock, cover crops and fertilizer, but it is obvious that the cost of production will be greater.

It would be simpler to advise against certain soils than to recommend the many good soils in which grapes will grow. Heavy clay, high concentrations of salt, Boron and other toxic material, poor water drainage and very shallow soils should be avoided.

However, some grape varieties respond more favorably as to color, quality, character, etc., in infertile soil than they do in what is considered very good soil.

Considerable research has brought to light specific climates combined with certain soils and approved cultural practices that are required by some grapes to bring them to perfection.

The range and type of temperatures in a location

should be known before a variety and market is selected. Dr. A. J. Winkler of the University of California introduced a suitable guide for California conditions referred to as degree days. Briefly it is determined by subtracting 50° F. from the monthly mean average, and multiplying that figure by the number of days in that month; for example:

$$May\ 85° - 50° = 35° \times 31 = 1,085$$

Do this for each month from April 1 through October 31 and then total them. These total degree days then translate into regions; for example:

less than 2,500	cool region	Napa Area-Coastal	I
2,501 to 3,000	moderate cool	St. Helena	II
3,001 to 3,500	warm	Paso Robles	III
3,501 to 4,000	moderate hot	Modesto	IV
4,001 upwards	hot	Fresno	V

The degree day heat index does not apply to all other states and countries as well as it does to California, primarily because of the difference in latitude. Oregon, for example, being farther north, has longer summer days, which results in more radiant energy from the sun. Some of the northerly latitudes of Europe, where grapes are grown for their fine wines, have between 1,700 and 2,000 degree days, while California's comparable grapes grown for similar wines are grown at 2,000 to 3,000 degree days.

The Evapotranspiration Index developed by Thornthwaite is used to compare world climates as they relate to plant responses. It is a rather complex equation based on monthly mean temperatures and yearly temperature patterns as well as latitude. This index is useful in selecting climate in terms of a plant species' specific needs and could also be used as a guide in selecting climate for grape growing.

There is still controversy in California over the arbitrary lines designated as borders for these regions such as county roads, rivers or certain topographical ranges. A problem as a result of these arbitrary boundaries is that they are also used to some extent as grape pricing guides. For example, a Zinfandel, or other premium wine grape, can differ in price anywhere from $10 to $25 per ton, all other conditions being equal, with perhaps only 100 yards separating one region boundary from the other. However, it is understandable to a wine connoisseur why a Zinfandel grown in Bakersfield, a hot region, as compared with one grown in the Napa area, a cool region, could differ by as much as $500 per ton.

Recent investigations have indicated that areas within regions need to be re-evaluated as they are quite broad and do not necessarily recognize temperature changes, area cooling influences or new areas of production as they relate to a complete quality grape.

However, growing the right variety in the right area may explain why the north coast plantings in California account for 16 per cent of the state acreage in premium wine grapes but for the past few years the crop value has been as high as 34 per cent.

The Americas and Their Grapes—Origin

The grapes of the Old World (vinifera) can be traced directly to the Eastern Hemisphere, specifically Asia Minor as recorded in the *Bible,* in fossilized remains and in folklore. There are many informative written accounts as to their origin and subsequent relocation. Many pleasant hours can be spent reading about grapes and wines of the Old World.

Some native American grape varieties are also used to some extent in Europe and Asia as rootstock.

They have been used in hybridization to improve negative conditions such as pests, soils and climate problems in the Americas as well.

Selecting Grape Varieties

Generally speaking, a grower should select the variety to plant after he has carefully checked with markets, processors, packers, shippers and wine brokers.

Significant new plantings of wine grapes in the past few years in California are Barbera, Cabernet Sauvignon, Petite Sirah, Ruby Cabernet, Zinfandel and Grenache in the black varieties, and French Columbard, Chenin Blanc and White Riesling in the white varieties. Rubired is a grape used for color.

Thompson Seedless and Muscat of Alexandria are the leading raisin-type grapes, although it must be remembered that both are used also in wine making and for table grapes.

Popular table grapes are Emperor, Tokay, Ribier and Malaga, used also to some extent in wine making, and Perlette.

The bulk of Michigan's and Washington's grapes are Concord, although sizeable vinifera plantings of Cabernet Sauvignon, Chardonnay, Rieslings and Pinot Noir are recorded. New York and other eastern states are planting some of the vinifera type grapes also with measurable success. However, other than experimental, other grape growing states for the most part continue to plant grape types native to their area.

Grape Trellis and Supports

Vinefera

As mentioned in Chapter V, grapes are planted

on the rectangular system (8 to 10 feet) or in rows from 10 to 12 feet and plants down the row from 6 to 8 feet apart. Each plant needs to be trained up a support of some sort. Many old wine and some table varieties have no support when they are older other than the trunk itself. Of course, cane- or cordon-pruned grapes must have a stake and at least one wire, in some cases two or three. With vigorous growth and anticipated mechanical harvesting on wine grapes, two to three wires are recommended for both vertical and horizontal trellising. The wires, other than support wires, help to spread out shoot growth for more light exposure to leaves as well as controlling twisting vines. This results in improving quality, keeping heavy growth from near grapes and aiding in harvesting and in applying pesticides.

Supports

Wood supports for vines in the past were mostly

Courtesy, Pacific Agrilands, Modesto, Calif.

Fig. 25.2—Vigorous growing wine grapes on a three-wire trellis prepared for mechanical harvesters. Note spread of foliage up and away from grapes.

redwood and cedar. However, because of shortage and expense, growers are using such material as other types of treated softwood and hardwood and imported hardwood as well as metal and plastic. These supports are driven in by hand or by hydraulic-operated machines, and some are installed by water pressure by blowing a hole down into the soil.

WINE GRAPE VARIETIES

Cane-pruned varieties such as Sauvignon Blanc, Pinot Noir, White Riesling and Cabernet Sauvignon have a wire trellis. Many new plantings use the three-wire vertical trellis. The bottom support wire is normally 42 inches from the ground, the second wire 10 to 12 inches above the support wire and the third wire near the top of a 7-foot stake or 10 to 12 inches above the second wire. Stakes should be in the ground at least 18 inches. Some growers use a 5-foot stake set between each 7-foot stake. The second and third wires

Fig. 25.3—Good quality vinifera wine grapes such as these are part of the reason for the increasing consumption of wine.

are stapled or nailed only on the 7-foot stakes.

Cordon-pruned grapes can be staked and wired the same as cane-pruned types. Head-pruned vines can use most any length stake from 4 to 6 feet and can be removed if desired when a strong 3- to 4-inch trunk has been developed. In the case of some grafted resistant rootstock, such as St. George, the supports should remain. Some growers also use a short cross arm trellis on wine grapes, mostly as an aid in harvesting.

TABLE GRAPE VARIETIES

Large growing vines use a wide top trellis. This is developed by attaching a cross arm to the top of each 6-foot stake or every other stake. Usually the arm is 36 inches long and placed off center on a stake at a 30° angle to the ground, the lower end about 15 inches from the stake and the upper end 21 inches. Commercial arms of metal and plastic are available that are simple and convenient to attach. A support wire (11 or 12 gauge) is placed just below the cross arm, and three 12-gauge wires are strung equal distances apart on top of the cross arms.

RAISIN VARIETIES

Most are Thompson Seedless and whether for raisins, fresh or wine market are trained on a 6-foot stake using a single 12-gauge wire. Parts of the permanent head are trained slightly below the wire, and the one-year-old canes are wrapped down the wire from each side. A few growers have another wire about 16 inches below the top wire and develop and wrap a cane or two here also. Quality becomes questionable, although this system can increase tonnage.

Fig. 25.4—Table grapes trained on a trellis showing early spring growth. Note slant on cross arms.

American-type Grapes

Basically all are patterned after a cone-type system. Trellising grape varieties such as Concord differ in some areas. However, most plantings have posts up to 30 feet apart, wire is strung across posts and anchored at the row end to a deadman or more often, a bracing system. The grapes planted between posts are secured to the wire or wires depending upon the system used. The four-cane Kniffin system uses two wires and the 6-cane type needs three. A stake to every mature vine is not practiced as in the vinifera and some Muscadine vineyards.

Deadman

A deadman is a type of an anchor. Its function is

Fig. 25.5—Raisin grapes. Thompson seedless before and after being picked. Note raisins on paper trays and those rolled ready for delivery to processing plant.

to keep the support and trellis wires firm. The wires help in supporting the crop as well as parts of the vine. Anchors can be made from such items as wooden or cement posts, railroad ties, iron stakes, iron rods with an eye on one end and a screw-type flange on the other, buried cement pieces or perhaps an old car fender or so. Whatever does the job is the right selection!

Many new vineyards in California are using a 30″ x ½″ mild steel rod with an oblong eye on one end and a 3-inch split washer welded 2 inches from its other end. The washer is attached in a manner that results in the rod's resembling a large bit. It is drilled into the ground about 26″ at a slight angle to the row with a ½ h.p. electric drill. Installation is fast and economical.

Wire

High tensile steel vineyard wire is replacing the

Courtesy, Pacific Agrilands, Modesto, Calif.

Fig. 25.6—Metal deadman. One is in the ground with wires attached. Note twist-on attachment upper right.

more expensive (but easier to work with) galvanized wire. Plastic materials are also being used. An 11- or 12-gauge support steel wire and 13- or 14-gauge trellis wires are satisfactory combinations, although often a grower will select one gauge for all purposes.

Steel wire is difficult to cut and bend. Twist fasteners, splicers and other devices are available to splice wires together and to secure wire to the deadmen.

Training—Pruning Grapes

Materials published in detail through the state universities on training and pruning are excellent and are recommended.

It takes from three to four years to properly train a vineyard. Training involves a pretty well established procedure in that growth must be directed by disbudding, suckering, tying, topping and pruning to force the vine to react in the manner desired.

The first year a grower should give preference to developing a good root system through well cared for vines. There are occasions in the warmer areas on good soil where it is possible to develop a cane up, or partially up, the stake the first year, depending upon the vigor and diameter of the cane.

The second year a single, vigorous cane should be selected and tied loosely to the stake and all others should be removed. Some growers like to leave an additional lateral with the cane, but this usually slows down the growth of the cane being trained. Disbud all other shoots (rub or break) from the lower half of the cane. Future trunk canes should be tied each time growth reaches 10 to 12 inches. When the shoot has grown 12 to 16 inches above the area where you plan to develop the head or cordon point, top (cut) the cane. When possible retain one node above the division point.

Fig. 25.7—These young grape rootstocks have developed good roots and top growth.

After the second year, training for head and cane differs from the cordon. Only laterals on the upper third of the vine are needed. The top of the permanent trunk should be cut off slightly above the area planned for the head. On large vines three or four spurs spaced properly (in the head area) with two or three buds can be left at dormant pruning. If the trunk is less than 5/16 inch, the cane should be cut down to two buds at ground level.

The third season bears crop. Still important is continued training and care. Shoots must be removed from the lower half or third of the vine. Allow shoots to continue growing on the upper part where the head will be. The dormant pruning year (third) a vine is well on its way. Cut four to five well placed canes back to spurs of from two to five buds.

Fig. 25.8—Young grapes that have been topped, allowing laterals on upper third of vine to develop.

Fig. 25.9—Young vine cut back to good caliper size.

The cane-pruned vines at this stage are similar to head-pruned vines except that several fruit canes are left with no more than 15 to 16 buds each (2 to 3 feet) and three or so renewal spurs properly located.

Cordon-trained vines at this point take a bit more attention. Select two (18 inches or more in length) laterals (canes) originating 6 to 10 inches below the support wire to tie down and develop as arms along the support wire. At the next dormant pruning cut them back to where they are about ½ inch in diameter. For a smaller diameter cut them back to a bud on each arm and regrow and train a new one. Add the proper amount of new growth each year to a slow developing arm until the desired length is obtained. Usually this

Fig. 25.10—The third year a vigorous vineyard will normally produce about 2 tons of grapes. The three-year-old vine above is not vigorous enough to carry this many grapes. This overcrop will adversely affect this year's quality and plant growth as well as next year's production.

Fig. 25.11—Well developed, uniform, cordon-trained vineyard.

is about 3 feet on a 7- or 8-foot row spacing. Keep all foliage clear between dividing point of trunk and support wire. Of special significance is overbearing. Thinning may be necessary.

During continuing years train and prune cane, head and cordon vines so they result in producing consistent maximum crops of good quality. Water sprouts from the trunk and suckers from below the ground must always be removed, preferably before they are 6 inches long.

Once the framework is developed it is a routine matter to develop sufficient new wood for the following year and to reduce buds enough to produce a good size crop. The vigor of the vine determines how much new wood and the number of buds to leave.

American grapes

As in the case of dormant *vinifera* rootings,

Fig. 25.12—Well developed cane-pruned Thompson seedless vine.

Fig. 25.13—Nicely balanced head-pruned vine.

whether being transplanted or grown in place, current growth—other than extreme vigor—should be cut back to a single healthy cane at the end of the first growing season, leaving one or two buds at its base.

The buds are allowed to grow until shoots are 10 to 12 inches long, then the most vigorous, properly located shoot is tied to the support if one is there or secured to the bottom or top wire of the trellis with string or wire. All other shoots and laterals are removed. Go through a vineyard several times to tie up the selected shoot (cane) and continue to remove all others. When this cane has reached the desired height (top wire, usually) allow laterals to develop on the upper third. After the cane has grown 10 to 12 inches above the top wire, top the vine slightly above the wire to encourage lateral growth. Any cane after the first training that lacks vigor resulting in a spindly diameter should be cut back again to two to three buds and trained up the following year. However, if good growth and diameter reach the first wire only, circumstances could warrant developing the single cane to that point the first year. All laterals would be removed and growth encouraged from the top bud for continued training for the next year.

The second-year laterals are allowed to develop along the wires on a vigorous vine. Suckers and water sprouts are removed.

The third training involves cutting properly located laterals, depending on vigor, to the desired length and number of fruiting buds. Generally, this would result in one cane with four to six buds, going in each direction along the usual two-wire Kniffin system. It must be remembered that Muscadine training can differ in that the trunks are often trained up a 6- to 7-foot support and grown overhead. Also the usual severe pruning for fruiting wood each year is not necessary.

The fourth-season pruning leaves a fruiting cane

Fig. 25.14—Young Concord vine, nicely trained.

of up to 15 buds down each vine plus one renewal spur of two buds for each cane. Extreme caution must be used in selecting fruiting canes. Those too large (bullwood) or small, long spaces between nodes and small buds should be avoided. Continuing years of pruning should look nearly repetitious of the fourth.

The grape industry in the Americas, for the most part, is in its infancy. The production of grapes as well as other fruits is going through great changes. The hope is to keep abreast of developments and in the near future to follow this work with an addition emphasizing this industry.

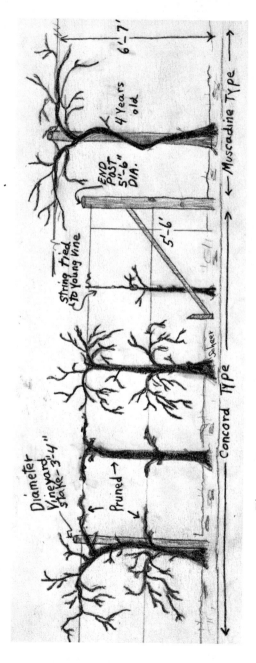

Fig. 25.15—Training, supporting and trellising American grapes.

INDEX